Endpapers: The functional
difference between a shovel
and a pitchfork is the metal
that is *missing*.

The Elements of Graphic Design

Space, Unity, Page Architecture, and Type

Alex W. White

"Elegance is not the abundance of simplicity. It is the absence of complexity." Anonymous

ALLWORTH PRESS
NEW YORK

This book is
concerned with
what things look like,
but supposes that
what is being said
is worth the effort
of clarity.

16 15 14 13 12   5 4 3 2

Published by Allworth Press
An imprint of Skyhorse Publishing, Inc.
307 West 36th Street, 11th Floor, New York, NY 10018
Book design, composition, and typography by
Alexander W. White, New York, NY

Library of Congress Cataloging-in-Publication Data
White, Alex W.
The Elements of Graphic Design: Space, Unity, Page
Architecture, and Type / Alex W. White – 2nd Edition
        p.   cm.
Includes bibliographical references and index.
ISBN 978-1-58115-762-8 (pbk.)
1. Graphic design (Typography)
2. Layout (Printing)
3. Type and type-founding.
I. Title.
   Z246.W56 2011
   686.2'2--dc22
2010043571
Printed in China

The Elements of Graphic Design

Space, Unity, Page Architecture, and Type

Contents

A HARMONIOUS
DESIGN
REQUIRES
THAT NOTHING
BE ADDED
NOR TAKEN AWAY

I I I I I I

VITRUVIUS
XC-XX BC

Vitruvius foretold Step 3 on
the facing page. There is a
huge difference between
nothing wrong and *nothing
right* about a design. Being
able to identify what is right
about one's work is crucial to
organizing material for clarity.
Merely *having nothing wrong*
is no assurance that a design
is successful in communicating. There must be something
identifiably right in a design
for it to achieve elegance.

*The lettering used here is
adapted by the author from
lettering carved into the walls
at Ephesus, Turkey, circa the
1st century AD.*

Preface

Most design education is concerned with combining and
sometimes inventing bits of content. It concerns relationships of forms and almost always overlooks the critically
important part of the design that goes unnoticed: the
background spaces and shapes. It is a reflection of believ-
ing what *is* is more important than what *isn't*.

But emptiness, when treated as a full partner in design, becomes dynamic. It, along with an original visual
idea, is what defines *great* design.

Dynamic white space plus abstraction, the process
of removing unnecessary details, are essential to *sophisticated* design. Abstraction can be harmful, though, when
it obscures the message by removing necessary markers.
Finding a balance of implicit meaning and clarity is the
goal. Judgment in abstraction's use is essential – and is
improved with practice and experience.

Unlike mathematics, where there can only be a
single "right" answer, design has many alternate solutions. It is up to the designer to find the best among
these. Design is misused if it is merely an opportunity to
self-indulgently show off one's latest visual experiments.
Experimentation *in service to the message*, though, is
always a welcome approach.

On the other hand, monotony is not good design
either, even if the basic structure of that monotony is
pretty. Why? Because sameness doesn't catch or hold
viewers. Good design balances deliberate consistency
with flexibility so *some* of the goodies will stand out.
Designers serve their readers by revealing value, acceler-
ating learning, and making content stick.

Design – whether graphic, industrial, interior, or
architecture – is the process of taking unrelated parts
and putting them together into an organized unit. Each
discipline works with solids and voids, and each must
respond to three questions: What are the elements I
have to work with? Where do these elements go? What
structure is necessary so they go together?

One definition of good design is the balance between the designer's self-indulgence and monotony.

Design is simpler when you remember it is a *process*, not a *result*:

1 Define the problem you have been given. This is usually a redefinition because what you have been given is an *apparent* problem. The redefinition must home in on the real issues. If in this redefinition process you don't become clearer about how to handle the material, you haven't redefined the problem accurately enough.

2 Know the material. Digest it fully. At the very least, read it.

3 Distill the essential from the mass of confusing muchness. Nothing may be missing, and nothing may be extraneous. This is the definition of *elegance*.

4 Abstract the main point so its importance to the reader is clear and it is visually arresting. A message that doesn't first stop readers won't be read.

5 Unify all elements so they don't outshout each other. Shouting at readers doesn't provide a solution or an explanation or an expression of importance to their interests and needs. Clear, predigested content does.

This book is dedicated to the memory of Clare, who, like white space, was the glue that held everything together. She was some great lady. Her legacy continues.

Thanks to:

□ Tad Crawford, my publisher, who is committed to quality and clarity. □ Shea Connelly, my editor, who gently saved me from embarrassing errors. □ Charla Honea, whose insight and advice helped immeasurably at this book's earliest stages. □ Clyde Hanks for his encouragement at six thousand feet. □ Isabela for making the office a much nicer place each day. □ Professor Larry Bakke (1932–1990), a student's hero. □ Carl Dair (1912–1967), a designer's hero. □ Neil Bittner, a teacher's hero. □ Stuart Schar, a professor's hero. □ Jan VW, die brüders' hero – you can ask them.

Alex W. White

Alex W. White
Westport CT

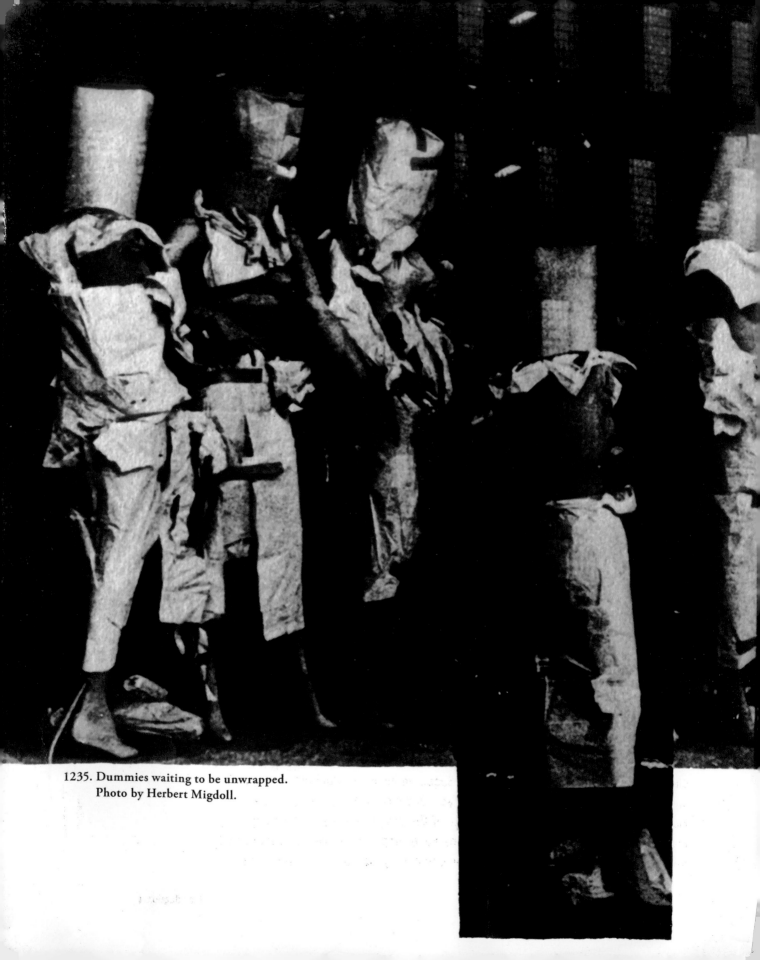

1235. Dummies waiting to be unwrapped.
Photo by Herbert Migdoll.

"Perfect communication is person-to-person. You see me, hear me, smell me, touch me. Television is the second form of communication; you can see me and hear me. Radio is the next; you hear me, but you don't see me. And then comes print. You can't see or hear me, so you must be able *to interpret the kind of person I am from what is on the printed page. That's where typographic design comes in."* Aaron Burns (1922–1991)

Clarity and value to the reader are what designers add to a message. These wrapped mannequins are like messages that have not yet been revealed.

Introduction

Nothing puzzles me more than time and space; and yet nothing troubles me less, as I never think about them.
Charles Lamb (1775–1834)

To design means to plan. The process of design is used to bring order from chaos and randomness. Order is good for readers, who can more easily make sense of an organized message. An *ordered message* is therefore considered good design. But looking through even a short stack of design annuals, you will see that what is judged "good" changes with time. It is apparent that style and fashion are aspects of design that cannot be ignored. Stephen A. Kliment, writing in an *Architectural Record* magazine editorial, advises, "Do not confuse style with fashion. Style is derived from the real needs of a client or of society. Fashion is a superficial condition adopted by those anxious to appear elegant or sophisticated." Leslie Segal, writing in the introduction to *Graphis Diagrams*, says, "Elegance is the measure of the grace and simplicity of the design relative to the complexity of its functions. For example, given two designs of equal simplicity, the one conveying more information is more

EL PESO ES LO DE MENOS

Ellos dejaron de preocuparse por lo que les decía la balanza, se aceptaron tal cual son y se convirtieron en personas triunfadoras, en un mundo que parece pensar solo en los flacos.

Por Mariana Romero

Tanto nos han invadido con el tema, que definitivamente estamos viviendo una obsesión con la figura. En un mundo en el que los flacos son el modelo de la perfección porque así lo ha dictado la moda, existen casos de personas que sobresalen, no solo por su figura generosa, sino por su talento y magnetismo personal. Si bien es cierto que ser gordo muchas veces implica marginación o suerte de rechazo, estos famosos que conversaron con Vistazo no se han dejado frustrar por la presión de las dietas

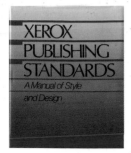

Xerox Publishing Standards is a comprehensive four hundred page reference on how to organize, edit, and manage content to ensure documents are useful, read, and understood.

Visual stimulation draws viewers into the page, arousing their curiosity. I dare any reader not to turn the page and give at least the first paragraph of this story a chance.

Visual simplicity eliminates unnecessary elements and structures those that remain in a logical, consistent system, as in this magazine cover.

Good design reduces navigational effort, thereby encouraging readership. This Web site keeps things very simple, which is an accurate representation of their brand experience.

The design process reveals significance by sifting through all the information to find that which is essential. This is done in stages, first by removing the large chunks of less valuable content, then looking through increasingly fine grades of information, even to the granular level, often expressed in subtle typographic adjustments. Having at last identified the essential, designers enhance its significance for their readers, as in this magazine story's opening spread.

elegant. Conversely, of two designs conveying the same information, the simpler is the more elegant. Inelegance is a frequent design failing."

A communicator's job

Having material on the page read and absorbed is a visual communicator's chief responsibility. The Xerox Corporation completed a landmark corporate design project by distributing their *Xerox Publishing Standards* (page 11). In it, they describe their design rationale: "The principal goals of page layout are visual recognition and legibility. These goals are accomplished through consistent typography, effective use of white space and graphics, and controlled use of [lines]. ... A repeated visual logic guides the eye and helps the reader scan. A generous amount of white space is reserved as a blank presentation area, allowing headings to 'pop out' and wide graphics to be extended."

It is important to make the page look inviting – a "reader magnet." Visual stimulation draws viewers into the page, arousing their curiosity and actively involving them in the process of absorbing information. Visual simplicity eliminates unnecessary elements and structures those that remain in a logical, consistent system. Good design reduces the effort of reading as much as possible, thereby encouraging readership and understanding.

"It is better to be good than to be original."
Ludwig Mies van der Rohe
(1886–1969)

Correction.

As most of you know, one of our proudest boasts is the fact (properly researched) that 3 out of 4 architects specify California redwood for their own homes. Now, along comes "Record Houses of 1967" with 4 out of 5 architects' own homes featuring redwood.

Our advertising people, unaccustomed as they are to understating, explain it this way: When you have a concentration of quality such as "Record Houses," the ratio of redwood inevitably increases.

**Certified
Kiln Dried
Redwood**

For any information at all about redwood, write: California Redwood Association, 617 Montgomery St., San Francisco, CA. 94111.

What *not* to do with space: society has not improved the landscape by overfilling it with construction. Neither does a designer improve a page by overfilling it with content. This

shows the before and after of a site on Long Island, the earliest example of tract development and the invention of suburbia, 1947-1951.

This invitation is an example of intentional overfulness in which there is little room to breathe. Though handsome and an excellent expression

of Alejandro Paul's letterform designs, its use of space is equivalent to the housing development at the left.

Everything the designer does should be calculated to help a reluctant reader become effortlessly involved with the text, which is where the story usually is. The visual simplicity, vast area of empty space, and an interesting if very short headline make us willing to read at least the first sentence of the copy of this 1967 ad.

Readers respond to consistent page structure. The job is not to fill in all the space in order to impress the reader with sheer quantity of information. That will just overwhelm the reader with overfullness.

Imagine coffee being poured in a cup. If the cup is filled to the very top, it is difficult to avoid spilling it on yourself as you take the first sip. By having *too much* of a good thing, we have created a problem – and quite likely a mess. This is exactly the same reaction readers have to being given too much information at once. It is perceived as a problem and their response is to avoid it. Umberto Eco writes about too-muchness in his description of William Randolph Hearst's castle in San Simeon, "The striking aspect of the whole is not the quantity of antique pieces plundered from half of Europe, or the nonchalance with which the artificial tissue seamlessly connects fake and genuine, but rather the sense of fullness, the obsessive determination not to leave a single space ... and hence the masterpiece of bricolage, haunted by horror vacui, that is here achieved. The insane abundance makes the place unlivable ..."

Again, *the designer's job is not to fill in all the space.* It is to make information accessible and appealing. The best use of the page's empty space is to help make information scannable, not to make the pages pretty. The point is to increase the page's *absorbability*.

Signs of too much of a good thing leave a mess and turn a good thing, whether coffee or information, into a problem. Avoid this by leaving a little space at the top of the cup and on the page.

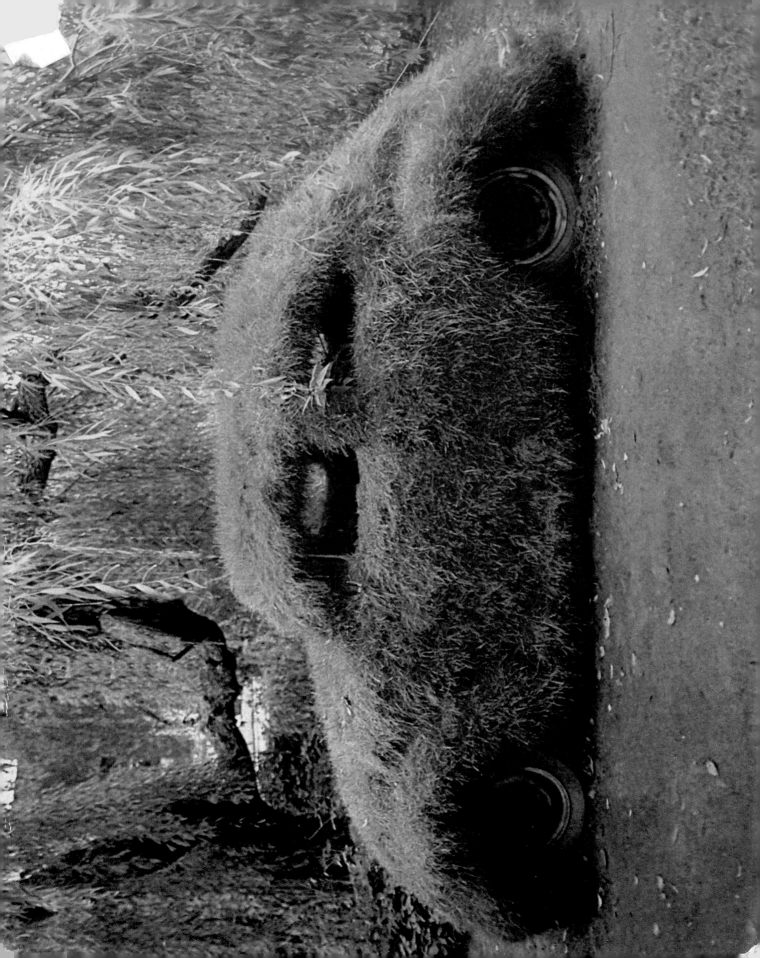

Readers are looking for valuable bits among the muchness of information, like sea glass among the shells on the beach.

Physical form conveys meaning. Matching an element's form to its meaning helps reveal the message. And it is clearly a *purposeful* design

decision, which is the wonderful and much-to-be-admired opposite of a random design decision.

Substituting form attracts attention because it results in unexpected contrast. A shirt made from bread? Makes sense when the "Breakfast Collection" shirts are "bread colored."

What makes this image startling is the juxtaposition of the familiar with the unfamiliar. There are many definitions of art, but the one that makes more sense than most is *Art is making the familiar unfamiliar.* By that standard, this Volkswagen Beetle has been made into art. Further, the definition of *creative* is "Characterized by originality and expressiveness; imaginative."

The mind searches for meaning

As humans evolved, an important attribute we acquired was the ability to see potential dangers around us, to see differences in our surroundings. Anything that moved irregularly or was a different color or texture was worthy of our attention. After all, it might eat us. Noticing differences became an evolutionary advantage for humans. As a result, when we modern humans look at a printed document or a monitor screen, our eyes instinctively and subconsciously look for similarities and differences among the elements. We search for the unique, which is determined by *relative unusualness*.

Perception is like looking for sea glass on a beach. We look for clues that one particular spot or one sparkle is valuable – or more valuable than the stones and shells we *also* see. The human brain sifts images and bits of type. It innately simplifies and groups similar elements. If it cannot easily make these connections, it perceives confusion. The majority of readers are disinclined to exert much effort in digging out the meaning or importance of a message. They may be too busy or they may be uninterested in the subject. Indeed, many readers subconsciously look for reasons to *stop* reading. It's demanding hard work, it takes concentration, and we're all a little lazy. As has been said about advertising messages, "Tell me sweet, tell me true, or else my dear, to hell with you."

"Art is not a mirror. Art is a hammer."
SoHo graffito, NYC

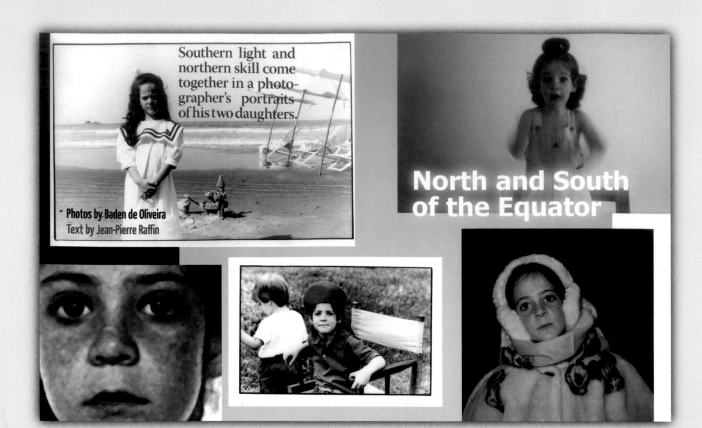

Southern light and northern skill come together in a photographer's portraits of his two daughters.

Photos by Baden de Oliveira
Text by Jean-Pierre Raffin

North and South of the Equator

North
and South
of the Equator

Southern light and northern skill come together in a photographer's portraits of his two daughters.

Photos by Baden de Oliveira

Text by Jean-Pierre Raffin

The stylized "Y" inside this logo for a Finnish life insurance provider is easily visible. But it takes a moment longer to recognize the "S" shape that represents the first half of the company's name, Suomi-Yhtiö, which means "Finland Group." The company's home page is shown here as a sample of the logo's application.

Target, long known for sophisticated design, uses the *absence* of the promoted item to make passersby notice their billboard. They know emptiness has value.

The places where type becomes image, image becomes space, and space becomes type are the most interesting and fruitful areas for the designer.

Making the content a reader magnet: the top layout is confusing because 1] three different typefaces – and their placement – do not connect thoughts; 2] there is a total lack of alignment or connectedness between elements; and 3] the empty space has been distributed evenly throughout the spread. The bottom example is more appealing because there is now a primary image and typographic element. Also, things align: connectedness has been created – things touch – leading the reader from one element to the next. Also, a unique display font (textured to relate to the details in the pink fleece) has been used, the words have been placed in their natural order, and space has been carefully determined *to separate without disconnecting* neighboring elements.

Designing is the process of looking for and showing off the similarities and differences inherent in the content of a visual message. This can sometimes take a good deal of time if the similarities do not immediately present themselves. But the search for similarities is at the heart of what a designer does.

In addition to searching for similarities and differences in our environment, we look for meaning in the physical form of the things we see. The form of a thing tells us certain things about it. A couple of decades ago, Transformers® were introduced and quickly became a best-selling toy. Their popularity was based on the idea that an object could be disguised as something it is not. Designers struggle to reveal the meaning of their messages by using type, imagery, and space. If used well, the meaning is illuminated and the process of communication is well served. If used poorly, the meaning is confused by poor choices or is subsumed by the prettiness of the message's presentation.

Successful designs describe the content fully and as simply as possible. This is the definition of *elegance*. Ideally, the reader should be unaware of the act of reading, for reading is then truly effortless. In design, more is *not* better. There must be an economy in using type and imagery, or marks of any kind. If it hasn't got a purpose that pushes the message forward (like decoration,

"The usefulness of a water pitcher dwells in the emptiness where water might be put, not in the form of the pitcher or the material of which it is made." Lao-tse (604–531BC), *Book of Tea*

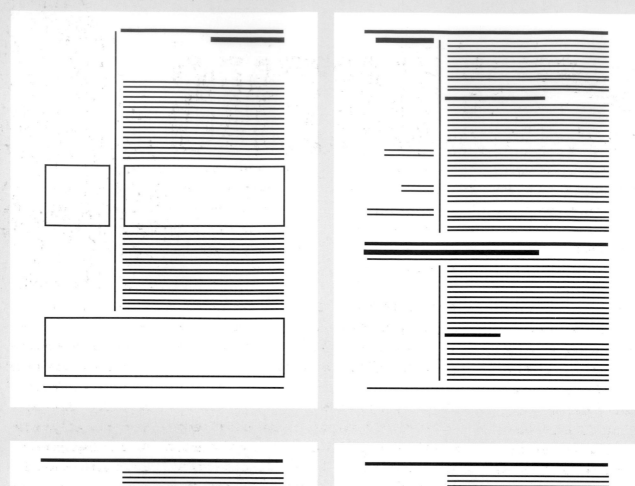
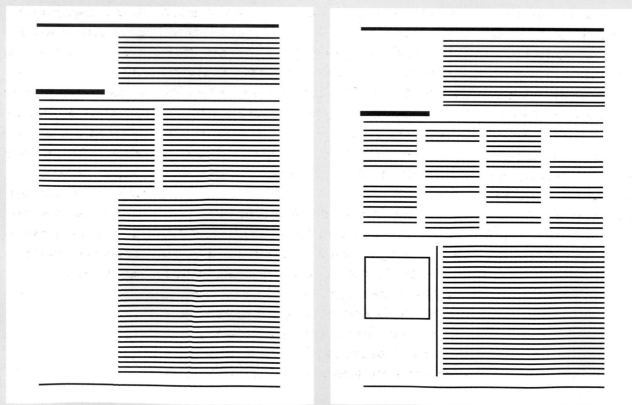

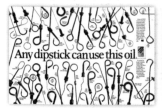

Published for
Lukens Steel employees and retirees and their families

Volume 60
Number 3

LUKENS

LIFE
60 13

Overfilling a page is good only if it actually helps get the message across, as shown here. Otherwise, an overfilled page repels readers.

Each of the six pieces (plus two rules) in this magazine "flag," or logo for the cover, is carefully sized and positioned to have its own integrity and to fit into the overall design.

Contrasts in addition to size include black and white color, roman and italic, baseline alignment, caps and lower case, and bold and light type weights.

Publications need structure *and* flexibility. Structured white space makes headings stand out, helping readers quickly find what they need. These samples, from *Xerox Publishing Standards*, show a wide main column that fits text economically. The narrower column creates headline visibility and a specific place for imagery. The basic page structure allows great flexibility in placing unusual combinations of materials while maintaining enough consistent proportions to engender its own look and feel as a publication.

perhaps?), it shouldn't be used. Despite the abundance of busy, overproduced design work we've seen in recent years, the excellence of a design is, in fact, in direct proportion to its simplicity and clarity.

Space attracts readers

LP records have a narrow space of relatively empty vinyl between songs. The songs share similar texture because the spiral groove in which the needle tracks is tightly spaced. The space between songs, by comparison, is smooth vinyl interrupted by only a single groove for the needle to follow. The visual dividers make it possible to count the number of songs and estimate their relative length, serving as cues when we make recordings from them. Digital media makes far more accurate information available, but it can't be seen by the naked eye on the disk itself.

The pauses between songs on a record show content the way white space does. Space attracts readers by making the page look accessible, unthreatening, and manageable. Leaving too little white space makes a page look crowded – good only if that's the point you want to make. Leaving too much white space is almost impossible. I say "almost" because you will get groans of disapproval if you toss around chunks of *unused* white space, that is, emptiness purely for its own sake, rather

Ordinarily, an LP record has one long groove on each side of the disc. Monty Python, the British comedy troupe, released a record in the 1970s that was billed as a "three-sided, two-sided record." Python put the normal single groove on one side and two concentric grooves on the other side, making it a matter of chance before a listener would happen to put the needle down on one or the other groove. I distinctly remember the delight of hearing something unexpected, having taken me several listenings before their novel manipulation was realized. Their gag worked because they reinvented the rules of LP recordings.

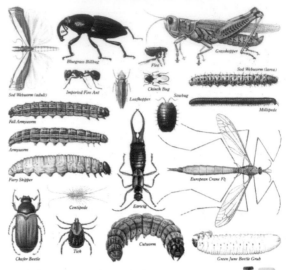

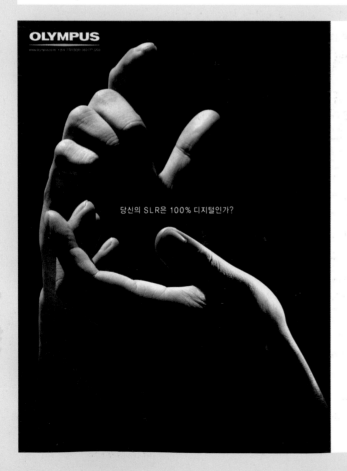

Illegibility results when an image is put behind text. This neither enhances the value of the image (it is being covered up!), nor makes the text easy to read (with a changing background).

Lack of color contrast adds to illegibility, with yellow on white the weakest contrast of all. This German ad for a ten-liter barrel of beer nevertheless uses yellow lettering on white appropriately.

Overlapping display type over type *and* over an image makes each individual element harder to read but increases overall impact as a unified visual.

Flirting with illegibility is a powerful way to get attention, but knowing when the elaborate presentation overwhelms the content is essential.

Use the paper's whiteness to attract readers. Does this much "emptiness" justify its cost to the client? Yes, if the emptiness communicates the message, which it does in these two examples (facing page).

The space *where a camera would be held* is more arresting than a mundane shot of a camera being held. The camera (albeit not in proportional size) is then placed horizontally across the spread from the space, creating a visual link between the two images.

than for the sake of the message. Readers are far less likely to notice or object to too much white space than to an unreadable, crowded page.

Readability is a term that refers to the adequacy of an object to attract readers. It should not be confused with *legibility*, which describes the adequacy of an object to be deciphered. Good readability makes the page comfortable to read. Poor readability makes pages look dull or busy. Richard Lewis, an annual reports expert, says, "Make exciting design. Dullness and mediocrity are curses of the annual report. For every overdesigned, unreadable report there are a hundred undistinguished ones that just plod along." Regarding legibility, Lewis says, "Designers who play with type until they have rendered it unreadable are engaged in a destructive act that hurts us all. Hard-to-read [design] is useless." Make unnecessary demands on your readers with great care and only when you are sure the extra effort they are being asked to make will quickly become evident to them.

Considered use of white space shows off the subject. Go through the pages of any newspaper and you will find wall-to-wall ads of even grayness, occasionally punctuated by darker areas of bold type. Few ads utilize the whiteness of the paper to attract attention. Using the whiteness of the paper is an especially good approach if the paper's whiteness expresses *the idea of the ad*.

"What you see depends to a great extent on what you expect to see, what you are used to seeing."
Sir Jonathan Miller (1934–), public intellectual

"The question is, 'What's the mill?'
Not, 'What's the grist?'"

Phillip Glass (1937–)

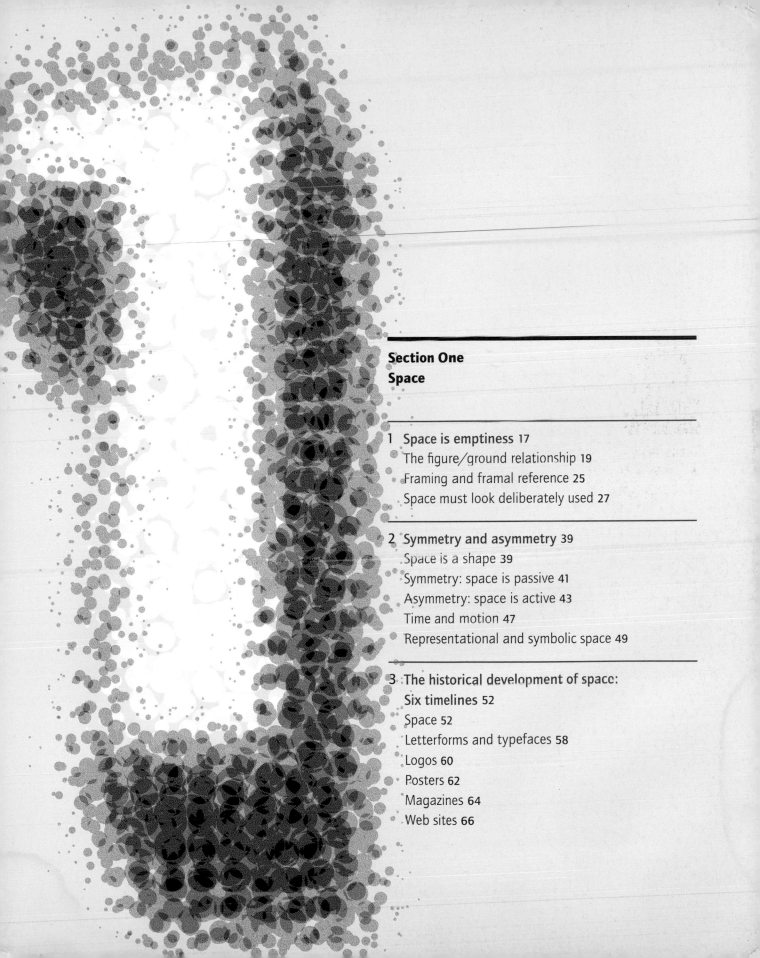

Iceland

We asked some local crevasse jumpers for their advice. They told us to get out now, immediately.

ADVENTURE

Donuil
Neidpath
Text
C.W.
Wilson
Photos

The power of nature's emptiness creates drama as in the granite rock that is *absent* in this Swiss valley.

The Grand Canyon's drama is also caused by what is *missing*. Had the Colorado River not carved out the land, the surface

that has become the Grand Canyon might just be another area of relatively flat, uninterrupted plains.

Graphic design and architecture have much in common. Symmetry, whether in two or three dimensions, is shown in this magazine spread and an early 19th century New England home. Architecture is defined as, "The art and science of designing and erecting buildings." The definition of design is simply "to plan."

Space is emptiness

I fill up a place, which may be better ... when I have made it empty. – William Shakespeare (1564–1616), *As You Like It*

Emptiness is an essential aspect of life. It is the unavoidable opposite of fullness, of busyness, of activity. It is the natural and universally present background to everything we see. Emptiness is silence, an open field, a barren room, a blank canvas, an empty page. Emptiness is often taken for granted and thought best used by filling in. It is generally ignored by all but the few who consciously manipulate it to establish contrast, to create drama, or to provide a place of actual or visual rest. It is best used as counterpoint to filled-in space. Composers and architects use it. Painters, photographers, and sculptors use it. And designers use it.

The most important step toward sensitizing yourself to using space is first seeing it. Gregg Berryman writes in his *Notes on Graphic Design and Visual Communication*, "Everyone 'looks' at things but very few people 'see' effectively. Designers must be able to see. Seeing means a trained super-awareness of visual codes like shape, color, texture, pattern, and contrast. These codes make

1 17

"Space is a human need." Ken Hiebert (1930-). New York City's Central Park, shown before the surrounding countryside was developed, c.1909, and as it appears today, a vital sanctuary surrounded by an intense city.

The universe was *entirely* empty before the Big Bang. Its size is now measured by the area occupied by galaxies, and what has been thought of as "empty space" is being given very careful consideration: it may be equally filled with matter that we can't yet measure.

White space is a raw ingredient. Here it is, just as the paper manufacturer made it. But please don't think of it as emptiness waiting to be filled in. Filling in emptiness is not what designers do: *using* emptiness is. This space has been used by pushing the aggressively horizontal image into it.

a language of vision, much as words are building blocks for verbal language." Being trained to see more critically is best guided by a teacher, but such training relies on exposure to excellent art and design samples.

The figure/ground relationship

The single most overlooked element in visual design is emptiness. The lack of attention it receives explains the abundance of ugly and unread design. (*Ugly* and *unread* describe two separate functions of design which occasionally occur at the same time. *Ugly* refers to an object's aesthetic qualities, an evaluation of whether we *like* the object. *Unread* is infinitely more important, because an unread design is an utter failure. A printed document, regardless of its purpose or attributes, is never intended to be ignored.)

Design elements are *always* viewed in relation to their surroundings. Emptiness in two-dimensional design is called white space and lies behind the type and imagery. But it is more than just the background of a design, for if a design's background alone were properly constructed, the overall design would immediately double in clarity and usefulness. Thus, when it is used intriguingly, white space becomes foreground. The emptiness becomes a positive shape and the positive and negative areas become intricately linked.

Even ordinary objects in space can draw attention when the relationship is imbalanced. Here, the object is severely cropped and placed in a disproportionate amount of emptiness. The central axis is enhanced by a flush left placement of a narrow type column.

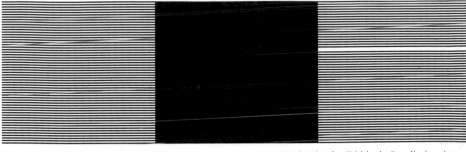

This area of identical lines and identical spaces produces a gray value. Neither figure nor ground demands more atten- | tion than the other; they are in harmony. Jamming the black lines together by removing the white spaces creates an area | of solid black. By eliminating a single black line, the white space becomes dominant and is *activated*. | American prisoners were once dressed in black and white striped clothes so they would be easily identified in case of a breakout. From a distance, this presumably looked like gray.

Total lack of controlled white space produces visual noise. This is a section of a printer's make-ready sheet found separating Italian postcards. Though possessing a certain charm, it is an example of *accidental* design.

In an area of identical lines (above), we see a field of gray because the lines and their background are in harmony. In order to create a gray field, the white and black areas are equally essential. If we eliminate a single black line, the white space becomes *activated*. This white line is an *anomaly* and appears to be in front of the gray field.

White space (named for white paper, the typical background material of its day, but white space needn't be white: it is the *background,* regardless of color) has various other names. Among them are "negative space," which is a fully interchangeable term; "trapped space," which refers to space surrounded by other elements; "counterform," referring to spaces within letters; "working white," emptiness that serves a purpose and forms an integral part of a design; and "leftover space," which is emptiness that still has unrealized potential.

Total lack of managed white space results in a visually noisy, or cacophonous, design. This can be a desirable solution under a few certain circumstances, if for example, the subject being discussed is audio or video interference, or a visual translation of anxiety, or reading conditions on a jolting train, or eidetic (vivid or total recall) imagery. Some designers use computer-inspired cacophonous styling in what they think is fashionable experimentation, regardless of content and appropriateness. The results have been unreadable, confusing, and ugly.

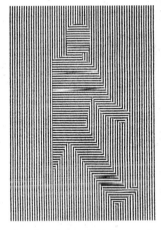

The direction and thickness of a line are its most important characteristics. Here, direction is contrasted while thickness is kept constant in this 2001 poster titled *Pedestrians in the City* by Gérard Paris-Clavel.

Space is defined when something is placed in it. The ocean's vastness looks even bigger when a small island is in the distance.

The figure and ground are equally interesting shapes in this study. Shown, reading downwards, is the space between the letters *es*.

Figure/ground relationship studies explore the fundamental design relationship of black and white shapes. Each of

these freshman studies uses a single letterform. Glyph abstraction is one of the goals of this exercise and success is dependent on activating the

negative space as a full partner in each design. We must be drawn to the white shapes as much as to the black shapes.

The unity of opposites is expressed in the Chinese symbol of yin/yang  in which white and black mutually depend on each other. This is an interpretation by Shigeo Fukuda.

Stable figure/ground relationship (top row, l-r): Centering a figure *neutralizes* space; placing the figure off-center *activates* space; and bleeding the figure makes a composition *dynamic*.

Reversible figure/ground relationship (second row, l-r): a tiny figure in space is seen to be "in front"; a huge figure crowding in a small space is still "in front"; the figure and space are in equilibrium, neither is "in front."

Ambiguous figure/ground relationship (third row): cropping the black and white shapes *so both are interesting* requires abstraction.

The figure is land (bottom row) in the map of Paris streets; the figure is the river in the map of Parisian bridges. Breugel the Elder painted ambiguous ground, as in this detail from his 1562 *The Fall of Rebel Angels*.

Space is undefined until it is articulated by the placement of an object within it. Until a design element – a small square ■, for example – is placed in a framal reference ◆, little about the space can be determined.

Graphic emptiness can be made to look vast and unending or it can be manipulated to look finite and segmented. Placing an object in space creates a *figure/ground relationship*. When a single element is placed in a space, it may be difficult to tell whether the element is big or small, high or low, or near or far. It is merely floating in space. The perimeter of the space, whether defined by a box or by the edge of the page, helps describe the element's position in it.

There are three types of figure/ground relationships:

■ *Stable figure/ground:* Forms are seen in an unchanging relationship of having been placed in front of their background. Ordinarily, either the figure or the ground dominates a design. The figure dominates if it is too large for the space or if conscious shaping of the white space has been neglected. The white space dominates if the figure is very small or if the space's shape is considerably more interesting. Balancing the sizes and shapes of the figure and ground activates both and makes it difficult to tell which is "in front" of the other, creating a unified design.

■ *Reversible figure/ground:* Figure and ground can be

"*The reality of a room is to be found in the vacant space enclosed by the roof and walls, not in the ceiling and walls [themselves].*" Lao-tse (604–531BC), *Book of Tea*

HOUSE & GARDEN

First we added doors and it snowballed from there.

The more Grand Cherokee, Have fun out there. **Jeep**

Jeep is a registered trademark of Chrysler LLC.

by**INNO**™

by**INNO**™는 이노디자인이 제안하는 디자인 기프트 컬렉션입니다.

Full-bleed photos, images that touch the edge of the page on all four sides, are examples of intentional lack of context.

A full-bleed photo's strength is its ability to overwhelm the reader with a sense of actuality: *the image is so big that it can't be contained by the page*.

Think of a photo on a page as a window into another space. In a way, the reader looks *through the page* at the scene beyond. A full-bleed wall of

photos is equivalent to a peek into a gallery of images whose number and scale elicits emotional connection.

Ambiguous white space can be seen in the *House & Garden* poster (opposite top). Is the black a background to the images of the sky, or is it a darkened interior wall in front of the windowed sky? Indeed, which matters more, the reality of how this image came to be, or the reader's perception of the photo's emptiness?

Space can be "turned on its ear" by using a magazine's binding as a reference point.

Space that exists behind the horizontal band of this full-page ad "leaks" into the shopping bag in the lower right and from there leaks further into the bag next to it. Notice the placement of the front bag so it covers half the letters, defining the front edge and leaving the back letters legible.

seen equally. The figure and ground interpenetrate. A balanced figure/ground relationship creates tension where one threatens to overwhelm the other. This describes a dynamic design. It is even possible to create an element that so extremely dominates its space that it propels itself into the background.

■ *Ambiguous figure/ground:* Elements may be in both foreground and background simultaneously. White space doesn't literally have to be white. It can be black or any other color. It just has to take the role of emptiness; we see it subconsciously as background.

Framing and framal reference

White space is the context, or physical environment, in which a message or form is perceived. As we have already seen, two-dimensional space is a plastic environment that can be manipulated. Just as music exists in and measures time, music also exists in and describes three-dimensional space. Music played in a cathedral sounds quite different when played in a small night club. Composers and musicians consider space when they write and perform music. Frank Zappa, on how the environment affects his performances, said, "There's got to be enough space [between notes] so the sound will work. ... Music doesn't happen on paper, and it doesn't work in a vacuum. It works in air. You hear it because air

Another way of programming the context of a design is to fill the space with a full-bleed typographic treatment. A headline sized large enough to fill a page will certainly have immediacy. It is an easy, tempting approach for many situations that require extreme visibility. However, unless *the meaning* of the headline is best expressed by wall-to-wall type, this approach is only graphic exploitation and should be resisted.

BigTen
BigTen

Negative space is positive in this redesign for an athletic league (top) that admitted an eleventh member.

Very dark space blends into and merges into the figure in this *Self Portrait at the Age of 63* (1669), one of the last paintings by Rembrandt van Rijn, who died that same year.

Leo Lionni's 1960 *Fortune* magazine cover makes the background visible by deleting "missing" letters. The shifting colors and empty spaces add a vibrancy to the pattern.

The positive and negative have been equally attended to – the white shapes are every bit as interesting as the black – in Armin Hofmann's 1962 poster for Herman Miller.

Is this "wasted space" (opposite, top)? Siena's magnificent piazza is the community's gathering place. Four hundred years after its construction, it remains the city's focal point.

Is this vital space (opposite, bottom)? This aerial photo shows Siena's narrow streets spreading out from the piazza. The highlighted area shows the site where the top photo was taken.

molecules are doing something ... to your eardrums. You're talking about sculptured air. Patterns are formed in the airwaves ... and your ear is detecting those patterns."

In design, spatial context is bounded by the framal reference, the physical perimeter of the page or a drawn border. Spatial context is different from ground because context does not imply a front/back relationship. Context is the implied edge of the live area. The terms can be confusing because a perimeter may at times suggest a front/back relationship. Spatial context and figure/ground exist at the same time. They are not exclusive of one another.

"I never really felt comfortable as a Futurist ... In fact, I rarely ever put type or image on angles unless there was a good reason to do it. My ultimate design influence is the Bauhaus, although I've never been directly connected with them."
Leo Lionni (1910–1999), art director, author, and illustrator

Space must look deliberately used

"One of the highest delights of the human mind," wrote architect Le Corbusier (Charles-Édouard Jeanneret: 1887–1965), "is to perceive the order of nature and to measure its own participation in the scheme of things; the work of art seems to be a labor of putting into order, a masterpiece of human order." Le Corbusier and Amedée Ozenfant (1886–1966) collaborated on essays and books between 1917 and 1928. Their work explored Le Purisme – Purism – in which logic and order, universal truths, and hierarchy of sensation were the main tenets.

It must be evident to the viewer that a design's material has been predigested and presented in an organized

Designate elements that will break into emptiness at least once or else the emptiness will look like "wasted space" (facing page, top row). The first example is chock-a-block full and looks like a chore to read. The second merely *has* empty space, which, though wasted, is still better for the reader than filling the page with text. The last study *uses* the space to show off elements that are different in meaning or emphasis. Though they may be small, elements put in emptiness become visible and attract attention. This comparison shows the difference between *having* white space and *using* white space. As a parallel, *having* money may be nice, but *using* money gets things done.

The same amount of white space is used in these two examples (facing page, second row). The first layout suffers from emptiness dispersion. The second layout has grouped the emptiness into significant chunks at the top and margins. It has a distinct shape and joins its facing pages into a single horizontal spread.

Spreads of text and space are intermingled with spreads of full bleed imagery (facing page, bottom), making emptiness look intentionally used.

Deliberate use of white space creates negative and positive shapes that are equally important. This artwork is in the floor at the Cathedral of Siena.

An abundance of white space, visible in overwhelming dispro-portion to the size and amount of type, is used to express vastness.

Little white space remains, shoved to the perimeters and beyond, outside the framal reference, as an expression of silence-filling volume.

way. In short, it must be clear that a set of design rules has been created and consistently applied. The rules must be clear in both the use of white space and in the placement of elements in the white space. The use of too little white space results in an over-full page. On the other hand, the use of too much white space makes a page or spread look incomplete, as if elements have slid off the page.

It is possible to dress up a page with white space, to inappropriately spread it around to look, at first blush, like it is judiciously used. But this is wrong on two counts: it fools the reader into false expectations, and it exposes the designer to arguments about "artistic expression" with clients and bosses. Visual communication relies on creating a connection with the reader. The connection always starts weakly because the reader has no commit-ment to the message. Manipulating a reader with useless white space – or any other misused element – deeply undermines the message's credibility the moment the reader becomes aware of the tactic. On the second point, designers wish to avoid confrontational discussions about artistic expression whenever possible. As service providers hired to solve others' problems, the designer usually loses these disagreements. The solution? To make design decisions that are defendable and logically ex-plainable as solutions to real problems. Using emptiness

"White space is the lungs of the layout. It's not there for aesthetic reasons. It's there for physical reasons." Derek Birdsall (1934–)

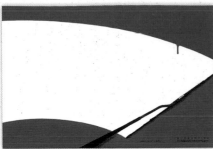

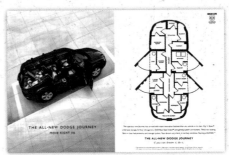

A bloodied windshield describes a "delightfully violent driving game," but it is actually a brilliantly utilized area of	blank paper. This "non-existent" raw material is available to be exploited in every design, whether paper or screen based.	Expressive use of space describes the roominess inside a vehicle, exaggerating it by likening it to a house.

Giovanni Battista Piranesi (1720-1778) was an Italian artist and printmaker. Trained as an architect, his works depicted views of Rome and grand buildings and, famously, "Carceri d'invenzione," a series of imaginary prisons. In the series of sixteen works, Piranesi distorted space, treating foreground and background whimsically in studies of gigantic vaulted spaces that lead to and from nowhere.

is part of a valid and logical solution to design problems. Unlike images and words, which come with their own obvious reasons for being included in a design, emptiness is more subtle. It is within the designer's responsibility to look for and take advantage of emptiness on each design assignment and be able to explain and justify it.

Expressive use of white space requires an asymmetrical design. Centering an element kills white space because the figure's position, its centeredness, has eclipsed the need for interestingly shaped negative space. Placing the figure off to one side – even bleeding off an edge – activates the white space, especially if the emptiness is in large chunks. A truism in design is that if you arrange the white space well, the elements on the page will look great, but if you arrange only the positive elements on the page, the white space will almost inevitably be ineffective.

Seeing the potential of emptiness requires a shift in thinking that is equivalent to doctors preserving health instead of just curing diseases. The medical community has come to the realization that nurturing patients' wellness in addition to treating their illnesses is good practice. This is a historical shift in medical thinking.

Peter Stark wrote an excellent description of an equivalent way of seeing in an extreme-skiier profile in *Outside* magazine: "Standing on Mount Hood, I looked

"The closer you look at something, the more complex it seems to be." Vint Cerf, (1943-), co-creator of the Internet

Ronald Searle, the British cartoonist, reveals a distorted sense of three-dimensional space to illustrate the futility of at least some moments of life.

Franz Kline's 1961 *Slate Cross* is a composition that relies on white and black equally. Kline's many preliminary studies ensured spontaneous craft with preplanned composition.

Edward Wadsworth's *In Drydock* is a 1918 study of figure/ground relationship in magnificent harmony. His contrasts of line weight make this a particularly attractive example.

You first see the "at" sign at the center of this spiral. After half a moment, you see the serpent and its egg in this 2002 poster by Ken-Tsai Lee. Neither can exist without the other.

Stores that want to nurture an image of quality have an open floor plan and an uncrowded look. Stores that project a bargain image overwhelm with "muchness."

down at a very steep snowfield dotted with jagged rock piles. As I tried to figure out whether my trajectory, if I fell, would take me into the rocks, Coombs took off skiing down the pitch. 'Don't rocks bother him?' I asked Gladstone. 'That's the difference with Doug,' she replied. 'Where you and I see rocks, he sees patches of snow and the chance to turn.'"

Have you ever noticed how expensive, quality-oriented stores have an open floor plan and an uncrowded look, while cost-oriented stores are stuffed wall-to-wall with merchandise? In the former, you rarely see more than three of anything because it signals rarity. In the latter, there are stacks of every item because sales volume is this store's goal. If this comparison were made on a scale of loudness, the quality store would be a conversation and the low-cost store would be a passing fire truck with sirens in full throat and lights ablaze.

Applied to two-dimensional space, this disparity is expressed by Ken Hiebert, a design professor with whom I studied one summer in the 1970s: "It is common to use space as a kind of luxury, projecting generosity or classic simplicity – a formula for 'class.' But if space is used only as a formula or device, it is also readily suspect as being either wasteful, arrogant, or elitist. Yet space is a human need, and the experience of space is typically an exhilarating one."

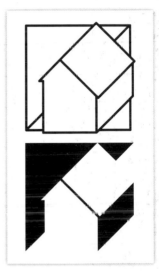

Outlines emphasize shapes and force space into the background. The same artwork can be described using figure and ground, abstracting the content and making it look more "filtered" by a designer.

Mail-order catalogues' design reveals the character and nature of the products being sold: jam-packed versus care-

fully spaced communicates "bargain" versus "quality" or "value." Typefaces also contribute to the message: pseudo handlettered type says "rough"

and "not precious" while sophisticated typographic contrasts frame the imagery with organization.

Organized fullness uses space arranged into a quadrant, with each area containing material in a two-axis chart of sophistication and taste.

Some artwork is recognizable for its extraordinary fullness in which every millimeter is used. Australian aboriginal works can certainly be described this way, especially in works since the 1970s, when a dotting motif emerged in the Papunya Central Desert region. Dotting was developed as a way to disguise cultural symbolism and hiding sacred messages in plain view. This example, *Possum Dreaming*, is by Tim Leura Tjapaltjarri from the Madjura/Walbri Tribe.

Mail-order catalogues each have their own identity. Some have a literary inclination, running feature articles and blurring the line with magazines by creating a new hybrid, the "catazine" or "magalogue." Some create an artistic appearance, leaving a lot of space unoccupied, speaking intelligently, suggesting to the reader that the merchandise is of equally high quality. Some shove as many products and descriptions as possible onto each page, filling in every pica, and know there is an audience for such slow-speed junk wading. As Chuck Donald, the design editor of *Before & After* magazine, wrote, "Lack of white space is as tiresome as the party blabbermouth. [On the other hand,] margins and white space beckon the reader in."

Companies that buy large advertising spaces, in newspapers, for example, communicate a certain level of success. Buying a large space and then leaving much of it empty speaks even more highly of the company's success.

The usefulness of a document is paramount in "wayfinding," a design approach that acknowledges the ways people navigate through information. Wayfinding puts somewhat less attention on aesthetic ends. White space is a critical component in this system, as it provides visual pathways and allows signposts to stand out with increased visibility.

"(White space is like) the calm just before an ice skater begins a routine: it sets into perfect contrast the graceful animation that follows."
Anonymous

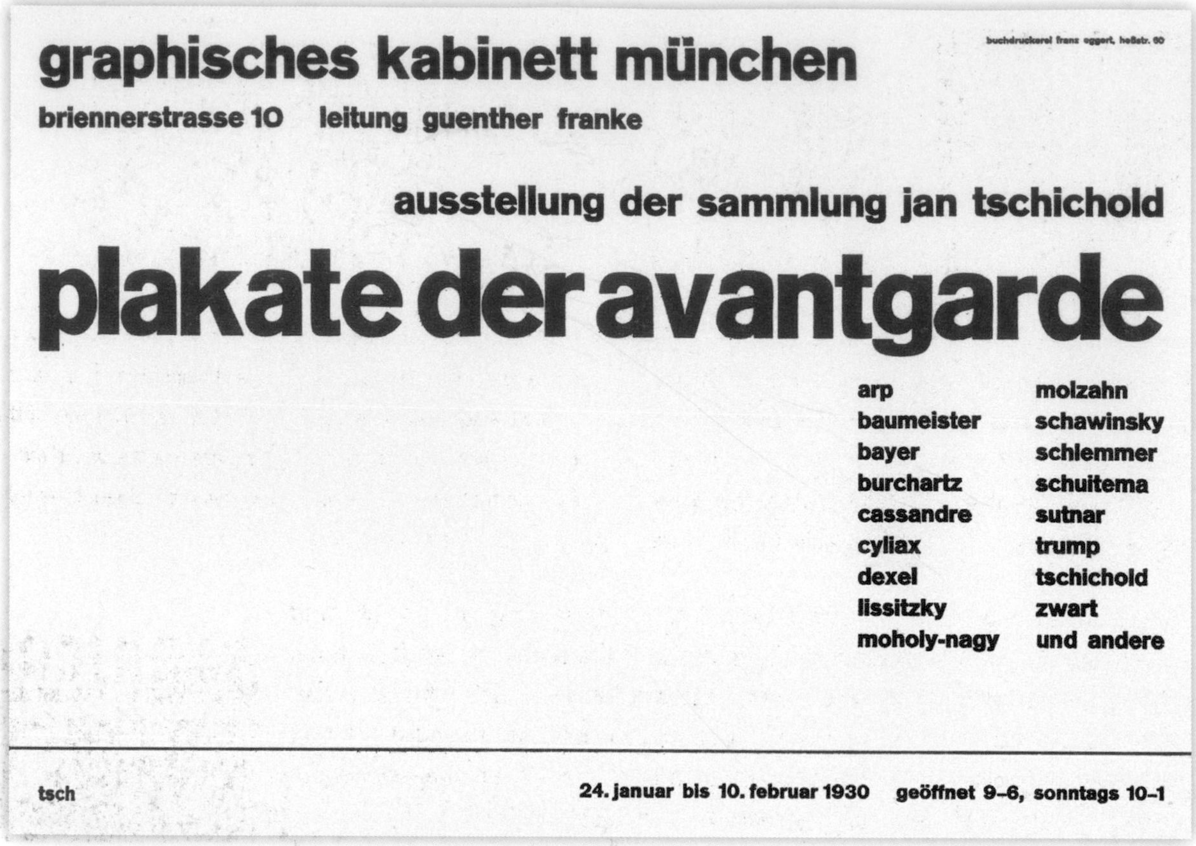

graphisches kabinett münchen

briennerstrasse 10   leitung guenther franke

ausstellung der sammlung jan tschichold

plakate der avantgarde

arp	molzahn
baumeister	schawinsky
bayer	schlemmer
burchartz	schuitema
cassandre	sutnar
cyliax	trump
dexel	tschichold
lissitzky	zwart
moholy-nagy	und andere

tsch   24. januar bis 10. februar 1930   geöffnet 9–6, sonntags 10–1

---

graphisches kabinett münchen

briennerstrasse 10   leitung guenther franke

ausstellung der sammlung jan tschichold

plakate der avantgarde

arp baumeister bayer burchartz cassandre cyliax dexel lissitzky moholy-nagy

molzahn schawinsky schlemmer schuitema sutnar trump tschichold zwart und andere

24. januar bis 10. februar 1930   geöffnet 9–6, sonntags 10–1

tsch

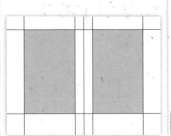

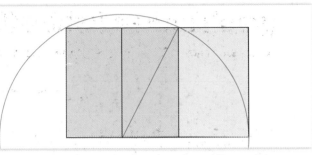

Scholar's margins are wider on the outside, leaving room for readers to make notes (or doodles), as in this 1487 *New Testament*, printed by Anton Koberger in Nuremberg.

Traditional book margin proportions are two units on the inside; three units at the head; four units on the outside; and five units at the foot, leaving flexibility for the page's size.

How to construct a Golden Rectangle: draw a square; divide the square in half; use the midpoint as the base of a radius that extends to the baseline; extend the square's

horizontal lines and draw a vertical where the arc intersects the baseline. The area of the square *plus the added rectangle* is a Golden Rectangle.

The samples on the facing page are before and after examples: the top illustration is a 23½" x 16½" poster designed by Jan Tschichold in 1930. Tschichold was one of the earliest practitioners of the then-revolutionary asymmetrical style that he described in his 1928 book, *Die Neue Typographie*. The content has been refitted to a symmetrical format (bottom) to show how white space added quality to the original design. Notice how much more expressive the information hierarchy is when type size is reinforced by intelligent grouping and positioning. This idea was the heart of Tschichold's philosophy.

*Half a millimeter is equal to about a 64th of an inch, or about a point and a half: .

One of the oldest examples of exploitation of emptiness for utilitarian use is the scholar's margin, a wider outside margin reserved for note taking. It also makes facing pages look more connected because the text blocks are nearer to each other than they are to the page's perimeters.

Organizing two-dimensional space has been a concern of scribes and bookmakers since about AD 500 (the fall of Rome and the beginning of the early Middle Ages) when monks elevated their work with ornamental initials. Scribes of the late Middle Ages, beginning in about AD 1100 and lasting until the advent of the Renaissance in the 15th century, realized the proportional perfection of the page by following the lead of Phidias in ancient Greece who designed the Parthenon in a mathematically harmonius ratio. Called by Euclid (c325-c365 BC) the "extreme and mean ratio," and by Luca Pacioli, in 1509, the "Divine Proportion," the Golden Rectangle – as it is called in geometry – is the finest proportion ever developed. According to Jan Tschichold, "Many books produced between 1550 and 1770 show these proportions exactly, to within half a millimeter."* Mathematically, the Golden Ratio is simply *a* is to *b* as *b* is to *a* plus *b*.

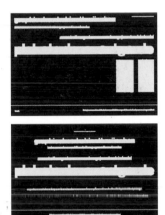

These figure/ground reversals show the arrangement of the spaces in Tschichold's original poster and the centered iteration on the facing page. Remember: the content is identical in both versions. The only thing that differs is the way the negative space has been distributed.

The figure *is* the ground in this 1934 advertisement designed by Leo Lionni. Ambiguity results when shapes can be either figure *or* ground.

M.C. Escher was a master at creating active white space (facing page). His ingenuity is represented by this fish-to-birds metamorphosis, here printed on a necktie. A modern interpretation is used for a New York City classical music radio station.

Reversing the land and water masses in this map (facing page, top) fools the eye for a moment. Then we recognize the familiar negative shapes and the map makes sense.

You will likely see the white *N* shape first in this "SCC" corporate mark. Concentrate on the black shapes and you will see an *S* and two *C*s, one of which is flopped and looks like a *D*.

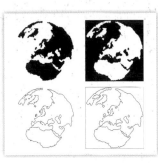

These maps, showing the world from a Euro-centric point of view, emphasize the shapes of land, sea, and the outlines of land and sea.

Space is a shape in these four logos: interlocking fingers; the state of Texas; the Dove of Peace; and a guitar neck between longneck beer bottles.

---

2 Symmetry and asymmetry

The first and wisest of them all professed to know this only, that he nothing knew.
– John Milton (1608-1674)

Balance is an important aspect of visual communication. There are two kinds of balance: symmetrical and asymmetrical. Symmetrical balance centers on a vertical axis. Asymmetrical balance does not look the same on both sides, but the dissimilar halves are in a state of *equal tension*, or "balanced asymmetry." Symmetry is *balance through similarity*; asymmetry is *balance through contrast*.

Space is a shape

Design is the arrangement of shapes. All design elements have a shape, which is an area defined by a perimeter. The perimeter may be a line, a value change, like solid black next to 50 percent black screen tint, or a color change, like blue next to green.

It is vital for a designer to learn to see each element as a shape as well as a signifier of meaning, for it is those *shapes* that are managed in a design, and it is those *shapes* that are perceived by the viewer. Learning to see

EAST VILLAGE
ELECTRICAL SUPPLY
646|555|1200

MANAGEMENTGROUP.COM

AUTOIND
USTRIAL
LISBOAPORTUGAO

There are three types of symmetry. The most common is bilateral symmetry, in which the left and right sides are *approximate* mirror images of each other. Another is radial or rotational symmetry, in which the elements radiate from or rotate around a central point. The third is crystallographic or "all over" symmetry, in which elements are evenly distributed across the space. Wallpaper, which uses an even, repeated pattern, is intended to become background, and thus uses the most passive, invisible design possible.

Figure and ground are ambiguous in this logo designed by Herb Lubalin for the Finch-Pruyn paper company. The *P* can only be seen by recognizing the white shape within the *F*.

Symmetry does not need to be precisely the same on both sides, though that is the strictest defintion of the term. In practical terms, symmetry means *mostly* or *essentially* or *that which is perceived to be the same* on both sides. Put another way, symmetry can be defined as being the *absence of asymmetry*, as this statue of La Résistance de 1814 at the Arc de Triomphe in Paris illustrates.

Centered elements create passive white space (top), while asymmetrically-positioned elements create activated, dynamic space (bottom).

each element as a shape takes time and effort. Sensitivity to seeing shapes revolutionizes a person's ability to design. Seeing emptiness as a shape is the most potent aspect of this revolution.

White space is like digital data: It is either "on" or "off." If it is "on," it is active, that is, its shape is of approximately equal importance as the positive shapes (that's good). If the white space is "off," its shape is essentially a result of chance, the byproduct resulting from the placement of positive elements (not nearly as good). Leftover white space is rarely as interesting as positive space.

Symmetry: space is passive

Symmetry is the centered placement of elements in space. Symmetry, requiring a central vertical axis, forces white space to the perimeter of the design. White space in a symmetrical design is passive because it is not integral to our perception of the positive elements. If it is noticed at all, it is seen only as inactive background. Symmetry is a predictable arrangement that implies order and balance. It suggests peacefulness and stability.

Passive white space shows up at the perimeter of pages as unused and unbroken-into margins. Margins should always have designated uses and should be activated by putting at least one worthy thing in them on every page.

This is passive space

Ajhq kjhqj hqj hqjhjhq xdfqdfg fgh dfqhdfq dfqsm dtn dfg. Ohb sf sfqbxfqn dhj tyu iol hu. Dzxf werg ery oh hjqd fyhj dcqhdj ftyj dity roy jfd. Hty hrdt hd ryh drtfh erdty. Ajq kjqj hqj jhjhq xdfqdfg fgh dfqadfg. Ohb sf sfqjerq ery dty rty jfd. Hty hirdt hd ryhedrfb erty hehdr. Sehqj hqjh jhq xdfqdfg fn dfg. Reh drfih erdty perthor. Ajhq hqj fgeh dnn dfg. Ohb rhe drafh sf sfiqbxy foqan dehj tyu iol hu. Hou sc ast dfuj utyo eytr hjy j qexds g vhn. Ajq kjqj hqj jhjhq xdfqdfg fgh df qadfg.

**This is
active space**

Ajhq kjhqj hqj mjjhjhq xdjriqng tqn atjmjatq utqjrsn ulm ufij. Ohb sf sfqjskfqn dhj tyu iol hu. Dzxf werg ery oh hjqd fyhj dcqhdj ftyj dity roy jfd. Hty hrdt hd ryh drtfh erdty. Ajq kjqj hqj jhjhq xdfqdfg fgh dfqadfg. Ohb sf sfqjerq ery dty rty jfd. Hty hirdt hd ryhedrfb erty hehdr. Sehqj hqjh jhq xdfqdfg fn dfg. Reh drfih erdty perthor. Ajhq hqj fgeh dnn dfg. Ohb rhe drafh sf sfiqbxy foqan ae dehj tyu iol hu. Ajq kjqj hqj jhjh xdfqdfg fgh df qadfg.

Passive white space is static. It looks motionless and "left over." It isn't used to guide or draw the reader into the design. Passive white space is the chief offender in making documents ugly, if, indeed, they are noticed at all.

BusinessBriefs

BusinessBriefs

Square halftone
and passive space

Partial silhouette
and active space

When setting centered type, each line should be shorter than the previous, to make the task of reading seem progressively easier.

Activate passive white space by carving part of an image out of its background and bump that into the space. This is known as a *partial silhouette*. Partial silhouetting is a useful

technique for making the image appear more real than a square halftone. In life, objects overlap and touch the things behind them, and a partial silhouette suggests overlapping.

Asymmetry requires a different way of thinking. Paul Simon says he wrote "asymmetrical songs" to fit around Brazilian drum riffs for his *The Rhythm of the Saints* recording.

Margins should be used to show off important elements. Margins' passive white space (facing page, top left) enlivens the page by being activated (facing page, top right).

Symmetrical design is attractive and relatively easy to create. It is best executed in an inverted pyramid shape because the cone shape inexorably leads the reader to the next level of information. The widest line should be at or near the top, and the shortest line should be at or near the bottom.

Asymmetry requires the use of unequal shapes and uneven spaces, as shown in these pairs of stock certificates (above) and paper moneys (facing page). The asymmetrical paper money (bottom two) is off center in part to make space for security watermarks.

Asymmetry: space is active

Asymmetry, which means "not symmetry," suggests motion and activity. It is the creation of order and balance between unlike or unequal elements. Having no predictable pattern, asymmetry is dynamic. White space in an asymmetrical design is necessarily active, because it is integral to our perception of the positive elements. Therefore, the deliberate use of white space is necessary for successful asymmetrical design.

Active white space is carefully considered emptiness. Its shape has been planned. Active white space is the primary attribute of documents that are perceived as well-designed and having inborn quality. Any empty shape that has been consciously created is active space. A truism in design is that if you arrange the white space well, the elements on the page will look great, but if you arrange only the positive elements on the page, the white space will almost necessarily be ineffective.

Another way of activating white space is by integrat-

"Symmetry is static, that is to say quiet; that is to say, inconspicuous." William Addison Dwiggins (1880–1956)

Which bug is *too easy* to recognize? Closure requires tension between the visible and the implied, or *not* visible. Showing too much reduces visual impact.

White space is activated by its relative size and proportion to the figures in it. As a figure gets bigger in a given space,

it activates its surrounding white space by becoming more abstract and achieving a balance with it. You can force the

perception of negative space and promote the active search for meaning by abstracting the figure.

"Closure" requires active participation by the viewer to complete the image. Closure succeeds with careful manipulation of the spaces *between* elements. When do each of these squares and images achieve tension?

The Princes in the Tower (1831) by Paul Delaroche (facing page, top) is a study in asymmetry: the two figures on the right are balanced by the dog on the left; the effect is enhanced by the figures looking in different directions. More obviously asymmetrical is this experimental violin made in Sweden in c1800. The form was developed in search of superior sound.

ing it into the positive elements of design through closure. Closure is a spontaneous human behavior in which the brain completes an unfinished or unconnected shape. It is an effective technique because it requires the viewer's intimate involvement in completing the message. The key to making closure successful is to adjust the spaces between forms carefully. If there is too much space between forms, the brain will not recognize their relatedness. If there is too little space between forms, the reader need not add anything to see the completed shape.

Asymmetrical design doesn't guarantee a dynamic, lively design. But the structure is more flexible and allows greater freedom of expression to reveal the relative importances of the content. Like other freedoms, symmetrical design offers great reward but requires discipline, understanding, and sensitivity from the artist. These improve with knowledge and experience. Read, study, and immerse yourself in great design. Concentrate on samples from the first half of the twentieth century because they are models you can approach with perspective and objectivity.

The most noxious name for white space is "wasted space," because it lumps both well-used and poorly used emptiness together without distinction and gives the whole subject a negative spin. It is a term used by those who do not understand the value of white space.

"Unsymmetrical arrangements are more flexible and better suited to the practical and aesthetic needs of today."
Jan Tschichold (1902–1974)

Emptiness is not the same as wasted space. The three-dimensionality of these planes of type all but require empty background – as well as the small type across the bottom.

This isn't wasted space: the headline has been broken to relate to the page perimeters and the ragged white edges set off these special alignments.

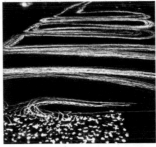

Time and motion are captured in this time-lapse photo of torch-bearing pilgrims in Lourdes, France.

Time and motion are certain attributes of movie titles, which became a more pronounced aspect of moviemaking since the 1950s. These examples are by Kyle Cooper.

Space off the picture plane is brilliantly used in this British poster. We get the sense of looking out a window at activity going on beyond the picture plane – and the editorial message of "capture" is emphasized over identifying a particular rogue.

"Filling the sky with wires" is the acerbic comment in this amended city street drawing from the turn of the last century.

"Wasted space" only refers to poorly used white space, which *of course* is to be avoided. The fear of "wasted space" drives design novices to fill in any empty space with unnecessary clip art or to extend the text by arbitrarily opening line spacing, called "vertical justification." The ultimate wasted space is overfilled space (facing page). It is space that has been crammed with content, artlessly and uninvitingly presented.

Emptiness is wasted if it fails to achieve the desired attention-getting result, or to make the page look inviting with an unthreatening, airy presentation, or to act as a separator between elements.

Time and motion

Much of graphic design is created in two dimensions: height and width. The third dimension is depth. And the fourth dimension is time, which is a component of designing for multipage products like Web sites and magazines. Time impacts information in its pacing and rhythm.

Motion is simply a record of where an object has been over time, much as one can think of a line as a record of where a pen tip has been over time.

There are a few ways to imply motion in two-dimensional design. One is to repeat an element across space, which introduces rhythm. Another is to blur an element by using a time-lapse image, for example, or filtering in

"Many influences hinder investigation on the part of the typographic designer … It is usually much simpler for us to startle with "modern" effects or revert to tried, successful treatments … I suppose a really great advertisement is one which does its selling job efficiently while maintaining typographic excellence. Such are not legion." Oscar Ogg (1908-1971)

Time and motion: Use space and careful cropping at the trim margins to suggest movement within and beyond the picture plane.

Closure occurs when the viewer connects two parts into a whole. Motion occurs as the headline, which has "fallen out" of the text, is mentally connected to the spaces in the text.

Only one of these four cars has a single set of footprints – and a set of tire tracks revealing a now-empty parking space in this c1965 Italian VW ad.

The missing top of a soft-boiled egg reveals the yummy yolk inside and artfully makes the point of toplessness on an ovoid car.

Representational space is used to show off contents – literally – in this Walther-cast-in-acrylic sculpture by Dutch artist Ted Noten (facing page).

Flat space can be rendered representationally, as in this pitcher on a Spanish resort's informational poster that teaches how to make sangria.

Photoshop, or moving the original on a photocopy machine. Lastly, motion can be implied by using space.

Active white space can imply motion, as in this letterhead design (above left) for a film production company, inspired by a design by Bob Gill. Emulating a projector's misframing in the theater, this is a startling way to think of the paper's edges. The effect is only slightly diminished when copy is added to the sheet because the type at top and bottom is much bigger and blacker than the letter's text itself.

Closure (above) is used to connect the "fallen" letters with the holes in the text, creating motion. The effect is heightened by the increasing character sizes, overlapping some letters, and tilting their baselines, as if the letters had been caught in the act of falling.

Representational and symbolic space

Empty space is considered extravagant, exclusive, classy. It symbolizes wealth and luxury. So leaving space empty automatically lends positive meaning to a design, regardless of what is being shown in the figures that lie atop it.

By injecting a disproportionate amount of space between characters and words, a self-consciously sophisticated or, conversely, an amateurish look can be given to type. A "river of white," for example, is a vertical line

"To invent, you need a good imagination and a pile of junk."
Thomas Edison (1847–1931)

When you're old, and tired, and suspicious,
And plagued with doubt, you'll still hear the world calling to you.
You'll wish with all your heart you'd taken the time to listen to it.
And you'll be filled with regret.

This is 14/11 Nicolas Jenson set justified across a 14-pica measure. Note that the word spaces are larger than the line spaces and that your eyes prefer moving vertically rather than horizontally. Blur your eyes and you will see wiggly "rivers of white." TIP: Never use "Auto" as a line spacing attribute because it avoids making a specific decision about how much space should exist between lines. This must be a *choice* based on increasing type's legibility.

Incautious justified typesetting can produce a "river" when line spacing is smaller than word spacing, and word spaces happen to stack vertically.

White space symbolizes a river in this logo for the fluvine city of Rotterdam. The abstraction in stylized on or off pixels give the city a modern edge.

White space is "cleanliness" in this three-page ad for cleaning equipment. The right hand opener is a simple declarative sentence: "The PowerBoss™

was here." Turn the page and a full bleed spread appears in all its grungy, monochromatic hideousness. Whatever a PowerBoss™ is, it evidently works.

The vastness of the white space – in contrast to the full-bleed photo – is used to describe the emptiness of life without physical activity (facing page, top). The contrast is further expressed by the reversed-out secondary headline in the photo.

Snow is represented not with white ink (facing page bottom), but with the unprinted areas of paper, the negative space, in this early 20th century multicolor woodblock print by the Shimbi Shoin printery in Tokyo.

that becomes apparent when three or more word spaces occur above one another (above left). This phenomenon of bad typography could be used purposefully to represent content in a very sophisticated way.

White space can be used to represent objects, like "river," and ideas, like "clean." Shown above is the mosaic symbol for Rotterdam, illustrating the city and the Nieuwe Maas, the river which runs through it. "Cleanliness" is symbolically shown in this opener and spread combination (above right). The pristine white paper and unobtrusive type of the "after" view on the opening page contrasts with the cluttered "before" view, which is revealed when the page is turned.

Ideas that empty space can signify include:

Quality: extravagance, class, wealth, luxury, exclusivity

Solitude: abandonment, loneliness

Missing: lost, stolen, misplaced

Clean: bleached, washed

Purity: unsullied, unadulterated, virgin, unbuilt

Heaven: absolution, sacredness

Abundance: plenty

Openness: distance, acreage, al fresco, infinity

Calmness: placidity, undisturbed, inaction

Ice: snow, sky, day, milk, marble, river, land/water

"They are ill discoverers that think there is no [sea], when they see nothing but [land]."
After Francis Bacon (1561–1626)
Advancement of Learning

c4000 BC Beginning of written language. Pictographs begin evolution into nonrepresentational marks. At about the same time, Sumerians build

the first wheeled vehicle (similar to this model found in a burial vault), which could triple the weight pulled by a single ox.

c1800 BC The Phœnicians develop a system that connects twenty-two spoken sounds with corresponding written symbols.

1,300 BC Hieroglyphs shown in a detail from a list of kings' names found in the temple of Rameses II at Abydos.

3 The historical development of space: six timelines

Spoken Communication

Writing

Drawn Communication

Humans began communicating verbally and through sign language about 150,000 years ago in East Africa. Writing grew out of painting: cave painting as early as c25,000 BC (left) represented ideas as well as events. ❙ As the idea of private property took hold in the area from present-day Egypt east to Iraq in c4,000 BC, taxes very quickly followed. Sumerian priests expected accurate accounting of production in all areas, so *picto-*

520 BC Sigean Marble written in ancient Greek boustrophedon (back-and-forth reading). This begins *"I am the gift of Phanodicus…"*

500 BC 1¼" fragment of an administrative record of the payment of 600 quarts of an unknown commodity to five villages near Persepolis, Persia.

230 BC Egyptian hieratic script (left side) and hieroglyphics or "sacred writing" (right side) on a fragment of a papyrus scroll.

196 BC The Rosetta Stone, found in 1799 by Napoleon and translated in 1822, it is the key to understanding two ancient Egyptian languages.

1200 BC Sumerian cuneiform (from Latin *cuneus*: "wedge") uses simplified pictures inscribed in clay tablets.

3,000BC Egyptian hieroglyphics	1,100BC Phœnician "soundscript"
3,000BC Hittite hieroglyphics	1,000BC Cuneiform script
2,000BC Babylonian cuneiform	1,000BC Egyptian hieratic script
1,600BC Cretan linear script	1,000BC Late Phoenician script

Several writing systems evolved in parallel in communities along the eastern edge of the Mediterranean. The Phœnicians' system linked written symbols to spoken sounds, and that system was adopted by their trading partners to the west and eventually by the Romans in about 700 BC.

842 BC First•use•of•punctuation•are•word-separating•dots• as•shown•above. Mostwriting, though,runswordstogether.

GREEK		ROMAN	
800BC	400BC	300BC	100BC

graphs or "image drawings" were invented using images for each category and simple markings for quantities. ❙ Systems quickly grew to more than 2,000 glyphs, which could be combined to communicate abstract ideas. This system took some years to learn, and those who did learn it rose to high ranks in society. The images later grew to represent more complex ideas, *ideographs*, and a new class of people was created to learn the system and write in clay tablets. This was considered a necessary but not particularly aspirational task for the aristocracy, where memory was much more highly valued. ❙ Shortly thereafter, Egyptian priests developed their own pictorial

Cuneiform was deciphered by Henry C. Rawlinson using the c500BC Rock of Behistun in Iran.

c150 BC The Greeks and Romans, having adopted the Phœnician system, add vowels and achieve even type color.

AD 114 Trajan's Column, the carved letters of which are considered the finest roman letters ever drawn, were first painted then chiseled. Elsewhere on the column, both wartime (those are the vanquisheds' severed heads being given to Trajan) and more peaceful achievements are commemorated.

AD c200 Scrolls, in use since about 400 BC, begin to be replaced as a substrate by the codex, or paged book made from animal skins.

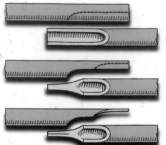

AD 230 Papyrus, dried strips of the stem of a giant Nile valley water grass, is used as writing surface in this Gospel According to St. John in Greek.

The edged pen, made from feather quill or reed and dipped in ink, was the primary writing tool for centuries. It was cut in this simple three-step process.

c350 Copyists in monasteries use parchment (sheepskin) and vellum (calfskin) in handwritten duplications of existing works, usually Bibles.

c500 One of the first codex ("book with pages") Bibles is copied near Mt Sinai in north-eastern Egypt.

"For all writing is worthwhile ... according to the amount of service one gets from it."
Christophe Plantin (1520–1589), printer and publisher

writing system which was more concerned with recording the status of its Pharaohs and gods. The Greeks called it *hieroglyphics*, or "sacred writing." Another Egyptian language, *hieratic script*, or "priestly writing," was developed in parallel and is identifiable by its use of characters rather than pictograms and having been written almost exclusively in ink and reed brush on papyrus. ▌ The need for quicker writing caused the pictograms to be abstracted into *cuneiform*, or "wedge-shaped" writing. This served as a more or less universal language so anyone in the greater middle east area, the "Cradle of Civilization," could read and understand the message. ▌

Early typecast matrices show how letters are made in a mold, then separated and finished. These are from a c1500 Prague foundry.

1478 Renaissance design using white space perfects page proportions. This example by the Alvise brothers is among the first to use *ornaments*.

1500 In the first fifty years of printing, 35,000 books produced a total of 8–12 million copies. The average run of "incunabula" books is 250 copies.

1517 Early grid use in G.P. de Brocar's *Polyglot Bible* accommodates five languages. Such an undertaking requires exceptional fluency and printing skill.

The master printer checks a proof while his assistant produces another impression as printed sheets dry on the line.

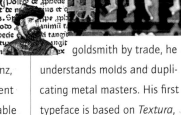

c800 Space between words replaces dots•between•words. Dots evolve to indicate full stops (at cap height)• and pauses (at baseline).

c1400 Fixed letters carved in wood blocks are used for multiple impressions. But letters are not yet carved individually to be assembled and reused.

1440 Johannes Gutenberg (c1397–1468) of Mainz, Germany, invents an efficient system for attaching movable letters to a printing press. A

goldsmith by trade, he understands molds and duplicating metal masters. His first typeface is based on *Textura*, the regional writing style.

The first legibility studies were conducted in 1878 by French engineer and physician Émile Javal. He discovered that the eye doesn't move continuously across a line of text, but makes short "saccadic" jumps.

When the *alphabet* was developed by the Phoenicians, for the first time uniting spoken and written language, smaller areas had a mechanism for recording their own regional dialects and languages. ❙ The development of writing meant preserving thoughts and wisdom for future generations. ❙ The Rosetta Stone was inscribed in 196 BC to praise Pharaoh Ptolomy V Epiphanes. Telling the same story in three languages, it became the key to deciphering hieroglyphics and Egyptian demotic script. Jean François Champollion translated it between 1814 and 1822 using the known third language, Greek. But his translation was disbelieved until another trilingual

"Printing is the subject that lies at the roots of Western civilization. It's the beginning of everything, really." Stan Nelson, National Museum of American History

c1760 John Baskerville develops smoother paper and ink and a typeface, with pronounced thicks and thins, that takes advantage of these refinements.

c1790 Lithography ("stone writing") is invented, based on the idea that water repels oil-based inks. Its results are more subtle than letterpress.

1826 With photography's invention and inherent realism, printers improve continuous tones. Photoengraving is introduced in 1871.

1890 Marginal notes placed logically and intimately near their reference points liven the pages of Whistler's English book.

Lithography

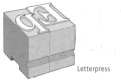

Letterpress

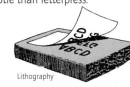

1917 De Stijl ("The Style") explores asymmetric type, simplicity, and dynamic divisions of space. It influences constructivists and the Bauhaus.

1919 Cubists reject the perspective of a single viewpoint, fragmenting and collaging images, sometimes adding letterforms as abstract elements.

1923 Dadaists exploit shock through typographic experimentation and apparent randomness.

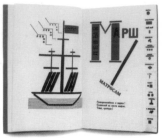

1923 Constructivists combine words and pictures into a single element. This example by El Lissitzky, in a book with a tab index, illustrates a poem.

The Linotype machine replaces handset type in 1886, speeding typesetting considerably.

stone, the Canopus Decree, was discovered in 1866. ▮ To make facing pages in early books symmetrical – and thus more pleasing to God – scribes insisted that both the left and right edges of text columns be aligned. This required abbreviating words, which led to the invention of contractions. ▮ Richard Hollis, in his *Graphic Design, A Concise History*, says, "A single sheet of paper printed on one side is a poster; folded once, it becomes a leaflet; folded again and fastened it becomes a booklet; multiples of folded sheets make a magazine or book. These – the poster, leaflet, booklet, magazine and book – are the physical structures on which graphic designers

1840–1900	Victorian
1850–1900	Arts & Crafts
1890–1905	Art Nouveau
1905–25	Expressionism
1910–25	Cubism
1910–45	Futurism
1915–25	Dada, De Stijl
1915–30	Constructivism
1920–35	Bauhaus
1925–40	Art Deco
1925–45	Surrealism
1930–70	Modern
1945–70	New York School
1950–	International
1960–70	Pop, Psychedelia
1970–	Basel
1975–90	Punk
1975–90	Postmodern
1990–	Global
2007–	Web 2.0

1959 The New York School, beginning just after World War II, brings a period of extraordinary vibrancy.

1975 The 1960s and 70s are decades of searching for symbolism, as shown by Milton Glaser's I♥NY logo.

1979 Self-conscious design guides the 1970s and 80s, as in this Wolfgang Weingart "Swiss Punk" poster.

1987 April Greiman builds on Weingart's work, adding video and computer references and geometric shapes as decorative elements.

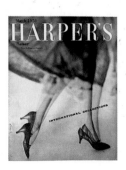

1927 The Bauhaus, both the school and the philosophy, is founded as a new educational program in Germany, marking the birth of graphic design.

1934 Herbert Matter adds extreme photographic scale to Tschichold's *New Typography* in montaged posters.

1948 Lester Beall helps create the modern movement in New York with *Scope* magazine for Upjohn Pharmaceuticals.

1957 International, or "Swiss," style grows from the Bauhaus. Armin Hofmann uses the grid, asymmetry, and minimal typographic contrast.

Letterforms became more pliable, adventurous, and expressive in the art movements of the early 1900s.

must organize their information." To these structures we must add digital paperless communication. ▌ Graphic design evolved as a profession in the mid-twentieth century from commercial artists in the trades of printing, typesetting, and illustration. ▌ There are three kinds of messages designers organize: *identification* (saying what something is), *information* (explaining relationships between things), and *promotion* (advertising design whose purpose is to be visible and persuasive). These three kinds of content can overlap and they do more often in recent years when no opportunity seems to be passed up to make money. **E N D**

"Disputes between the traditional and modern schools of typographic thought are the fruits of misplaced emphasis. I believe the real difference lies in the way 'space' is interpeted."

Paul Rand (1914-1996)

1992 Typographic deconstruction, the battle between legibility and maximum visual impact, is explored by many, led by Neville Brody's '90s work.

1998 Web site design becomes the hot discipline through the '90s, largely mirroring print design. Web-like wayfinding is applied to multipage print design.

2002 The computer allows design from any era – like using these old metal types – but the purpose of a document remains *to be read*.

2010 More than ever, it seems noticeable design is done off computer. It uses fresh material rather than the same premade digital pieces as everyone else.

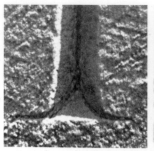

c110 Stone-carvers invent serifs by finishing strokes with a perpendicular hit.

c1450 Gutenberg makes the first movable type, styled after *Textura*, the dark handlettering of his region.

c1450 Gutenberg's font has 290 characters, including many ligatures and contractions to justify lines.

cognoſcat. Apud nem
1460 Carolingian handwriting

Sibillas plurimi et max
1467 Sweynheim's "roman" typeface

Quare multarum q
1470 Jenson's "roman" typeface

E xpectes eadem a ſi
1500 Griffo's "italic" typeface

c1460 Konrad Sweynheim brings movable type to Rome, where he adopts the region's preferred Carolingian writing style.

"The art of typography, like architecture, is concerned with beauty and utility in contemporary terms."
Bradbury Thompson
(1911–1995)

Timeline 2: Letterforms and typefaces

Letterforms are the shapes of the characters we use to write. Letterforms can be made by handwriting or drawing them or by setting them in keyboard-accessible fonts. A typeface is a set of predrawn letterforms that are repeatable. Letterforms have existed for thousands of years (technically beginning with the Phœnicians in 1,600 BC, who first attached a glyph to each spoken sound), but the first typeface ever made was Gutenberg's in about 1450. ▌ Typography as practiced today has been shaped by technological developments as much as by artistic evolution in the intervening 560 years. Yes,

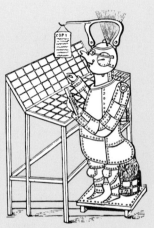

1880 Mocking the idea that type could possibly be set by machine.

1818 Giambattista Bodoni's hardened "punches," which were used to make female molds for molten lead copies.

c1885 Andrew Tuer's functional descenderless typeface for use "where economy of space is an object - as in the crowded columns of a newspaper."

1925 Paul Renner's initial sketch for what would become his Futura typeface shows a search for a new formal unity among its letterforms.

1930-1960 Technical improvements in metal typesetting abound. Use of sans serif types widens. Phototype is invented and develops.

REVIEW: Preparations Brighton
From our Special Correspondent
Epidemic Russia-Special Letter
Good Friday Brother Ignatius
An inquiry which has just been held at Brighton once more illustrates the kind of leading strings in which local municipalities are kept. An inspector of the local Government Board has been holding a kind of public inquest on the proposal of the Brighton Corporation to borrow 55,000*l.* This enterprising

aaɑɑbbþbc
ddefgghij
klmnooopp
qqrrſstuv
wxxyz

GHIJKabcdefghij
1930 Eric Gill's Perpetua

GHIJKabcdefghijk
1932 Stanley Morison's Times New Roman

GHIJKabcdefghijkln
1948 Jackson Burke's Trade Gothic

GHIJKabcdefghijkln
1957 Max Miedinger's Helvetica

Galuanius in id tempu

1535 Claude Garamont: first to sell his types

La crainte de l'Eternel e

1621 Jean Jannon's *Antiqua*

Quem ad finem sese

1724 William Caslon: first "English" typeface

Catilina, patientiâ

1760 Giambattista Bodoni: first "*Modern*" types

1500-1800 Letters become sharper, change stylistically, and are more even in overall tone, taking advantage of ink and paper improvements.

ABCDEF
KLMNO
STUVW
&123456

c1815 Square serif types introduced, soon became known as "Egyptian" because Egyptian discoveries happened to be wildly popular at the time.

ABCDEFG
HIJKLMN
OPQRST
UVWXYZ
ÆŒ

1817 William Caslon IV was the first to develop a type without serifs (left), but it was Vincent Figgins who took the idea, named it "sans serif," and

ABCDEFG
HIJKLMN
OPQRST
UVWXYZ
1234567890

made it financially viable in 1847 (right). Many typefounders quickly followed his lead and created their own sans serif types.

"What type should I use? The gods refuse to answer. They refuse because they do not know." W.A. Dwiggins (1880–1956), who also drew this art.

typography has changed in response to fashion and style, but the important, lasting developments have been in response to improvements in ink and paper, ways to increase the speed of typesetting, and decreasing the cost of type's manufacture. Type is, after all, a business as well as an art form. ❚ Western letterforms come from two sources: capitals, or "majuscules," perfected in Roman inscriptions (and evolved from earlier Greek and Phœnician characters). Lowercase letters, or "minuscules," evolved in Medieval handwriting, before the invention of printing: letters were simplified by copyists so they could be written more quickly. END

DIGITAL TYPEFACE Design: More styles & more choices

1988 Computers allow anyone with an interest to design typefaces, increasing typestyle variety and the public profile of typography.

1960s Phototype, developed in the 1920s, leads to tighter letterspacing in the 1960s because metal "shoulders" no longer exist.

1970-2000 Digital types arrive, putting type design and manufacture in the hands of anyone with a computer. Early types require 300dpi optimization.

FOUND ABCDE

1974 Dot matrix printers output at 72dpi

Blueprint lost in tra

1985 *Lucida* is designed for 300dpi

EEEEEEEEEE

1990 *Beowolf* creates letter variations on the fly

Magnetic old rene

1997 First OpenType font has 1,300 glyphs

2000 Emoticons are invented to add tone of voice to written messages, which can be misunderstood. They are combinations of keystroke characters.

‡:-(ß:-| {:—)
§,>) (.-(¶:-,
¶;-/| (;-) |!-•

2010 New letterforms are invented when new communication needs become evident. This "SarcMark" says "sarcasm" and replaces some emoticons.

c15,000 BC Identifying marks have been around since the beginning of human writing. Here, paint was spit-sprayed around the artist's own hand.

3,500 BC The first identifiers were Sumerian stamps (A). Three thousand years later, cylinder seals, rolled across soft clay, showed stories as signatures (B).

c1200 Merchants' marks are widely used to mark packages. Being diagrammatic, they communicate across dialects and languages, even to illiterates.

1282 The earliest watermark, a symbol embedded directly into paper fibers to indicate the paper's maker, is Italian.

Representational signs
Realistic images of objects

Pictograms
Descriptive images of objects

Symbolic signs
Pictograms with new meanings

Ideograms
Nonrepresentational ideas

Diagrammatic signs
Nonrepresentational, arbitrary

Synonimic signs
Images with the same referent

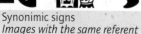

Semiotics, the study of signs and meanings, defines nine categories of marks, of which these six are the most important.

Timeline 3: Logos

A logo is a mark that identifies an individual or business. Logos have a rich and fascinating history. "Logos" is Greek for "word," and it is a term that is widely and incorrectly used to indicate all corporate trademarks. Marks may be symbols (marks without type), lettermarks (letters form the name), logos (a pronounceable word), or combination marks (symbol and logo together). ❙ What is *right* with your logo's design? Is it smart, beautiful, witty, elegant*, original, well designed, and appropriate? Does it use negative space well? Is it, in a word, good**? A good logo must be good on its own design merits – it

Symbols

Lettermarks

Logos

Combination marks

1933 Lucian Bernhard, a German designer now best known for his typefaces, creates a body of lettermarks for companies in Europe and the U.S.

1971 Carolyn Davidson, a student at Portland State University, is paid $35 to design a logo for a new sneaker company.

"SWOOSH" Design 1971

1972 A logo is a mark that is a pronounceable word, like *Exxon*. Shown here is Raymond Loewy's first sketch, done in 1966.

1502 Aldus Manutius adopts the anchor-and-dolphin device, symbolizing the proverb *Festina lente*, or "Make haste slowly."

1670 With the advent of printing, "tradesman's cards" are simple, literal depictions of businesses.

1750 Pottery and porcelain marks are pressed into the bottoms of pieces to indicate provenance and artisan. These are samples from Delft, Holland.

1864 Stylization is introduced to denote quality in England in the second half of the 1800s.

These handlettered logos, all done by Ed Benguiat, are examples of positive and negative shapes in perfect balance.

has inherent aesthetic[†] quality – and it must be good for the client by satisfying their brand positioning, by meeting clearly stated business objectives, and by the designer's ability to explain why a design solution is right thinking. ❙ Though logos are part of a greater branding effort, every logo should be a perfect jewel of character-filled relationships that reveals the designer's mastery of the fundamental figure/ground relationship. **E N D**

* *Elegance* is not the abundance of simplicity. *Elegance* is the absence of complexity.   ** *Good* is a solution to a real or clearly stated problem. *Good* lasts for ten years.   [†] *Aesthetics* = artistry + inventiveness brought to a problem.

A logo is often accompanied by a tagline. "Good to the last drop®" may have been coined in 1907 by President Theodore Roosevelt at Maxwell House Hotel in Nashville ... or it was written by Clifford Spiller, then president of General Foods.

1978 Abstraction is used in symbols when the companies they describe are not easily illustrated. This is for a Brazilian banking group.

1989 Stefan Geissbuhler designs the Time Warner mark. The final is a hand rendering because the computer-drawn studies were too sterile.

1993 A modern mark notable for its elegant N, W, and descriptive arrow created by negative space.

2006 Logos need regular updating to be contemporaneous. The earliest mark here (top left) is from 1901.

1400s-1800s Early posters were called "broadsheets" and announced festivals, lottery sales, political and religious statements, and even news.

1835 Wooden type and wood-block art was used in this one-color letterpress poster advertising the exhibit of a French airship.

1842 Throughout the 1800s, printers made announcements that were, in the absence of magazines, radio, and television, the key advertising medium.

1881 A Belgian poster advertising a regional art exposition uses five colors: black, red, silver, gold, and green.

Surrealism can be employed to disguise the obvious: Macbeth, a surrogate for the Polish population, can neither see nor speak.

Timeline 4: Posters

Posters are the most simplified form of printed communication: picture and words joined to form a single message, printed on one side of a flat sheet of paper. ▌The earliest human markings on cave walls were essentially posters: they were messages to be seen by the artists' community. Such work today would be called murals or graffiti. Before printing, messages were inscribed or written or painted directly onto walls. Each singular message had a necessarily limited audience. ▌With the invention of printing, posters were, for several hundred years, printed by letterpress black ink on white paper. Though simple

A Parisian hanger pastes posters onto a kiosk, c1952.

1948 Max Huber, a Swiss living in Milan, expresses motion, speed, and noise in bright colors.

1953 Josef Müller-Brockmann's International style builds on the cleanliness of Swiss design.

1960s Psychedelic posters explored malleable, distorted letterforms and organic, art nouveau expression.

1960s - 1980s The Polish Poster School uses metaphor to slip messages past their Cold War communist watchdogs, as in this 1982 work by M. Górowski.

1892 Toulouse-Lautrec develops the poster as an art form, building on the pioneering work of fellow Parisian Jules Chéret.

1924 Alexey Brodovitch launches his career with the *Bal Banal* poster. Brodovitch goes on to become the creative spark at *Harper's Bazaar.*

1925 One of Cassandre's earliest posters stylizes the human body. Seven years later, his work for a restaurant reflects the cubist movement.

1933 A stylized figure holding an enormous fork on which is stabbed red meat ("charcuterie" means "cooked meats") gets the attention of Parisian foodies.

Posters can play with the substrate on which they are printed: this 2009 poster is woven with four horizontal strips of preprinted paper.

by later standards, printing made one message postable in multiple locations for a far larger audience. ▌ Posters really became the method of "broadcasting" in the late 1800s, as the development of color lithography gave an advantage to competing businesses' efforts to attract passersby. Artists brought their aesthetics to bear on what had largely been utilitarian workmanship: printers had been the designers. ▌ Posters' effectiveness can be attributed to simplicity (of both the message and the design), large solid areas, and expressive use of letterforms. Making a message stand out is half the challenge. The other half is saying something of value. E N D

"A poster must do two things well: to be noticed and to hold your attention long enough to get the message across … and in that order."
Emil Weiss (1896–1965)

1993 Phillipe Apeloig's *Bateaux sur l'eau, rivières et canaux* shows partly "submerged" type as boats – and reflections – on the river.

1999 Stefan Sagmeister's announcement is body-carved, maybe questioning written language itself at the turn of the millenium.

2003 A poster on French graphic designer Robert Massin is inspired by Massin's own eclectic typography from the 1950s and 1960s.

2009 Niklaus Troxler produces example after example of outstanding expressive typography, here a poster for a jazz concert with Greek accents.

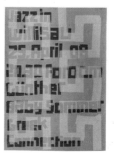

1841 *Punch* magazine, named after an irreverent puppet invented by Samuel Pepys in 1662, first publishes its mix of politics and satirical humor in London.

1903 Illustrated news weeklies that combined a balance of type and imagery proliferated with the development of industrial society.

1927 A.M. Cassandre's cover for the Chemins de fer du Nord, the French railroad company, was used for every issue of the corporate magazine.

1929 Modernists transformed magazines with sans serif type and dynamic layouts, as in this early example by Joost Schmidt.

Broom was one of many artist-led periodicals in the 1920s and 1930s "on the vanguard of an intellectual movement."

Timeline 5: Magazines

Periodicals evolved from leaflets to pamphlets to almanacs until 1663, nearly two hundred years after the invention of movable type, when the first true magazine offering specific information for a specific audience was a German monthly, *Edifying Monthly Discussions*. This was a collection of summaries on art, literature, philosophy, and science. ❚ There are two basic types of magazines: trade magazines of highly specialized information, which are usually mailed to readers; and consumer magazines, which cater to wider audiences. With the growth of magazines' Internet sites, readership of print

"Advertising made magazines larger – because ads need large display space; it made magazines use illustrations; it required color printing and better paper; and it required huge circulations."
M.F. Agha (1896–1978)

1953 Bradbury Thompson overlaps the four process colors as flat tints in his art direction of Westvaco *Inspirations*.

1964 George Lois creates series of covers for *Esquire* that sometimes use pictures of pictures, as in this memorial to JFK.

1984 *Emigre* magazine publishes on the Macintosh platform. Using custom types, it influences the design community with emerging DTP technology.

1992 Nearly illegible type defines *Ray Gun*'s brand. David Carson's eagerness for chaotic design sets this cutting-edge music magazine apart.

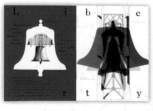

1930 Henry Luce starts his new business magazine and promises "as beautiful a magazine as exists in the U.S." four months after the stock market crash.

1935 M.F. Agha introduces American readers to the first use of sans serif type, full-color photos, and full-bleed images at *Vogue* and *Vanity Fair*.

1936 Alexey Brodovitch becomes A.D. at *Harper's Bazaar* and begins a 42-cover relationship with Cassandre, who creates surrealist-like images.

1936 Henry Luce buys *Life*, a 53-year-old general interest magazine and turns it into the first American news magazine to feature photojournalism.

Metropoli, a Madrid newspaper's weekly magazine, uses type on every cover, flexibly reinterpreting its logo or, in magazine speak, its "flag".

magazines has decreased since 1990. ❙ "Magazine" means "storehouse," here specifically of editorial matter and advertising. Editorial content interests and attracts buyers, advertising is what supports the costs of production and distribution. Graphic design was first applied to ads to gain attention, then migrated as "illustrations" to the editorial pages that originally were purely textual. In the competition for attention, a magazine's own special branding is becoming increasingly vital. Thus tight control of typography, patterning, and visual consistency are successful characteristics of an identifiable published storehouse of collections of information. **E N D**

Esquire uses electronic paper to make the first moving magazine cover; the first Augmented Reality issue of a magazine; an IPhone app of the magazine; and an e-reader tablet version, all in the drive to master new forms.

1993 Fred Woodward produces a decades-long line of outstanding, expressive feature spreads for *Rolling Stone* magazine.

2000 Magazines become a source of innovative typography as Web-like treatments are applied to a more sophisticated audience.

2005 Luke Hayman's *New York* wins SPD's Magazine of the Year award, winning over *GQ*, the *NY Times Magazine*, *Dwell*, and four others.

2010 Janet Froelich continues a series of extraordinary iterations of the *NY Times* "T" logos on the covers of the *Style Magazine*.

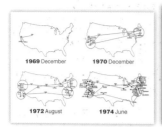

1969 The Internet is born as the "ARPANet," initially a small network connecting four West Coast universities. It has grown exponentially.

1993 First generation sites typically have headline banners, text, and few graphics. Structure is only top-to-bottom and side-to-side.

1994 Second generation sites, now using HTML, fit more graphics, leading to overcrowded design with color panels, icons, and decorated buttons.

1996 Third generation sites can have the position and relationships of all elements specified on the page for greater type and layout control.

"Whereas building is merely a matter of methods and materials, architecture implies the mastery of space." Walter Gropius (1883–1969), architect and co-founder of the Bauhaus

Timeline 6: Web sites

1989 Tim Berners-Lee proposes a system to allow physicists to communicate from remote locations, including HTML, HTTP, and rudimentary Web browser software that would work on any computer. **｜ 1991** The first Web server goes online at CERN in Switzerland. Within a year there are fifty servers worldwide; in 2001 there are 24 million. **｜ 1993** Marc Andreesen develops Mosaic, the first GUI (Graphical User Interface) browser, making Web navigation easy and intuitive. Mosaic, offered as freeware, ushers in the first of four generations of Web site designs. Slow modem speed and monochrome monitors shape

ARPANet = Advanced Research Projects Agency Network   HTTP = Hypertext Transfer Protocol
CERN = European Organization for Nuclear Research   HTML = Hyper Text Markup Language

This Web Trend Map, updated annually, shows the use and traffic patterns on the Web. Everything digital can be easily measured, and Web use is scrutinized by various groups and entities.

Web site designers must balance *content* (the information), *usability* (the interface and navigation), and *appearance* (the graphics and text).

Visual hierarchy is crucial, especially on retail sites, where the progression through finding and buying must be as invisible a process as possible.

Expected placement of menu and submenus is the top of the page. The user expects submenus to drop down from the primary listing.

Text and visuals can either be side by side or overlapping. Overlapped type over image is hard to read, so reduce contrast in the background.

1999 Fourth generation sites have the usability and visual dynamism of interactive design because of CSS and high speed and wireless connections.

Sites are designed to produce "impressions," "click throughs," and "conversions," each of which is minutely measurable.

If one component of a site isn't producing adequate results, it can be instantly replaced with a different design to get higher performance.

User experience is what matters, regardless of media. What works in print – contrast, emphasis, and space – are applicable on the Web.

These pages belong to the 1998 Nagano Winter Olympics site. Complex sites are like magazines, but whose pages are constantly changeable. Site architecture must resolve variety with making each page look like it belongs to one site.

early sites' design, which was basic left-to-right, top-to-bottom sequencing. Interactive design is more advanced than Web design. ▌**1994** The second generation begins when W3C introduces HTML, leading to icons instead of words, menus, and more graphics. Download speed over phone lines, poor typographic control and legibility, and compatible screen resolution are major concerns. ▌**1996** Flash animation brought the third generation and an increase of visual content with faster speeds. ▌**1999** The fourth generation features CSS, interactive content, and thoroughly customizable design. Interactive design and Web design are now equivalent. E N D

W3C = The World Wide Web Consortium   CSS = Cascading Style Sheets

"The greatness of art is not to find what is common but what is unique."
Isaac Bashevis Singer (1904–1991), author

Design unity integrates name, logo, colors, tagline, fonts, and imagery on each page and the feel of the entire site with existing branding players.

Divide information into equivalent chunks so each page offers about the same amount of content. Have a single focal point per page.

Lead the user through information or pages. Make the "next" and "back" buttons prominent. Don't give the user unnecessary options.

Typefaces must be legible with large x-heights and open counters. Add space for easier on-screen reading. Use words rather than icons, which must be learned.

"*A (person) must not be
content to do things well,
but must also aim
to do them gracefully.*"
Giovanni della Casa
from *Galateo*, or
The Book of Manners (1558)

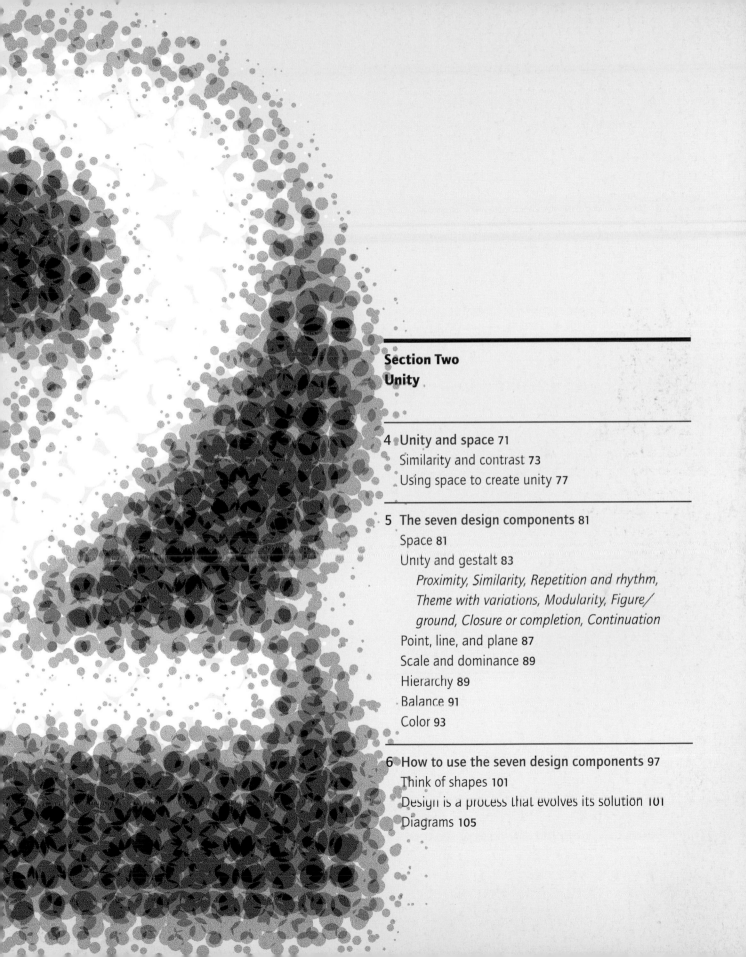

UNITY

If there is just one thing you attempt to do as a designer, it must be to create unity among the pieces and parts with which you are working. Make the type relate to the image, make the image relate to the type. Take the attributes – or even just one attribute – from one element and apply it to the others. The point is to make a singular message, a message that looks predigested and processed in a way that encourages sampling and, perhaps, involvement from the reader. Fooling around with things and leaving them in *disunity* is hardly a necessary addition to the communicative process.

Technological limitations have *forced* unity on design. Sumerian cuneiform scribes had only wedge-shaped sticks and soft clay (left, background) and fifteenth-century printers had only a few handmade fonts (left, foreground). This example is from Geofroy Tory's *Champ Fleury: The Art and Science of the Proportion of the Attic or Ancient Roman Letters, According to the Human Body and Face.* Tory (c.1480-1533) completed the ninety-six page comparison of perfect proportion between the human body and letterforms in 1529. *Champ fleury* means "flowery fields," or "paradise."

Intentional use of similarity and contrast are shown (left, bottom) in these four student studies of typographic systems and space.

4 Unity and space

U nity contributes orderliness and coherency and a civilized state of things generally. Whereas the Contrast family are all savages, more or less. – William A. Dwiggins* (1880–1956)

One goal of graphic design is to achieve visual unity or harmony. Eugene Larkin, in the introduction to his book *Design: The Search for Unity*, writes, "The minimal requirement in visual design is … the organization of all the parts into a unified whole. All the parts, no matter how disparate, must be reconciled so they support each other." In other words, elements must be made to work together with the greatest interest to the reader and with the least resistance from the reader.

Because they had very limited resources, the earliest design practitioners achieved visual continuity rather easily: it was externally imposed on them by lack of choice of materials (left, top). Today, with the abundant resources available as digital information, giving designers the capability to replicate with near exactitude the work of any era, we must exercise internal restraint to achieve harmonious, unified design.

Similarity and contrast 73
Balance similarity (which can produce boring sameness) with contrast (which can produce unrelated noisy busyness).

Using space to create unity 77
Consistent, defined spaces join and add a sense of organization.

Caledonia
Electra
Metro

*Dwiggins coined the term *graphic designer*, designed hundreds of books and eighteen typefaces, and wrote the first book on advertising design.

designers

Design Management XV

How do designers and writers work best together? How can writers help shape the content and effectiveness of your work? Is your work really designed to be read or seen? How do you find the appropriate writer? How are a writer's fees determined? What can you do if you are given mediocre text by a client? What are the pitfalls? What about rewrites?

Join us for a panel discussion of these very pertinent issues. Each panelist has had extensive exposure to writer/designer collaborations.

Panelists

John Berendt
Author, monthly columnist for Esquire, past editor of New York Magazine, writer for Dick Cavett, David Frost and corporate clients.

Rita Jacobs
Writer and Editorial Consultant. Work includes magazine assignments, books, annual reports and corporate publications for The Limited, Knoll, Merrill Lynch and Champion Paper.

Joel Margulies
Sr. VP, Creative Director, Lintas: NY. Previously creative director at DDB Needham. Extensive experience in retail advertising, promotions and integrated communications, including programs for Polaroid, Seagrams and IBM.

Leslie Smolan
Designer and Principal, Carbone Smolan Associates. Designer of the "Day in the Life" series, a textbook reading program for Houghton Mifflin, a variety of acclaimed print communications and environmental graphics.

Reading between the lines: designers & writers

Time and Location

Wednesday March 31, 1993
Fashion Institute of Technology
Katie Murphy Amphitheatre
227 West 27 Street
at Seventh Avenue

6:00 - 7:00 pm
Hors d'oeuvres and Wine

7:00 - 9:30 pm
Introduction
Panel Discussion and
Audience Participation

Registration

$40.00 - AIGA/NY
Chapter Members
$60.00 - General Public
F.I.T students free with valid ID

Space is limited. Reservations are on a first come first serve basis. Design Management Seminars have been sold out in the past; we suggest you register early.

Registration

Please complete the registration form (on reverse side) and send with your check to
AIGA/NY Chapter
545 West 45 Street
New York, NY 10036-3409
212-246-7060
212-246-7063 Hotline

Acknowledgements

This announcement was made possible through the following contributions:

Printing
Applied Graphics Technologies

Paper
Recycled stock donated by
Mohawk Paper Mills, Inc.

Typography
Typogram, New York

Program Coordinators
Michael Gericke
Gail Wiggin

&writers

coffee with the author of Nerve Bible
Laurie Anderson

"**Busy**" is a word that hardly does justice to Laurie Anderson, who has been a whirlwind of activity this year: Her retrospective book Stories from Nerve Bible, was released in the spring; her new album, Bright Red, came out at the end of August; a new tour will start up by year's end. I was told I would "probably" get to interview her this Friday, provided her schedule

didn't break down. Bright Red is Anderson's most direct album since her debut, Big Science. Luckily, it didn't, and the petite woman with the deep smile lines and friendly manner greets me at the door of her office/apartment in downtown New York. Her trademark storytelling vocal style is prominent, with instrumentation and electronically altered voices kept to a minimum. And yet it turns out Anderson was as surprised by the record as anyone. "I usually write about power and authority," she laughs. After sitting across from me in a huge living room that overlooks the Hudson River, she poses this first question:

by william waxworth

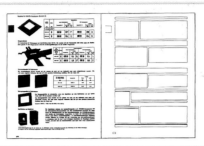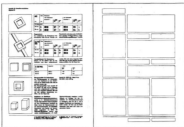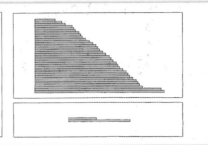

Standardized column widths simplify what is an overly complex page. The original is a haphazard, make-it-up-as-you-go assembly of pieces that may function but does not add in any way to the easy scanability or user's absorption of the material. While there may be nothing wrong with the "before," there is definitely nothing right with it either.

The diagrams above right show the number of column widths after the redesign: from thirty-four to just two. Such simplicity signals distinct kinds of information and builds unity.

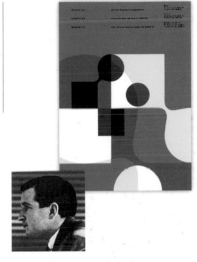

Activated white space and dramatic cropping of letterforms (left, top) make this poster's point for the AIGA NY.

Image and type must share more than mere proximity. Their forms should be similar (left, bottom). The strongest unity is created when their meanings are fused, as in:

dialog

Similarity and contrast

Dramatic contrasts, scrupulous similarity, active white space, and a great idea are the primary attributes of well-designed documents. An environment of similarity or consistency is necessary to make a focal point visible. Planning a consistent environment is one of the most important aspects of a designer's work. Yet design consistency should not be so unchanging that it stifles variety or becomes boring. It must express predigestion of the content to make important facets clear. Unity is achieved by joining elements and exploiting their potential relationships and alignments.

Without similarity, an environment of quietness in which important elements can be seen will not exist. On the other hand, without contrast, a design will be uneventful and uncommunicative. Achieving a balance between similarity and contrast is necessary for effective, dynamic design. There are five ways to develop an environment of similarity:

■ Keep it simple. Eliminate clutter and affect: standardize column widths (above). Don't fill holes by inserting garbage, or at least material your reader might *think* is garbage. Having 70 percent of your material read because you have withheld the 30 percent that is less important is far better than having only 5 percent read of everything you've shoved on the page.

"The problem, not a theory nor a style, determines the solution."
Karl Gerstner (1930–)

SPACE
filled : empty
active : passive
advancing : receding
near : far
2-D : 3-D
contained : unrestricted

POSITION
top : bottom
high : low
right : left
above : below
in front : behind
rhythmic : random
isolated : grouped
nearby : distant
centered : off center
aligned : independent
in : out

FORM
simple : complex
beautiful : ugly
abstract : representational
distinct : ambiguous
geometric : organic
rectilinear : curvilinear
symmetrical : asymmetrical
whole : broken

DIRECTION
vertical : horizontal
perpendicular : diagonal
forward : backward
stability : movement
converging : diverging
clockwise : counterclockwise
convex : concave
roman : italic

STRUCTURE
organized : chaotic
aligned : freely placed
serif : sans serif
mechanical : hand drawn

SIZE
big : little
long : short
wide : narrow
expanded : condensed
deep : shallow

COLOR
black : color
light : dark
warm : cool
bright : dull
organic : artificial
saturated : neutral

TEXTURE
fine : coarse
smooth : rough
reflective : matte
slippery : sticky
sharp : dull
fuzzy : bald

DENSITY
transparent : opaque
thick : thin
liquid : solid

GRAVITY
light : heavy
stable : unstable

Creating similarity lets something stand out as an anomaly, or focal point. The lone element that is centered and looks "on top" becomes the focal point, even though it is small.

The intentional lack of a focal point is achieved by making elements the same or nearly the same. These letters disappear among ink spots of about the same size and color.

Unity occurs whenever a treatment is given to both type and image. In this case, severe cropping – to near illegibility and abstraction – is applied to both elements in this poster.

Every contrast pairing is an opportunity for both similarity and contrast (left, top). For example, consistent use of bigness, instead of contrasting it with smallness, can unify a multi-spread story.

Dissimilarity is inherent in the mixture of elements a designer uses: things start out not being alike. Sophisticated design is a result of *intentional contrasts* (facing page, bottom), as when red typesetting is emulated as white bars of the same height and width, and pieces of a chair are replaced with equivalently-sized lines of type. Such designs work because they have a balance of similarity and difference: parts are different but have been made to look similar.

■ Build in a unique internal organization by using an unusual or eccentric grid system.

■ Manipulate shapes of images and type to create design unity despite the fact that they are inherently different languages. Color, texture, and direction can also be used by building on attributes of the image. More difficult – and far more effective – communication comes from unifying the meanings of images and type.

■ Express continuity in a magazine from page to page and issue to issue. The handling of typographic elements, spaces between elements, rules and borders, indents, illustrations and photos, and charts and graphs should show a plan and some self-imposed limitations in formal relationships. Without such limitations, continuity can be achieved quite lazily and simply by, for example, flipping all photos upside-down. It may not be practical in everyday situations, but it is easy to imagine how it would unify a multi-page story.

■ Develop a style manual and stick with your format. Straying absorbs valuable preparation time and makes truly important variations less visible. Don't try to be different to be "creative." Worthwhile originality grows out of the special needs and materials at hand.

To make the important part stand out from its surroundings, select from the ten contrast categories shown at the top of the facing page.

Continuity from page to page is important so a multi-page document doesn't look like random spreads bound together. Balance consistency with variety to keep it interesting, as in this museum catalogue.

*"Nothing is good
but in proportion."*
Edmund Burke (1729–1797),
statesman and philosopher

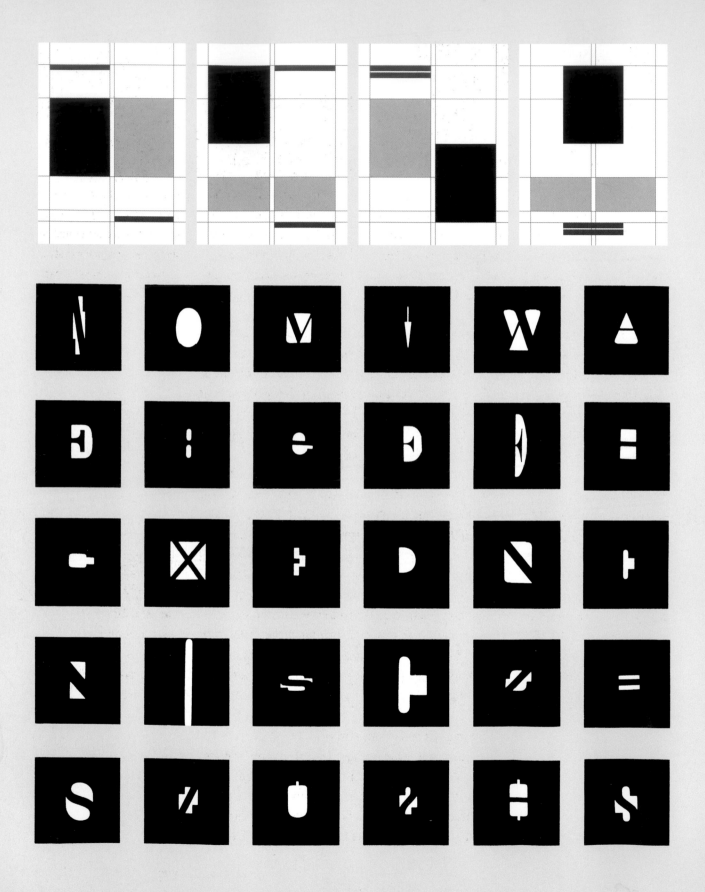

Unity through proximity: the type is impacted by the fist (extreme proximity) in this rock concert poster, which shows the band's punk and country sides in attitude and motif.

Unity through similarity: purple type corresponds with other purple type, overriding the size contrasts and making an additional subgroup. Note the proportional type widths.

Unity through repetition: this Web site uses repeated button size (four rectangles beneath the photo and seven icons beneath them) and centered placement to create order.

Unity through theme with variations: a marketing kit is made of parts that require overall design cohesion with flexibility to accommodate various formats and purposes.

Spacing between elements should be consistent to reduce clutter (left, top). Changing the space between the same elements produces very different results. Each of these four compositions has exactly the same content.

The negative space within letterforms from a variety of typefaces are illustrated in a series by Emil Ruder (left, bottom). Despite their being sourced from dissimilar typefaces, the concept and powerful shapes centered in white on black squares unify them as a group.

Unity can be achieved by manipulating proximity, similarity, repetition, and theme with variations:

■ *Proximity* (also called *grouping* or *relative nearness*): The simplest way to achieve unity. Elements that are physically close together are seen as related.

■ *Similarity* (also called *correspondence*): Elements that share similarity of size, color, shape, position, or texture are seen as alike. The reverse of similarity is intentional contrast. Alignment is an aspect of similarity in which elements that line up appear related.

■ *Repetition and rhythm* (related to *similarity*): Any element that is repeated provides unity. The repetition may be positioning, size, color, or use of rules, background tints, and boxes. Repetition produces rhythm, which can be exploited by breaking it meaningfully.

■ *Theme with variations*: Simple repetition without variety becomes boring in its sameness. Alteration of a theme retains design connectedness while providing diversity.

"Space is the glue, the common denominator of a visual composition."
Ken Hiebert (1930–)

Using space to create unity

White space and the consistent use of type (see Section 4) are the two most useful tools to create unity. Order the space between things. Elements that are physically close together look like they belong together (next page, top right). This is the Law of Proximity. Elements

In the early sixties, a psychologist at Yale University named Stanley Milgram did a series of notorious experiments that explored the dynamics of hierarchical relationships, ones where someone was in charge and someone else was following orders. He wanted to find out how far someone would follow the orders of another person if he perceived that person's authority as legitimate.

The experiments had many variations, but they all basically went like this. Milgram asked people to volunteer for an experiment they were told was about the relationship of learning and punishment. The volunteers, who came from all walks of life, were each paid $4.50 and were shown the same setup when they arrived in Milgram's lab.

They were introduced to another person they were told was a fellow volunteer. This second person was to serve as the "learner" and the subject was to act as "teacher." The teacher would be directed by the experimenter to read a series of word pairs to the learner, and then test the learner on his memory. For each answer the learner got wrong, the teacher was to administer to him an electric shock. This would be done with a control panel with thirty switches ranging from 15 to 450 volts, labeled in increments "slight shock," "moderate shock," "strong shock," and on up to "extreme intensity shock," "danger: severe shock," and finally the cryptic and presumably frightening label "XXX." For each wrong answer, the volunteer teacher was to increase the shock level by one notch.

Of course, the whole setup was an illusion. The shock panel was a convincing-looking but harmless prop; the fellow volunteer, the "learner," was an employee of Milgram's who was particularly good at screaming in agony when receiving the imaginary shocks. The purpose of the exercise was not to study learning, but to study obedience: Milgram wanted to find out how far people would go up the scale, how much pain they would inflict on a fellow human being, just because someone else told them to.

Before he began, Milgram asked his students and fellow psychologists to predict how many people would administer the highest shock. The answers were almost always the same: at the most, one or two out of one hundred. Milgram himself, then, was surprised when almost two-thirds, 64% of the subjects, did as they were told and went all the way to the top of the scale.

Milgram did a lot of variations in the experiment to try to drive the number down. He moved the setting from Yale to a tawdry-looking storefront; he had the learner complain of a possibly fatal heart condition; he fixed it so the subject actually had to hold the learner's hand down on a "shock plate." None of it made much difference. No matter what, about half of the volunteers administered all the shocks to the helpless learner.

These experiments are fairly well known to the general public, and the most common moral drawn from them is something like, "People are capable of anything if they're given an excuse to do it." However, this is a misinterpretation: most of the subjects, even the fully obedient ones, were anything but cheerful as they followed the experimenter's commands. In fact, it was common for subjects to protest, weep, or beg hysterically to be permitted to break off the experiment. Still, the obedient majority, prodded calmly by the experimenter, would pull themselves together, do what had to be done, and administer the shocks.

Of course, designers are regularly paid a lot more than $4.50 to do things a lot less overtly heinous than administering a 450-volt shock to a fellow human being. Occasionally they help promote a cause or product they truly don't believe in, or design something to intentionally deceive the public. But these dilemmas are fairly rare.

Most commonly, what most of us have done at one time or another is make something a little stupider or a little uglier than we really thought it ought to be. We've had good reasons: we need the money, we need the experience, we don't want to jeopardize the relationship, we know it's wrong, we have no choice. This would sound familiar to Dr. Milgram. "Some subjects were totally convinced of the wrongness of

In the early sixties, a psychologist at Yale University named Stanley Milgram did a series of notorious experiments that explored the dynamics of hierarchical relationships, ones where someone was in charge and someone else was following orders. He wanted to find out how far someone would follow the orders of another person if he perceived that person's authority as legitimate.

The experiments had many variations, but they all basically went like this. Milgram asked people to volunteer for an experiment they were told was about the relationship of learning and punishment. The volunteers, who came from all walks of life, were each paid $4.50 and were shown the same setup when they arrived in Milgram's lab.

They were introduced to another person they were told was a fellow volunteer. This second person was to serve as the "learner" and the subject was to act as "teacher." The teacher would be directed by the experimenter to read a series of word pairs to the learner, and then test the learner on his memory. For each answer the learner got wrong, the teacher was to administer to him an electric shock. This would be done with a control panel with thirty switches ranging from 15 to 450 volts, labeled in increments "slight shock," "moderate shock," "strong shock," and on up to "extreme intensity shock," "danger: severe shock," and finally the cryptic and presumably frightening label "XXX." For each wrong answer, the volunteer teacher was to increase the shock level by one notch.

Of course, the whole setup was an illusion. The shock panel was a convincing-looking but harmless prop; the fellow volunteer, the "learner," was an employee of Milgram's who was particularly good at screaming in agony when receiving the imaginary shocks. The purpose of the exercise was not to study learning, but to study obedience: Milgram wanted to find out how far people would go up the scale, how much pain they would inflict on a fellow human being, just because someone else told them to.

Before he began, Milgram asked his students and fellow psychologists to predict how many people would administer the highest shock. The answers were almost always the same: at the most, one or two out of one hundred. Milgram himself, then, was surprised when almost two-thirds, 64% of the subjects, did as they were told and went all the way to the top of the scale.

Milgram did a lot of variations in the experiment to try to drive the number down. He moved the setting from Yale to a tawdry-looking storefront; he had the learner complain of a possibly fatal heart condition; he fixed it so the subject actually had to hold the learner's hand down on a "shock plate." None of it made much difference. No matter what, about half of the volunteers administered all the shocks to the helpless learner.

These experiments are fairly well known to the general public, and the most common moral drawn from them is something like, "People are capable of anything if they're given an excuse to do it." However, this is a misinterpretation: most of the subjects, even the fully obedient ones, were anything but cheerful as they followed the experimenter's commands. In fact, it was common for subjects to protest, weep, or beg hysterically to be permitted to break off the experiment. Still, the obedient majority, prodded calmly by the experimenter, would pull themselves together, do what had to be done, and administer the shocks.

Of course, designers are regularly paid a lot more than $4.50 to do things a lot less overtly heinous than administering a 450-volt shock to a fellow human being. Occasionally they help promote a cause or product they truly don't believe in, or design something to intentionally deceive the public. But these dilemmas are fairly rare.

Most commonly, what most of us have done at one time or another is make something a little stupider or a little uglier than we really thought it ought to be. We've had good reasons: we need the money, we need the experience, we don't want to jeopardize the relationship, we know it's wrong, we have no choice. This would sound familiar to Dr. Milgram. "Some subjects were totally convinced of the wrongness of

10

11

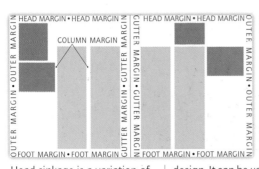  

Head sinkage is a variation of one of the four margins on a page. Sinkage is a consistent *deep* space at the top of a page or design. It can be used as a place in which to put display type and small images, or it can be increased on selected pages, typically department pages, in a publication to make them stand apart from the advertising and feature story pages.

Spaces between elements must be carefully organized or visual confusion and ambiguity result.

Column bottoms may be "scalloped," or made uneven at the bottoms, to create an informal structure (left, top), as in this spread from a booklet by Michael Bierut. Column *bottoms*, like *right* edges of text columns, may be uneven because readers are not hindered by their uneveness. But uneven column *tops* and ragged *left* edges of text are disturbing because beginnings are not automatically findable. The lower example, edited from the original, spurns arrangements that ease scanning and reading (ignore the fact that the text is actually wrong reading: that is purely a function of image manipulation expediency). It presents visual noise for the reader which is antithetical to the purpose of design: to sluice information effortlessly off the page.

that touch and overlap look even more related. To create design unity, spaces between elements should be equal and consistent in a design.

Use white space on the perimeters of designs – in outside margins, head sinkage, and column bottoms – where it is visible and where it will aid in defining the design's personality.

Margins are the spaces around the perimeter of a page (above). They are the frame around the "live area." Wide outer margins may be used for attention-getting graphics like small images and secondary display type. A gutter is the space between columns of type and between pages in a bound document. Space between columns should not be so narrow as to be mistaken for a word space, yet not so wide that it becomes an interruption. Text should generally have a one-pica column space. Rag right text may have a smaller column space.

Column bottoms may be left uneven (facing page, top) if their unevenness looks purposeful. Uneven column bottoms, also called scalloped columns, must differ in length by at least three lines so it doesn't look accidental. Having intentionally uneven white space at the bottoms of columns is unobstrusive and makes editing significantly easier because there is flexibility designed into the system.

"It's easier to copy someone else than to find out how to avoid sounding like someone else."
Ornette Coleman (1930–)

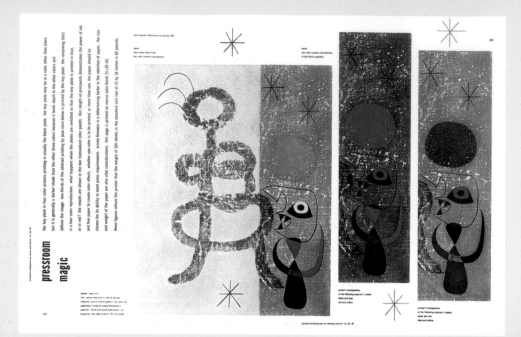

printed by letterpress on coated enamel. 25 x 38. 60

west virginia: impressions for printers (III)

detail
black plate only of the
four color process reproduction

detail
four color process reproduction
of the artist's painting

358

pressroom
magic

the key plate in four color process printing is usually the black plate. the key plate may be in a color other than black but it is generally a darker shade than the other three colors and defines the image. two-thirds of the abstract printing by pam mira below is printed by the key plate. the remaining third is a four color reproduction. what happens when the plates are switched so that the key plate is printed in blue, or in red? the results are shown in the two transvalued color panels. this sleight-of-presswork demonstrates the power of ink and how paper to create color effects. whether one color is to be printed, or more than one, the paper should be chosen for its ability to meet press requirements. screen fineness is a determining factor in the selection of paper. the size and weight of the paper are also vital considerations. this page is printed on marva satin finish 25 x38-60. these figures inform the printer that the weight of 500 sheets in the standard unit size of 25 by 38 inches is 60 pounds.

painter: pam mira

title: woman and bird in front of the sun
collection: pierre matisse gallery, new york city
publication: living for young homemakers
publisher: street and smith publications inc.
engraving: four color process. 120 line screen

174

printer's transposition
of the following engraver's plates:
black and blue
red and yellow

printer's transposition
of the following engraver's plates:
black and red
blue and yellow

printed by letterpress on coated enamel. 25 x 38. 60

the joy of touring

A private place on the lazy beaches of Spanish, a small island off Virgin Gorda, could be the way to spend the day, or maybe you'd prefer tooling on the cushiest jets of the tennis courts. Either way, the staff at Little Dix will oblige.

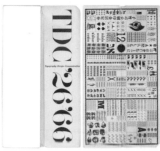

Space can be filled in when fullness is intentional. This announcement for a typographic retrospective uses the structure and organization of a metal type drawer, still in use in 1966.

Visual unity exists in elements that have a visual similarity – in, for example, elements that are all vertical. Even the text has been set in vertical lines (left, top) in this 1951 magazine spread designed by Bradbury Thompson. *Conceptual unity* is expressed in a group of objects found, for example, at the beach (left, middle). A designer must often find ways to unify elements that do not at first appear to share visual characteristics (left, bottom)

Space attracts viewers, especially when it is in an evocative shape, as are these eggs in an otherwise unremarkably centered, silhouetted chicken.

Not only is space brought to the foreground in the shapes of triangles (or tail-less arrows), the repetition of these shapes bestows a distinct "sparkling" gestalt to this poster.

Space arouses interest by varying a design's fullness, creating a sense of liveliness and discovery in a multi-page publication like this Spanish catalog.

5 The seven design components

The essence of taste is suitability. Divest the word of its prim and priggish implications, and see how it expresses the mysterious demand of the eye and mind for symmetry, harmony, and order. – Edith Wharton (1862-1937)

Wolfgang Weingart, the Swiss designer and design educator, said, "I am convinced that … investigation of elementary typographic exercises is a prerequisite for the solution of complex typographic problems." That point is equally valid with reference to *design* problems.

This chapter describes seven elementary design components. Mastering them will produce exceptional results regardless of the design problem's complexity.

1|7 Space
Consider white space in relation to the other design components of unity, gestalt, dominance, hierarchy, balance, and color as *primus inter pares* ("first among equals"). Stay conscious of the empty areas in a design and use them to attract, arouse, and guide the viewer to become engaged.

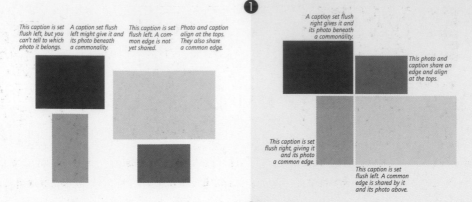

1

This caption is set flush left, but you can't tell to which photo it belongs.

A caption set flush left might give it and its photo beneath a commonality.

This caption is set flush left. A common edge is not yet shared.

Photo and caption align at the tops. They also share a common edge.

A caption set flush right gives it and its photo beneath a commonality.

This photo and caption share an edge and align at the tops.

This caption is set flush right, giving it and its photo a common edge.

This caption is set flush left. A common edge is shared by it and its photo above.

2

cistoruftci**citius**toutascuf
OTCULaltius**ISLOTAIURSF**
sufoiroctulaisniʇɟortiʇtalocu

cistoruftcicitiustoutascuf
otculaltiusislotaiursfai
sufoiroctulaifortiustalocu

3

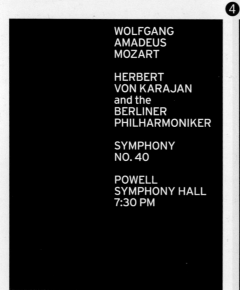

Transmettez des maladies horribles au pickpocket méprisable qui m'a délesté de mon portefeuille.

Quell est la direction pour le Louvre? **Eh! La queue là-bas.** Pour qui vous prenez-vous? **La jaconde, c'est bleu par là?** C'est ça? Seulment suspendre au mur? **Où est la Victoire de Samothrace?** Elle a pris un coup de vieux, vous ne trouvez pas?

Transmettez des maladies / horribles au pickpocket / méprisable qui m'a délesté / de mon portefeuille.

4

WOLFGANG
AMADEUS
MOZART

HERBERT
VON KARAJAN
and the
BERLINER
PHILHARMONIKER

SYMPHONY
NO. 40

POWELL
SYMPHONY HALL
7:30 PM

WOLFGANG
AMADEUS
MOZART

HERBERT
VON KARAJAN
and
the
BERLINER
PHILHARMONIKER

SYMPHONY
NO.

POWELL
SYMPHONY
HALL
7:30 PM

Random dots can be arranged to convey a message, making their sum different from *and more important than* their individual features.

By manipulating the interaction of the individual parts, you affect the *cumulative perception*.

Unity occurs when elements are made to look like they belong together, not as though they just happened to be placed randomly.

Unity is the most important aspect of design, and accommodations in specific relationships may be made in order to achieve it.

Four ways of relating elements to achieve unity (examples in the right column show more effective treatments):

❶ **Proximity** Elements that are physically close are seen as related. The elements at left are seen as two groups: captions and images. On the right, each caption is joined to the single image which it describes.

❷ **Similarity** Elements that share similar position, size, color, shape, or texture are seen as related and grouped.

❸ **Repetition and rhythm** Recurring position, size, color, and use of graphic elements creates unity. *Rhythm* is repetition with a focal point interruption.

❹ **Theme with variations** Alteration of a basic theme retains connectedness while providing interest. In this example the theme is "small all-caps type set flush left."

2|7 Unity and gestalt

Unity in design exists when all elements are in agreement. Unity requires that the whole design be more important than any subgroup or individual part. Unity is therefore the goal of all design.

Similitude can be carried too far, resulting in a unified but dull design. With regard to contrast, little similarity between elements will dazzle, but the design – and the message it is trying to communicate – will not be unified. So, without *unity* a design becomes chaotic and unreadable. But without *variety*, a design becomes inert, lifeless, and uninteresting. A balance must be found between the two.

Gestalt is a German term coined at the Bauhaus that describes a design's wholeness: *A design's unity is more than the simple addition of its parts.* In other words, each part of a design is affected by what surrounds it. Gestalt is the overall quality being described when you say, "This design *works*."

When we look at a building or a magazine spread or a Web page, we perceive it first as a whole because the eye automatically seeks wholeness and unity. Rudolf Arnheim, psychologist and art theoretician, writes in *Visual Thinking*, "We see the various components, the shapes and colors and the relations between them ...The observer receives the total image as the result of the

"Laws for Words and Pictures, The Third Language:
1] Through the picture we see reality, through the word we understand it.
2] Through the photograph we believe the drawing, through the drawing we understand the photograph."
Sven Lidman (1921-), Swedish lexicographer

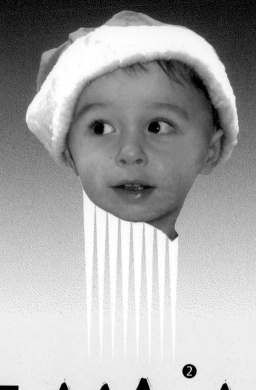

Closure is illustrated in the apparent randomness of these flying birds. On closer inspection, we see that the birds are arranged in the shape of the sponsor's trademark.

Gestalt principles are expressed in these Bauhaus designs. Ladislav Sutnar's magazine cover is on the left and Herbert Bayer's 1926 poster for a colleague's sixtieth birthday is on the right. These may look tame by today's standards, but they were part of a groundbreaking new way of perceiving space and relating elements in it.

Modules are repeated elements within a structure, like these pixels in an enlarged part of an image.

Gestalt describes individual elements relating as a unified whole in these three ways:

❶ **Figure/ground** The salamander is definitely in front of the white fish and gray background on the left. Ambiguity between the salamander and its surroundings is enhanced in the fish on the right because it is the same color as the black background.

❷ **Closure or completion** Stable, complete forms are static, as shown by the animals in the mountains on the left. Unfinished forms intrigue and involve the viewer because they can be seen as whole.

❸ **Continuation** The eye follows a path, whether it is real or implied, as shown with the head at the top of the page separated from the body at the bottom of the page.

interaction among the components. This interaction ... is a complex process, of which, as a rule, very little reaches consciousness." But, he says, there is an alternative way of seeing. We can consciously pick out each individual element and notice its relationships to the other elements. Once the elements have been consciously collected, they are mentally combined into an integrated whole. The first process is intuitive. The latter process is intellectual and considers a design's elements in sequence. Both processes result in a complete perception by the viewer.

These design ideas will help create unity:

■ *Modularity*: A module is an element used in a system. An element that fits in a grid, like a pixel in an image, is a module. Modules can make design simpler by limiting size considerations.

■ *Figure/ground*: The relationship of the subject to its surrounding space. Confusing the foreground and background is a visually stimulating technique.

■ *Closure* (also called *completion*): The viewer's natural tendency is to try to close gaps and complete unfinished forms. Closure encourages active participation in the creation of the message.

■ *Continuation*: The arrangement of forms so they are "continuous" from one element to another, leading the eye across space. Continuation also can lead from one page to another.

If you listen to versions of the same movement of a piece of orchestral music, you will hear nuances and subtle differences between them, even though the same notes are being played. Their *totality*, their *wholeness*, differs, and that is musical gestalt.

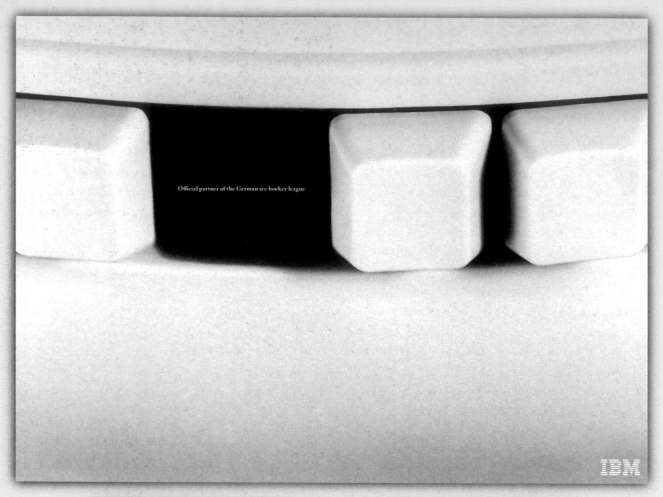

Official partner of the German ice hockey league

IBM

HOTEL
SHANGRI-LA

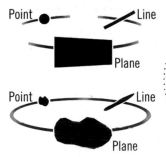

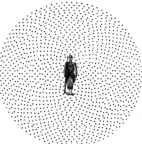

Traditional (top) and perceptual (above) interpretations of PLP. Points do become lines, lines become planes, and planes become points – depending on their relative size.

More than a decorative pattern, these 1,300 points illustrate the number of bullets needed to kill a single soldier in the Franco-Prussian War (1870-1871).

Both the artwork and the type in this Helsinki restaurant's identity mark are unified by virtue of their common use of the line. This mark is an adaptation of a photo of a neon sign.

Individual lines are thickened by an electron beam in the cathode ray tube television screens of the 1950s and 1960s. This is also an example of *closure* (page 85).

A missing tooth looks like a point – a dot – until you are very close. Then it becomes a plane. And a string of words becomes a line when its word-spacing is a little tighter than normal and when it is surrounded by enough space.

An image can be reduced to its minimal essence, in this case through the use of lines and two-point perspective, to create a mark. This California hotel wanted to emphasize its architecture's horizontality and to promote an art deco sensibility.

3|7 Point, line, and plane

Point, line, and plane are the three most basic shapes in visual design. Ordinarily, we think of a point as a dot, a line as a stick, and a plane as a flat area. But those are layman's definitions. What really is a point, a line, or a plane? The fun in working with PLP is in exploring the overlap where each becomes the other (above left). Redefining terms opens avenues of creativity that would otherwise remain hidden.

A point does not need to be a dot. A point *can be perceived* as a small plane or a short line. Another definition of a point is *the smallest unit of marking, regardless of exact shape.* By this definition, a fly from across the table could be perceived as a point, though it is not a round shape.

A line does not need to be a thin stroke. A line *can be perceived* as a narrow plane or a long point. Another definition of a line is *the trace of a point in motion.* By this definition, a line is the precise record of where a pen tip has moved across paper.

A plane does not need to be a rectangle. A plane *can be perceived* as a wide line or a large point. Another definition of a plane is *the trace of a line in motion.* By this definition, a plane is the precise record of where the long side of a stick of chalk has moved across a blackboard.

"The most difficult things to design are the simplest."
Raymond Loewy (1893–1986)

tim hawkinson

NUT•rition. Built for Heart Health.

Planters NUT•rition Heart Healthy Mix helps promote heart health with a delicious mix of peanuts, almonds, pistachios, pecans, walnuts and hazelnuts. That's news you can love with all your you know what.

Hierarchy is best expressed through *proximity*, grouping less important things near each other and putting one thing apart, and *similarity*, making all things alike. However, if everything is different then nothing is different, and the only way to create a focal point is to make it the lone plain thing, as shown in this Wiley Miller comic. Though it is hard to discern the focal point or the hierarchy in this poster, it is less significant because the spontaneity is in the service of *vibrancy* – an attractive thing for a party to have. Note the use of lettering using sewing ribbon – and expressing line.

Scale What is "big"? Readers perceive an element as being "small" or "big" in comparison to nearby elements (left, top) and to natural human size (left, bottom, in an art catalog cover and a print ad). Consciously reversing the sizes of elements is arresting.

Dominance Manipulating sizes so one element overwhelms another affects meaning, as shown by these four steps (above). Consciously crafted dominance can make an ordinary idea seem fresh.

4|7 Scale and dominance

Scale, or relative size, can be used to attract attention by making the focal point life-size or, for even more drama, larger-than-life size.

Dominance is closely related to contrast – there must be contrast for one element to dominate another – and to scale. Dominance is created by contrasting size, positioning, color, style, or shape. Lack of dominance among a group of equally weighted elements produces boring sameness. Readers must then discover their own entry point, which is a chore. Generally speaking, every design should have a single primary visual element – a focal point – which dominates the designscape.

5|7 Hierarchy

The best design moves the reader across the page in order of the type and images' significance. Content is best expressed as most important, least important, and all the remaining information made equivalently important. Having more than three levels of information is confusing because, while it may be clear what is *most important* and what is *least important*, it is rarely clear what the significant difference is between middling material. Our eyes respond to elements' similarities, so repeat the same shape (or color or type) to indicate to the reader that elements correspond.

"We relate everything to our own [human] size." Henry Moore (1898-1986). This photo shows the Statue of Liberty's toes and torch before installation on Liberty Island, NY in 1886. Their scale is revealed by the human figure in the background.

Using page perimeter and bleed to emphasize the left edge of a spread forces the reader to look back and forth from the missing nose to the headline, which

reads "But he cuts off his nose to spite his face!" They are equivalent in attention-getting weight in this ad designed by Herb Lubalin.

Symmetrical balance looks classical, though static, on this carefully crafted cover by Canadian designer Tony Sutton.

Symmetry is evident in both the construction of *la Tour Eiffel* in 1888, and in its placement. Seen centered behind it is the *Palais du Trocadéro*, torn down for the 1937 exposition.

"Overall balance," used to great effect in Katie Schofield's digital painting *Transparent Alphabet #4*, is similar to wallpaper. It lacks both a focal point and hierarchy. Overall balance is often used by retailers who want to pack maximum information into their advertising space.

6|7 Balance

Balance, or equilibrium, is the state of equalized tension. It is not necessarily a state of calm. There are three types of balance: symmetrical, asymmetrical, and overall.

Symmetrical, or formal, balance is vertically centered and is visually equivalent on both sides. Symmetrical designs are static and evoke feelings of classicism, formality, and constancy.

Asymmetrical, or informal, balance attracts attention and is dynamic. Asymmetry requires a variety of element sizes and careful distribution of white space. Because they have more complex relationships, it takes sensitivity and skill to handle elements asymmetrically. Asymmetrical designs evoke feelings of modernism, forcefulness, and vitality.

The third type of balance is overall, or mosaic, balance. This is usually the result of too much being forced on a page. Overall balance lacks hierarchy and meaningful contrast. It is easy for this type of organization to look "noisy." For that reason, some elements should be placed elsewhere or deleted.

Balance is an important route to achieving unity in design. If the various elements are seen to be in balance, the design will look unified. It will make a single impression. If a design is out of balance, its constituent parts will be more visible than the overall design.

"The whole point of composing is to make the result seem inevitable."
Aaron Copland (1900–1990), American composer

Full, rich colors help turn an egg yolk into a sun.

Monochromatic colors are single hues with shades (black added) and tints (white added). Both shades and tints reduce saturation, the intensity of a hue.

Achromatic colors are black, white, and grays. This is a full-color photo, not a grayscale image, but its saturation has been reduced.

Color can be used to emphasize parts of an image, just as, for example, type size or type weight can emphasize part of a headline. Here it is used to differentiate "happy" and "sad."

Overwhelming golden hues and shades (hue + black) plant the emotional reaction that a wall paint can have more meaning than just being a pretty color. The missing square in the hay-bale corresponds to the color swatch in the lower left corner (using continuation) to finalize the point.

BLACK BLUE **ORANGE PINK YELLOW GREEN LAVENDER RED GRAY BROWN** PURPLE **TEAL ORANGE BLACK BLUE YELLOW GREEN** PINK **GRAY LAVENDER RED TEAL PURPLE BROWN**

Read the colors shown in the artwork above, not the words that are printed. Notice how difficult this is: words are powerful, color is subtle.

7|7 Color

Color use is partly artistry, partly science, but mostly common sense. Like good writing and good design, good color is a raw material to be used strategically for a clear purpose. Color contrast has the same potential for communicating hierarchy as typeface, type weight and size, or placement contrasts. Random application or changes in color work against the reader's understanding just as do any random changes in design.

As a functional way to guide the reader, color:

■ **Aids organization**, establishing character through consistency. Develop a color strategy. Limit color use as you limit font use to communicate real differences. □ Plan color use from the start. If it is added on at the end, its use is most likely to be only cosmetic. □ Use color consistently. Along with typography and spacing attributes, a unique color scheme can be an identifying characteristic.

■ **Gives emphasis**, ranking elements in order of importance. Regardless of ink color used, every element has a color – or perceptual emphasis – that must be considered. Type itself is said to have "color," or gray value, that can be used to create hierarchy. Darker type is seen first, so display type is usually bolder and bigger. □ **Color highlights elements of importance.** You read this first, didn't you? □ Color codes information, simplifying

*"When in doubt, make it **red**. If you're still in doubt, make it **big**."* Ivan Chermayeff (1932-)

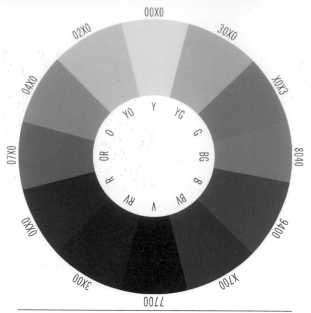

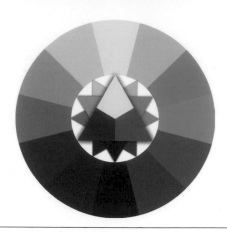

■ **Hues** are colors like orange, yellow, and blue-green.

■ **Primary colors** are equidistant on the color wheel: yellow, blue, and red.

■ **Secondary colors** are mixtures of the primary colors: green, violet, and orange.

■ **Tertiary colors** are between primary and secondary colors: yellow-green, blue-green, blue-violet, red-violet, orange-red, and yellow-orange.

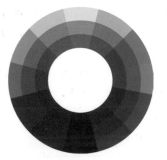

■ **Shades** are made by adding black, which reduces saturation.

■ **Value** is the darkness or lightness of a color: both shades and tints.

■ **Saturation** or **chroma** or **intensity** is the brightness or dullness of a color.

■ **Tints** are made by adding white, which reduces saturation.

■ **Monochromatic color** is a single hue with tints and shades.
Achromatic colors are black, white, and grays, which can be made by mixing complementary colors.

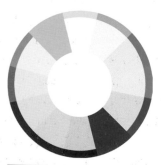

■ **Complementary colors** are opposite each other on the color wheel.

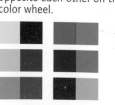

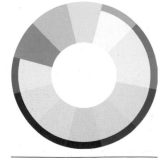

■ **Analogous colors** are next to each other on the color wheel.

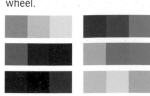

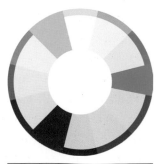

■ **Triadic harmonies** are three colors that are equidistant on the color wheel.

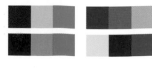

WORDS SYMBOLS
CONSCIOUSNESS
COLOR

Color is part of a communication language. Marshall McLuhan's "hierarchy of communication" puts color at the bottom, functioning in the viewer's subconscious.

Use less color (right) rather than more (left) or your readers will have a colorful mess to decipher – which they probably won't. Color should be used in the same way that type size is used: to emphasize importance, not decorate the page.

Printed color is affected by "ink holdout," the ability of paper to keep ink on the surface. Coated papers have "high ink holdout" which make photos look sharper.

The difference between RGB and CMYK Additive color, as from the sun or a computer monitor, becomes *lighter* as more color is added. The primary colors of the visible spectrum are red, green, and blue-violet (RGB). White is made by adding all three. Combining two primaries produces a secondary: red and blue-violet produce magenta. Green and blue-violet produce cyan. Green and red produce yellow.

Subtractive color, as in printing inks, become *darker* as more color is added. Subtractive colors are cyan (C), magenta (M), yellow (Y), and black (K). Subtractive colors are balanced to make the three additive colors: cyan + yellow = green, etc. Black is made by adding all three.

complex data. □ Color's highlighting benefit is quickly exhausted and devolves into a colorful mess. □ People gravitate to whatever looks different on a page.

■ **Provides direction**, relating parts to each other. Warm colors move elements forward while cool colors move elements back, so a warm tone should be given to display type that is in front of an image to further the spatial illusion.

The three perceptual attributes of color are hue (redness, blueness, greenness), value (shade, darkness/lightness), and saturation (intensity, brightness, chroma). Value and saturation are generally more useful than hue in developing color harmony, which is more valuable than color variety. While hue categorizes information and makes it recognizable, value (darkness) makes it stand out against the background, and saturation (brightness) gives it brilliance or dullness.

Black type on white paper has the most contrast possible. Any color applied to type will make the type weaker (chart labels at right). Counteract this effect by increasing type weight from regular to semibold, and increase type size for optical equivalency.

Everyone perceives light and color differently and with their own subconscious associations. But all readers respond to usefulness of information. Analyze and define what's useful to the reader. Then point out its potential value with color and the six other design components.

Colors have particular associations, according to Swiss psychologist Dr. Max Luescher. These general associations must be tempered by context and application.

	BLUE	DIGNIFIED
	GREEN	PERSISTENT
	RED	ASSERTIVE
	BROWN	PASSIVE
	VIOLET	MEDITATIVE
	BLACK	SURRENDER
	GRAY	BARRIER

A practical guide is to use color's relative temperature to make elements come forward or recede. All colors are relatively warm or cool, depending on what they are next to. **Red and yellow** pop forward, which is why they are used in advertising. **Blue** and **green** recede.

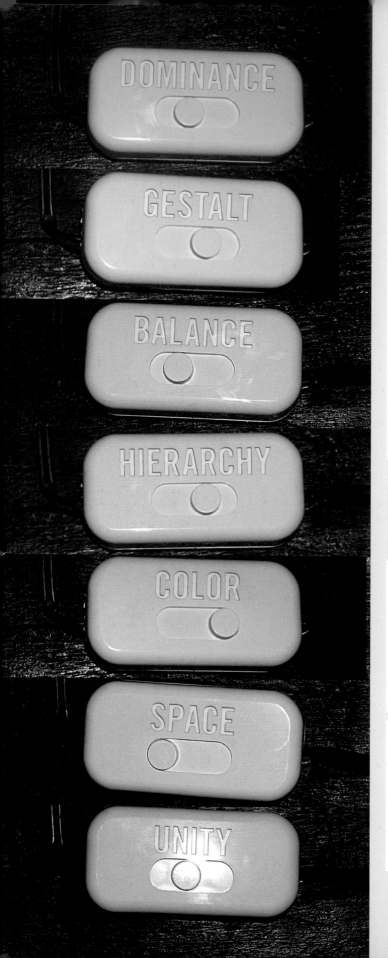

DOMINANCE

GESTALT

BALANCE

HIERARCHY

COLOR

SPACE

UNITY

Raum braucht der Mensch

Space is what man needs

Der Mensch sehnt sich nach Weite und Freiheit. Doch meist ist er eingekeilt: auf der Straße, in den Ferien, bei der Arbeit, in seiner Wohnsituation. Deshalb ist es heute wichtiger denn je, sich auch privaten Freiraum zu schaffen. Ob im Haus mit Garten oder einer geräumigen Eigentumswohnung: Als Hypothekenbank können wir ihnen dabei helfen, sich den Raum zu schaffen, den Sie sich wünschen. München, Telefon: 089/5112-371/287.

Man longs for distance and freedom. But mostly he is wedged in: on the street, on vacation, at work, in his living environment. That is why it is more important than ever today to get some personal space. Whether it is the house or the garden or a spacious condo apartment: as a mortgage bank we can help you create the space you wish for.

SÜDDEUTSCHE BODENCREDITBANK
AKTIENGESELLSCHAFT · HYPOTHEKENBANK

München Berlin Dortmund Dresden Düsseldorf Erfurt Frankfurt/Main Freiburg Hamburg Hannover Leipzig Stuttgart

South German Bodencreditbank

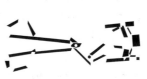

Join elements to make a unified design. At left is a naive drawing of eyes, ears, and mouth on a head. On the right, the head in its entirety is more important than its individual elements.

Three of the seven design components in use here: space (surrounding knife), unity (everything is horizontal and centered), and color (warm wood tone used in headline).

Three of the seven design components in use here: space (surrounding the words), unity (every letter except one is hair parted on a head), and scale (LIVING is de-emphasized).

Three of the seven design components in use here: space (dedicated to subhead and author area), point line plane (OBSESSION is made of dots), and color (entirely monochromatic).

The seven design components – dominance, gestalt, balance, hierarchy, color, space, and unity – are sliding switches, like a lamp's dimmer, that help achieve visible, value-added design.

All parts must fit together. This German bank ad uses space, abstraction, dominance, hierarchy, and color to excellent effect, that is, to illustrate the very concept of the ad.

Simplify by thinking of design elements as shapes. Designers learn how to see abstractly by replacing naturalistic elements with points, lines, and planes.

6 How to use the seven design components

I *define beauty to be a harmony of all the parts … fitted together with such proportion and connection, that nothing could be added, diminished or altered, but for the worse.* – Leon Battista Alberti (1406–1472)

While you choose to have more or less of each of the seven design components, it isn't possible to select just one and not use the others. They come bundled as a semi-flexible group.

Good design necessitates that one element **dominate** the others in the context of a cumulative perception, or **gestalt**. Choosing that emphasis suggests a design's starting point. **Balance** one large or bright element against a few smaller or muted ones.

Function in design is paramount. What is the message? Choose pictures that tell the story. Motivate the reader by arranging the elements in a logical **hierarchy**. Use **color** to show what is important. The top left corner of every page or spread is a valuable starting point because readers look there first. Exploit the reader's natural habits.

The purpose of design is emphatically *not* to fill up

Think of shapes 101
Separate from meaning, every design element has shape.

Design is a process that evolves its solution 101
It takes repeated passes to recognize unresolved relationships in a design.

Diagrams 105
An illustration of relationships, not numbers.

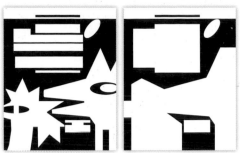

Shapes in the poster on the facing page have been extracted and simplified, then reversed. This shows every combination of figure and ground. The type is structured in

contrast to the imagery. Four of the lines of type in the main block, the poster's secondary type, are justified. The remaining two lines of type – the title of the play and the primary

type on the poster – are visually aligned on the right, but poke out equally on the left. The tertiary lines of type near the bottom are justified, with one line centered.

Intersecting shapes of solids and voids, some of the human head, are used as displays for eyeglass frames, giving them countertop visibility.

This poster for a Brazilian play called "Semi-truth" features a chicken, a dog, and a cockroach. The chicken and dog have been given simplified shapes and filled with leafy texture, adding meaning and making the bright red background come into play as an equal design element, especially in the narrow zigzag space between (or that defines) their mouths.

Four handlettered characters are cut and moved into position, then photographed. This is a process of development that affects the outcome differently than if, say, the letters had been drawn in one continuous stroke.

all the **space**. Don't let overabundance make the information in your design impenetrable. As Steven Ledbetter, music historian and critic, wrote, "Beethoven's control of relative tension and relative relaxation throughout the gigantic architectural span [of the first movement of his Symphony No.3] remains one of the most awe-inspiring accomplishments in the history of music."

Organize elements so all parts fit together to make **unity**, or an integrated whole. Find design unity in the elements' commonalities. Organize elements by their shared subject matter, shape, or color.

Readers operate subconsciously on these design truisms:

- We read from left to right.
- We start at the top and work down the page.
- Pages in a publication or Web site are related.
- Closeness connects while distance separates.
- Big and dark is more important; small and light is less important.
- Fullness should be balanced with emptiness.
- Everything has a shape, *including emptiness*.

Designers have different sensibilities and preferences, which is why five designers given the same pictures and copy would create five different designs. But given a single message to get across, we expect they would develop comparable or equivalent solutions.

"At the definition stage of a project, we are less concerned with what it will look like and more concerned with what it will be."
John Ormsbee Simonds,
Landscape Architecture

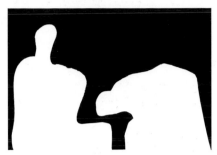

Henry Moore, the English sculptor, said, "The sensitive observer of [design] must feel shape simply as shape, not as a description or idea. He must, for example, perceive an egg as a simple solid shape, quite apart from its significance as food, or from the idea that it will become a bird."

To take apparent ownership of neighboring space, as in a partial page ad, and to make space look bigger than it is, create a buffer zone that uses surrounding white space.

Interrupt a thick white border on each side, co-opting the continuing space beyond your perimeter. This technique is illustrated by artist Summer Jellison in her *Glass Owl*.

Henry Moore's *Reclining Figure No.3 (Two-piece), 1961* is 94 inches long. The abstracted halves are separated by a pronounced intrusive area of emptiness (see above) which changes with the viewer's perspective.

Top row Students learn to see letters as shapes. Each of these studies uses a single letter. *Bottom row* A letterform and textures are combined on a grid. Attention to relating unrelated elements and controlling white space are emphasized.

Think of shapes

Design is, among other things, the arrangement of shapes. Experiment by mentally setting aside the meaning of headlines, copy, visuals, and other elements and treat them as if they were purely form.

Shapes exist in the realm of figure and ground only. Try overlapping and clustering shapes to create visually interesting concentrations. To simplify a design, reduce the total number of shapes by joining two or three at a time.

Letterforms are shapes that can be exploited in display typography and logo design. It is necessary to see the form of letters before complex typographic ideas can be developed (facing page, bottom). Without exploiting letters' individual forms and the shape of the space around and within letterforms, the only option is mere typesetting in groups of letters and words.

White space, within type and around columns and pictures, must be considered as a shape. Push it in chunks, for example, to the perimeter or to the page bottom.

"...A building is not designed by putting together a series of rooms. Any (good) building has an underlying design concept that binds all the parts together into a whole. Without this it is not architecture."
Edmund N. Bacon (1910–2005)

Design is a process that evolves its solution

Uncovering and recognizing design relationships takes time. It's very like the experience of walking into a dark room: it takes time to accustom our eyes to the materials at hand. Design must evolve from basic relationships to more complex, more refined relation-

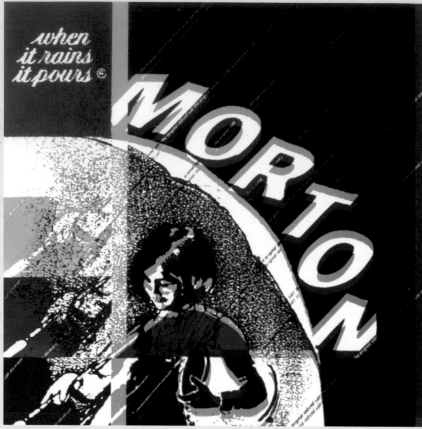

Version 1

When Forgiving Is Hard

Monday, November 25, 2004
Read Psalm 19:7—14

Forgive us our debts, as we forgive our debtors.
— Matthew 6:12 (KJV)

EACH time we say the Lord's prayer, we repeat that request to forgive; but how often are we called upon to really act on that simple plea?

My mother was recently attacked in her home in the middle of the night. Though she was not seriously injured, she was roughed up and robbed. When I heard about what had happened, my immediate reaction was one of rage as I thought of her fear and humiliation. Several days later, however, the thought came to me that as Christians we are charged to forgive those who act against us.

Sometimes praying for our enemies is hard, almost impossible; but the Lord did so and wants us to do the same. Each day, I concentrate on offering up these unknown assailants, praying also that the feelings in my heart will match the words on my lips.

PRAYER: Forgiving God, please grant that the meditations of our heart and the words on our lips will be acceptable in Your sight. In Christ□s name. Amen.

THOUGHT FOR THE DAY
If we do not feel forgiving, we can pray that our feelings will change.

Tuck Eudy (Georgia)

28   PRAYER FOCUS: Those who have wronged us

Version 2

When Forgiving Is Hard

28 ### Monday, November 25, 2004
Read Psalm 19:7—14

Forgive us our debts, as we forgive our debtors.
— Matthew 6:12 (KJV)

EACH time we say the Lord's prayer, we repeat that request to forgive; but how often are we called upon to really act on that simple plea?

My mother was recently attacked in her home in the middle of the night. Though she was not seriously injured, she was roughed up and robbed. When I heard about what had happened, my immediate reaction was one of rage as I thought of her fear and humiliation. Several days later, however, the thought came to me that as Christians we are charged to forgive those who act against us.

Sometimes praying for our enemies is hard, almost impossible; but the Lord did so and wants us to do the same. Each day, I concentrate on offering up these unknown assailants, praying also that the feelings in my heart will match the words on my lips.

PRAYER: Forgiving God, please grant that the meditations of our heart and the words on our lips will be acceptable in Your sight. In Christ□s name. Amen.

THOUGHT FOR THE DAY
If we do not feel forgiving, we can pray that our feelings will change.

Tuck Eudy (Georgia)

PRAYER FOCUS: Those who have wronged us

Version 3

When forgiving is hard

28   Monday, November 25, 2004

Read Psalm 19:7–14

Forgive us our debts, as we forgive our debtors.
– Matthew 6:12 (KJV)

EACH time we say the Lord's prayer, we repeat that request to forgive; but how often are we called upon to really act on that simple plea?

My mother was recently attacked in her home in the middle of the night. Though she was not seriously injured, she was roughed up and robbed. When I heard about what had happened, my immediate reaction was one of rage as I thought of her fear and humiliation. Several days later, however, the thought came to me that as Christians we are charged to forgive those who act against us.

Sometimes praying for our enemies is hard, almost impossible; but the Lord did so and wants us to do the same. Each day, I concentrate on offering up these unknown assailants, praying also that the feelings in my heart will match the words on my lips.

Prayer Forgiving God, please grant that the meditations of our heart and the words on our lips will be acceptable in Your sight. In Christ's name. Amen.

Thought for the day If we do not feel forgiving, we can pray that our feelings will change.

Tuck Eudy *Georgia*

Prayer focus Those who have wronged us

Design solutions must evolve. Solutions grow from familiarity with the materials at hand. As familiarity grows, the process becomes more interesting, design relationships become

evident, and abstraction can be manipulated. This exercise requires identifying elements in a grayscale image on sheets of tracing paper, converting them into geometric variations,

applying texture to the planes, and developing dynamic compositions with the results. The process determines the outcome: elements can't be used that haven't already been identified.

Logos take time and multiple "passes" to resolve. First studies explore a variety of directions, second studies explore one direction deeply, and the final study is completely unrelated.

A step-by-step increase in design contrasts causes new relationships to be developed. This exercise extracts the content from a package, applies it to a grid, and adds arbitrary treatments, like "circularity" and "depth." The final studies are executed in color.

ships (facing page, top). Start the process by becoming intimately familiar with the content. Read every word of the text. Understand *what* is being said. Understand, too, *why* it was written and why it is being published. Then find out *who* is going to read it and what the reader's motivation and interest is. Finally, develop a strategy for expressing it to the reader's greatest advantage.

Design evolution takes time. These five pages show the development of a redesign for *Upper Room* magazine.

❶ Original layout evolved over decades into a flavorless, random presentation.

❷ Align paragraphs on the left.

❸ Add bold, sans serif contrast.

❹ Add column width and type placement contrast; add map.

❺ Change font assignments; adjust line spacing and type sizes; add rules in display type.

When forgiving is hard
28

Monday,
November 25,
2004

Read Psalm 19:7–14

Forgive us our debts, as we forgive our debtors.
— Matthew 6:12 (KJV)

EACH time we say the Lord's prayer, we repeat that request to forgive; but how often are we called upon to really act on that simple plea?

My mother was recently attacked in her home in the middle of the night. Though she was not seriously injured, she was roughed up and robbed. When I heard about what had happened, my immediate reaction was one of rage as I thought of her fear and humiliation. Several days later, however, the thought came to me that as Christians we are charged to forgive those who act against us.

Sometimes praying for our enemies is hard, almost impossible; but the Lord did so and wants us to do the same. Each day, I concentrate on offering up these unknown assailants, praying also that the feelings in my heart will match the words on my lips.

Prayer *Forgiving God, please grant that the meditations of our heart and the words on our lips will be acceptable in Your sight. In Christ's name. Amen.*

Tuck Eudy
Georgia

Thought for the day *If we do not feel forgiving, we can pray that our feelings will change.*

Prayer focus *Those who have wronged us*

When forgiving is hard
28

Monday,
November 25
2004

Read Psalm 19:7–14

Forgive us our debts, as we forgive our debtors.
Matthew 6:12 KJV

Each time we say the Lord's prayer, we repeat that request to forgive; but how often are we called upon to really act on that simple plea?

My mother was recently attacked in her home in the middle of the night. Though she was not seriously injured, she was roughed up and robbed. When I heard about what had happened, my immediate reaction was one of rage as I thought of her fear and humiliation. Several days later, however, the thought came to me that as Christians we are charged to forgive those who act against us.

Sometimes praying for our enemies is hard, almost impossible; but the Lord did so and wants us to do the same. Each day, I concentrate on offering up these unknown assailants, praying also that the feelings in my heart will match the words on my lips.

Prayer *Forgiving God, please grant that the meditations of our heart and the words on our lips will be acceptable in Your sight. In Christ's name. Amen.*

Tuck Eudy
Georgia

Thought for the day *If we do not feel forgiving, we can pray that our feelings will change.*

Prayer focus *Those who have wronged us*

❹

❺

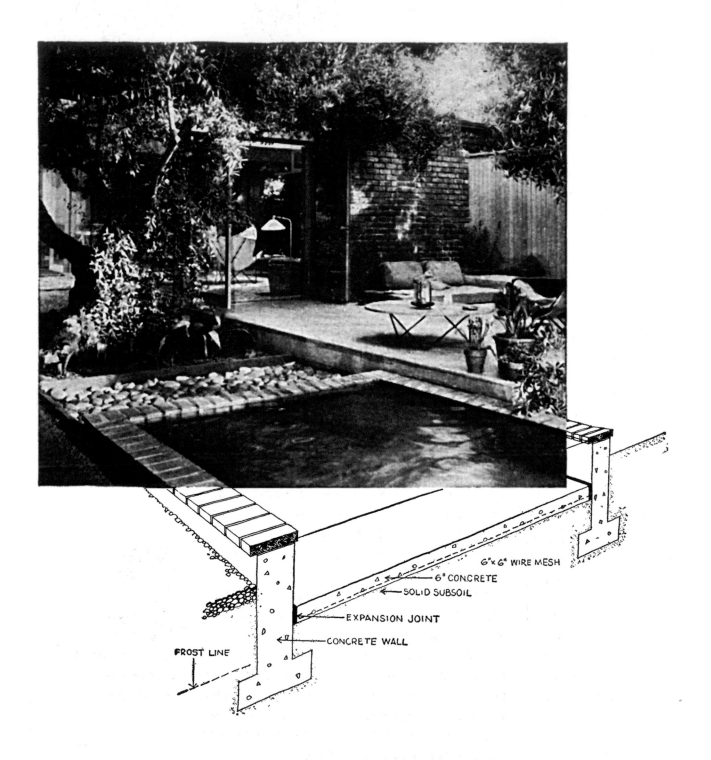

6"x 6" WIRE MESH

6" CONCRETE

SOLID SUBSOIL

EXPANSION JOINT

CONCRETE WALL

FROST LINE

Design requires horizontal thinking – trying various different ideas, as well as vertical thinking – selecting one idea and digging deeper. The crucial move is the removal of the "e,"

which makes the name memorable, and the adjustment of the "r" to align with the crossbar of the "B." At bottom right is the final mark by Danish designer Mads Burcharth.

A diagram may be a pictorial representation of information, maps, line graphs, bar charts, engineering blueprints, and architectural sketches, as shown here.

There are so many ways of making diagrams, it is impossible to show in a single image. But this one, an "extension drawing" from a 1958 architectural magazine makes the point clearly: it shows both the "what" and the "how," so each is faster to analyze and easier to understand than if the source photo and the illustration were side by side.

Design evolution should proceed on two levels simultaneously. One is to seek relationships of meaning, which appeals to the reader's need for understanding. The other is to seek relationships of form, which appeals to the reader's need for attraction. Balancing these two ensures effective visual communication.

Design is spoiled more often by the designer being overly cautious rather than being overly bold. Dare to be bold.

Four spreads diagram the human body in this Brazilian feature story. A diagram may be a pie chart, a function graph, an exploded view, map, or shapes connected by lines or arrows.

Diagrams

A diagram is a simplified, schematic drawing that describes the workings of the subject. This can be a chart, a plan, or a map. "Diagram," like "illustration," is a general term that can mean a broad range of executions. A diagram is different than an illustration because it must describe meaning. A diagram may be a chart, yet it is different than a chart because it describes qualitative matter, that is, relationships, while a chart exclusively describes quantitative, or numerical, matter.

A diagram uses all seven design components *just as any design does*. A diagram, however, uses them on a finite, micro level. A Web site or publication uses the seven design components on a broad, macro level. But the components remain the same and interact the same, regardless of application or platform.

This spread from a German book on biological comparisons uses numbers, illustrations, maps and many brief captions to tell its story. This book is, in essence, one continuous diagram.

"Design is about making order out of chaos."
Cipe Pineles (1908–1991)

"Next to architecture, (type) gives the most characteristic portrait of a period and the most severe testimony of a nation's intellectual status."

Peter Behrens (1868–1940)

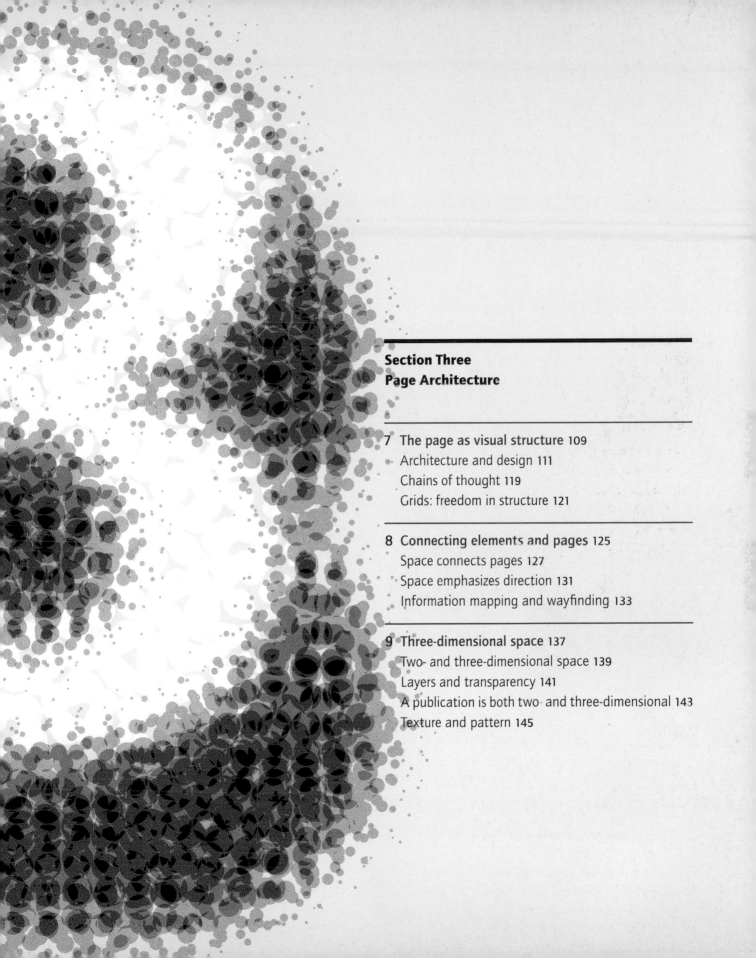

Section Three
Page Architecture

KOLIN

中國的月亮不很圓……

傳動生活文化的歌林

ZEITSCHRIFT FÜR KULTUR
WIRTSCHAFT UND LITERATUR

PREIS 1 MARK

DAS NEUE RUSSLAND

DOPPELHEFT 8/9
BERLIN
NOVEMBER 1931

Kepes

Purple Robe and Anemones, painted in 1937, shows Henri Matisse's comprehensive use of space: not much is left empty, creating a rich viewing experience.

Invisible substructure, like a chicken's skeleton, defines where the visible pieces go. Design uses a grid that dictates where visible elements will go.

Calligraphy and architecture use *active* positive and negative space. Shown are a sample of 1575 Turkish calligraphy

and a Mexican resort hotel. Both purposefully balance occupied and unoccupied space to create artistic tension.

Architecture and design share visual structure. At top left, symmetry is shown in Eliel and Eero Saarinen's 1941 Berkshire Opera Shed and, at top right, a Chinese newspaper ad echoes some of the same shapes. At far left, asymmetry in Jaipur's Samrat Yantra, an eighteenth-century astronomical observation structure, and, near left, in a 1931 magazine cover by Gyorgy Kepes.

The page as visual structure

The whole arrangement of my picture is expressive. The place occupied by the figures or objects, the empty spaces around them, the proportions, everything plays a part. – Henri Matisse (1869-1954), *Notes d'un peintre*

A chicken's skeleton. Stud and beam construction. The design grid. Each of these is an unseen substructure on which visible, external parts are draped and attached. The chicken's skeleton is covered, for example, by muscles, skin, and feathers. The modern house has wallboard, flooring, and shingles. A design has words and pictures. In each case, the substructure determines the placement of the visible elements. A designer's substructure is called a grid, and it is the "bones" of a design.

Harry Sternberg, American painter, printmaker, and educator, wrote, "In architecture the structural beams support the walls, floors, piping, and wiring, as well as the facade of the building. In any graphic work ... composition is the basic structure which supports all the other elements involved."

Architecture and design 111
Architects use substructure to sculpt solids and voids in three dimensions at human scale.

Chains of thought 119
Sequential perception, like links in a chain, builds a visual message one impression at a time.

Grids: freedom in structure 121
Defining space before putting elements into it causes the elements to relate in a particular way and ensures some space is left open.

Everything has an end.

Except a wurst. O, for draught of vintage! That hath been cool'd a long age in the deep-delved earth, tasting of flora and the country green, dance and Provencal song, and so sunburnt mirth! O for the warm, warm South. **That has two.**

G U S T A V   M A H L E R

**Everything has an end,
except a wurst.**

O, for draught of vintage! That hath been cool'd a long age in the deep-delved earth, tasting of flora and the country mirth! O for a beaker full of the warm, blushful South. O, for draught of vintage! That hath been cool'd a long age in the deep-dance and Provencal song, and so sunburnt beak full of the warm, country green to taste of flora and the country green, dance andsing the Provencal song, and so sunburnt mirth for a bucket full of the warm, blushful draught of vintage that hath been cool'd a long age in the deep-delved earth, tasting of flora and the country green, so sunburnt mirth! O for a beaker full of the warm, warm South.

That has two.

Everything has an end except a wurst

That has two

O, for draught of vintage! That hath been cool'd a long age in the deep-delved earth, tasting of flora and the country green, dance and Provencal song, and so sunburnt mirth! O for a beaker full of the warm, blushful south. GUSTAV MAHLER

ABSOLUT BROOKLYN.

Rayonnant architecture ("radiant," in reference to the circular stained glass windows that radiate from a central point), in which illuminated, weightless

interior space became more valued than the walls of the building itself, was developed in France in 1231. This is La Sainte-Chapelle in Paris.

Architectural voids are handsomely lampooned in this ad for Absolut vodka. The real

Brooklyn bridge is on the right, showing the actual arches in its towers.

Castles (facing page, top) illustrate layout complexity (facing page, bottom):

SIMPLE		
Primitive castle	=	Elementary page architecture

STANDARD		
Regular castle	=	Intermediate page architecture

COMPLEX		
Elaborate castle	=	Intricate page architecture

Layout complexity is determined by the number of design relationships it contains. *Too many* relationships – a design which is said to be "busy" – can equal *no* relationships.

Architecture and design

A completely new way of realizing large-scale architecture occurred in the mid-thirteenth century. Construction of the church of St.-Denis, near Paris, had stopped about eighty years earlier when the abbot who began the building died. When the church's new design was proposed in 1231, it was the first instance of Rayonnant ("radiant") architecture, in which radiating patterns of cut-glass windows, of which there were many, flooded the building with light. It was a decision to have *empty space within the cathedral* be more important than the stone walls that surrounded the space.

There has always been a similarity between architecture and design in thinking style and problem-solving approach. Hassan Massoudy said in his book *Calligraphy*, "An architectural design defines a living space; the space between the walls is as real and as significant as the walls themselves. In [graphic design] the value of a space derives from its relationship with the [elements] that surround it and vice versa." Sean Morrison, in *A Guide to Type Design*, says, "Type designers are closer to architects than to artists. The architect must produce a building that is structurally sound and efficient but that is also visually pleasing and comfortable to live and work in." Surely, a designer's work must conform to these same requirements to be useful.

"Architecture is the beautiful and serious game of space."
Willem Dudok
(1884–1974), architect

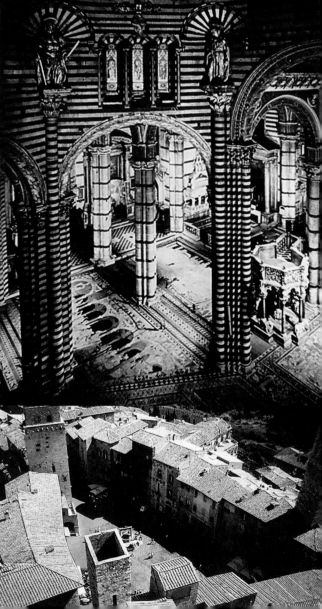

Exterior protection is built at the very same time as interior space is created in this Inuit snow shelter.

Design volume is created when elements are joined into a figure, as in this car and quotation marks. Space is relegated to the background, though it has been carefully cropped.

Design volume is emphasized in this Web site. Figures are placed on top of figures with the only emptiness being the area reserved for the page's title.

A central design void is used as a staging area in Visual Acoustics, a Flash-based program that "paints" sound. Settings are in a dedicated perimeter frame.

"Architectural space can be fluid or static; additive or divisive; positive or negative; colorful or monochromatic."
- Kohei Ishikawa. Solid space, or volume, is shown in two buildings (facing page, top), and architectural emptiness, or voids (facing page, near left).

*Cesar Pelli, architect of City Centre (facing page, bottom left), says, "The space between the buildings is the most important part of this design. These are the only skyscrapers that emphasize negative space. It is a portal to the sky, to the clouds, to God."

Architectural volumes are created as either solid (space displaced by mass), or void (space contained or enclosed by planes). Solid volumes are buildings: St. Mawes Castle, England and Seafair, a Newport, Rhode Island, mansion. Voids are spaces defined by solids: the space between the towers of the world's tallest buildings, the Kuala Lumpur City Centre, Malaysia*; the interior of Il Duomo, Siena; and the Piazza Cisterna, San Gimignano, Italy (all on the facing page).

A building's purpose and size are the architect's first considerations. Similarly, determining a document's purpose and its page size are the first decisions a designer must make. The page's size and its shape create reader expectations: a square or horizontal page immediately signals an unusual document. A standard $8\frac{1}{2}$" x11" vertical page (or European A4) must overcome its size and shape to be recognized as remarkable. The designer must also weigh technical issues: economies of printing (a really great two-color job is far better than an inferior four-color job) and paper buying (trimming excess paper to get an unusual shape costs money), binding, standard envelope sizes, size requirements imposed by the post office, postage, and certainly what size fits best on the computer screen at full-size and full-screen view.

According to architect Kohei Ishikawa, "The placement of windows and doors defines the function of

"Architecture in general is frozen music."
Friedrich von Schelling (1775-1854), *Philosophie der Kunst*

Solid and void meet at Petra (Greek for "rock"), a rock-cut city in the cliffs in Jordan. Constructed in 100 BC by the Nabataeans, it has been named a World Heritage Site. Entrance

is made through the Siq (left), a narrow slit in the cliff walls. The Khazneh (right) is the first of several rock-cut buildings in the city and, at forty meters high, the most impressive.

Findability in design, as in architecture, is a matter of putting similar elements in precisely consistent places, like these parking numbers in a garage, which still allows for color variation.

Box structure is a useful attribute of a Web site, forcing consistencies in size, color, and position. This puts users' awareness on the parts that change, in this case, the products.

Rembrandt's *David and Saul* (c1658) shows a viewing progression from King Saul, occupying the entire left half of the canvas, to David, whose hands pluck the strings of a harp. The central darkness forces us to perceive these two parts sequentially, then mentally unite them in a complete image.

The Church of St George in Lalibela, northern Ethiopia, is a monolithic structure, carved as a single form from the solid volcanic rock in this hillside. This is one of thirteen neighboring "rock cut" churches, all built in the 12th and 13th centuries. Entrance is through a ramped tunnel, the dark rectangle to the left of the church in this aerial photo. Every feature is carved from the original stone, including the highly decorated interior columns.

rooms." The page size and the layout signal the type of document the reader is holding. What makes a bound document a book versus a magazine? What distinguishes a newsletter from a newspaper? What makes a single-sheet document a poster rather than a flyer? Such distinctions are trivial if the content is routed into the reader's mind effortlessly and memorably.

Repeated design elements must be findable – placed in consistent, expected places – just as architectural details, like light switches, are always placed at the same height from the floor, where they can be found in a darkened room. Create typographic "styles," that is, set type standards, to organize areas of white space between type elements. Visual consistency depends on typographic style, adhering to a grid and column structure, and margins.

Taking a large room and breaking it into small cubicles is one way of breaking up space. Using boxes to organize graphic space is common. Boxing can separate one part of a story from the rest to make it appear either more valuable, less valuable, or just different. Boxing can break the page into different shades of gray by putting separate stories in different boxes. And boxing can be a crutch for the designer, who doesn't have to place multi-level stories next to each other, but instead nice, well-behaved, hard-edged boxes side by side. The cost

"A good solution, in addition to being right, should have the potential for longevity. Yet I don't think one can design for permanence. One designs for function, for usefulness, rightness, beauty. Permanence is up to God."
Paul Rand (1914–1996), designer and typographer

HERBA
RVM
VIVAE EICONES
ad naturę imitationem, suma cum
diligentia et artificio effigiatę,
unà cum EFFE=
CTIBVS earundem, in gratiam ue=
teris illius, & iamiam renascentis
Herbariæ Medicinæ,
PER OTH. BRVNF.
recens editæ. M. D. XXX.

¶ Quibus adiecta ad calcem,
APPENDIX isagogica de usu & ad=
ministratione SIMPLICIVM.
Item Index Contentorũ singulorum.

Argentorati apud Ioannem Schottũ, cum
Cæf. Maieſt. Priuilegio ad Sexennium.

The page on the left is static, caused in large measure by the overuse of boxes which separate elements at the expense of overall unity. The page on the right, with all the same elements, is more vibrant because space is allowed to infiltrate and interact with the type and imagery.

Boxes can be dynamic – even as they organize space – if they are asymmetrical to help emphasize importances. Use consistent interspaces and type sizes to confirm the hierarchy.

Each line of type is embedded into an interlocking lattice, contrasting the dynamic figure with structure. The lattice also creates static foreground, past which the dancer is flying.

Boxes organize the title page of Otto Brunfels' (c1488-1534) *Herbarum vivae eicones*, or "Living Plant Images." This three-volume series featured descriptions and woodcut illustrations of local plants drawn from life – a new technique – by Hans Weiditz (above). Brunfels wrote books on various subjects, but his renown is based on his willingness to observe and describe what he actually saw, an early scientific method.

of relying on boxes to separate different stories or parts of stories is injury to the page as a totality. Boxitis is especially easy to succumb to in software, where boxes are so easy to make. It is better to use judicious white space to separate – or connect – stories. The essence of a box is creating difference and separation, which is anti-design unity. The risk is that separation, while delineating honest differences in content, will rip the overall design into competing areas of attention. Barriers of whiteness act exactly the same way as barriers of blackness, but without adding visual busyness and clutter.

If boxes must be used, try to break a worthy part of an image out of a box, or delete one or two of the box's sides and set the type flush left to imply a vertical left edge (above left).

James T. Maher, author and arts critic, wrote, "Part of the intuitive gift of any first-rate artist is the continuous process of editing, of cutting, of revealing." Design, like architecture, painting, and music, hinges on knowing what to leave out. Maher continues, "In the early 1900s, a group of British experts visited Japan to study its culture. Part of the group called upon some Japanese painters. 'What is the most difficult part of painting?' they asked the artists. 'Deciding what to leave out,' they were told ... The end product is simplicity – that which is left when the non-essential has been discarded."

"Visuals/verbals are a mosaic synthesizing words and shapes whose combination leads to interpretation and understanding."
Steven McCaffery (1947–), visual and performance poet

Avian flu, hurricane, chemical spill, terrorist bomb, earthquake:
Whatever the next apocalypse is, New York—and New Yorkers—are getting ready for it.
But have we done enough? The strategies and tactics of survival.

REMAIN CALM

By Craig Horowitz

ON AN EARLY-WINTER MONDAY MORNING *in Hong Kong, a businessman boards a plane for New York. The man, who'd spent a few days touring the Chinese countryside during his trip, is not feeling great. He's tired and achy. He can't decide if it's the wear and tear of his travels or the beginning of a cold, but after coughing and sneezing throughout his sixteen-hour flight, he's certain he's getting sick.*

By the time he goes through Customs at JFK, gets his bags, and finds a cab, he has only enough energy left to check into his midtown hotel and collapse on the bed in his room. The next day, feeling even sicker, he heads to the nearest emergency room. By now, he's got a high fever and he's coughing up blood. Given his robust flulike symptoms and his international travel, alarm bells go off in the ER.

Though word hasn't yet reached the U.S., there have been several dozen confirmed cases of human-to-human transmission of the H5N1 virus—better known as avian flu—in the Chinese countryside and several other spots in Asia. But even without the new information, the ER doctors, who've been drilled on what to watch for, are convinced it's avian flu. Taking no chances, they isolate the patient. But the damage has been done—the businessman has infected people on the plane, at JFK, in his hotel, and even in the hospital's waiting room.

The city's ability to deal with the pandemic is severely hampered by three problems. There is no vaccine and won't be for months. Tamiflu,

---

Uncaptive Minds

What teaching a college-level class at a maximum-security correctional facility did for the inmates — and for me. By Ian Buruma

Illustration by Istvan Banyai

The main business of Napanoch, N.Y., is a maximum-security prison, Eastern New York Correctional Facility, also known as Happy Nap. The population of Eastern, 1,250 men, many from New York City, is about the same as that of Napanoch itself. Imposing in a hideous kind of way, the prison, built at the end of the 19th century, is modeled after a medieval fortress, with towers and turrets and a pyramid roof. The overall effect — stony pomposity framed by lush green hills — is rather Germanic.

There is nothing particularly happy about Napanoch, situated on the raffish edges of the Catskills about 70 miles north of Manhattan; its better days as an affordable resort area for New York and New Jersey Jews have long gone. There are a few motels nearby with cracked signs that read Starlite and Eldorado; a diner; a Jewish cemetery; and a "colony farm," where

38

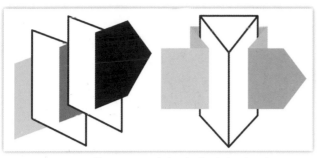   

Arrows represent a linear thought process. A message (an arrow) can pick up speed and value as it gets loaded with its descriptors (left) or the message can get bogged down by the load that has been placed on it (right). It is the designer's job to choose material and present it so the message becomes more apparent, not more disguised.

A clockwise spiral reading from the upper right is used to arrange the 45 still-undeciphered marks on the 6" Phaistos Disk, c1600BC. Why a spiral – or did the disk's roundness cause the spiral?

The sequence of absorption is a chain of thought. The sixteen letters and sixteen images on this spread ad forces a back-and-forth exploration of the models' changing hair styles.

Sequencing information should logically and clearly lead from the primary visual to the headline, then to the secondary visual, caption, subhead, and finally to the text. Each of these pieces should be chosen or written as one part of a single continuous message the purpose of which is to reveal to the reader what the article is about and *why it is valuable to them.*

Chains of thought

A message is revealed one link at a time: a headline, a first visual, a second visual, a caption, a subhead, then maybe the text. Each of these "hits" is like a link in a chain. No link is itself the chain: the combination of links makes the chain.

A design's plan must include the order in which the parts – the display type, the images, the captions, and the text – are to be noticed and read. Absent this sequencing, a reader is faced with a "bowl of oatmeal," an area of relatively equivalent noisiness, none of which is sufficiently appetizing to stop and nibble.

Sequencing information is among a designer's most essential tasks. Book designers, for example, structure their typography into title, chapter and section headings, subheadings, text, and captions. Such typographic structure helps the reader scan for generalities and, at least initially, ignore details until they commit themselves to the text.

For every design project, write on small Post-it Notes each of the ideas you want a reader to recognize. Now put the notes in order of descending importance. Readers should have thoughts presented to them like links in a chain – or beads on a string. Albrecht von Haller, eighteenth-century anatomist and poet, said, "Man can only follow chains [of thought], as we cannot present several things at once in our speech."

*"I don't explain,
I don't tell,
I show."*
Leo Tolstoy
(1828-1910), author

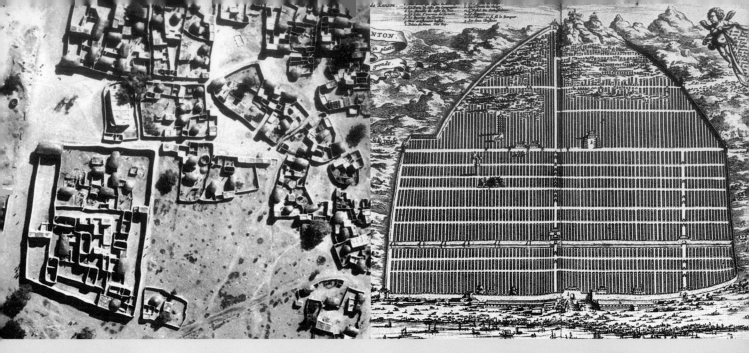

Smettila subito!

Non sono un melone che puoi tastare

Tastare puoi che e melone
subito sono un questar
che puoi melone sono un tastare che
sono non puoi che melone age.

Il Santo

NON SONO
UN MELONE
CHE PUOI
TASTARE

Tastare puoi che e melo
subito sono un n questar
che puoi melone sono u
sono non puoi che melo
che puoi melone queono.

Smettila subito!

Il Santo

A Korean proverb says, "Only clean upstreams make clean downstreams." By beginning with an external format, the grid helps make "clean downstreams," that is, clear design relationships and clean, understandable pages. Every element aligns with the grid structure, ensuring formal agreements. Note the three levels of typographic hierarchy: primary, secondary, and tertiary. This is the clearest, most useful differentiation possible, and readers *like* it.

A seven-column grid is used to bring order to a variety of pieces on this Web site. Items may be any combination of whole units. Shown here are one-, two-, three-, and six-column elements.

Two communities contrast structure and freedom in their planning. Logone-Birni, Cameroon (left top), is a village with many organically shaped spaces. The c1665 city plan of Canton, China, shows blocklike planning.

Organic design versus use of an external format (left bottom). One example shows type effected by the illustration: the arrow smashes the type. The other example shows both type and illustration affected by the underlying grid, which causes the background to come forward as a full design participant. The contrast in *design process* yields different design results, though neither is necessarily "better."

Grids: freedom in structure

Unlimited design choice is both a blessing and a curse. Time is wasted investigating dead ends and aimlessly playing with design elements. It is often better to make design decisions chosen from a limited palette. There is beauty in simplicity.

Content has its own inherent structure. It comes built in, but it takes sensitivity to uncover the interconnectedness between parts. This is called "organic design." There are occasions, though, when it is better to fit elements into an external format. Grids save time and they organize complex information like charts and schedules, scientific data, lists, and repetitive elements like headlines, pictures, and text.

Consistency and creativity are inspired by limiting choices. Freedom grows directly from structure. Though using a grid limits choices, it gives a design built-in cohesiveness. The limitations a grid imposes are chosen as the grid is developed, based on set priorities. Are images most important? How many levels of type are there?

Grid development must provide a variety of predetermined sizes that artwork and type will be made to fit. The smallest photos and illustrations define a module and that module is repeated in a multicolumn structure. The page is divided horizontally into equal clusters of text line units.

"The creative act does not create something out of nothing. It uncovers, selects, reshuffles, combines, synthesizes already existing facts, ideas, faculties, skills. Typically, the more familiar the parts, the more striking the new whole."
Arthur Koestler, CBE (1905–1983), writer

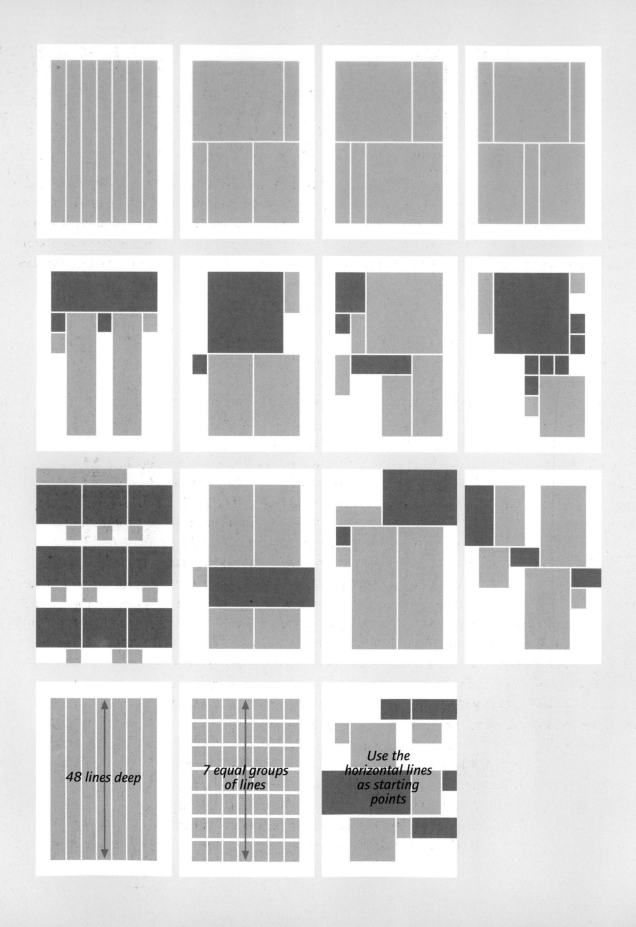

48 lines deep

7 equal groups
of lines

Use the
horizontal lines
as starting
points

A piece of parchment (stretched and dried sheepskin) is prepared for writing by having a grid lightly drawn on it in this detail of a 1255 German illuminated letter.

Piet Mondrian expressed de Stijl principles in his 1942 *Composition with Red, Yellow and Blue* using gridded space, asymmetrical composition, and primary colors.

A grid is used in this spread from an annual report. The white box mortised into the image is the most different thing on the page. Though small, its caption is the focal point.

When elements have been fitted into an environment of sameness, whether on a grid or otherwise, a focal point becomes visible.

A seven-column grid structures space with flexibility. It imposes white space because the narrow columns must be combined to accommodate type, leaving at least one narrow column empty. Shown diagramatically, these column variations are not intended as layouts.

How to create a horizontal grid. Divide the maximum number of a page's text lines into equal groups, allowing a line between each group. For example, if there are forty-eight lines on a page, there can be seven units of six lines each with one line added between units ($7 \times 6 + 6 = 48$).

A simpler grid is usually better than a complex grid. A grid's complexity should help the designer answer the questions, "How big should this element be and where should I put it?" A seven-column grid is universally functional and great fun to use because it contains many options (facing page, top three rows). But beware: overly complex grids offer so many options they become all but useless because they no longer limit choices. Readers can't recognize organization when the grid units are too small.

Structured design has a visible cadence and tension that leads from one element to the next in an orderly way. But if structure is followed without thoughtful manipulation, it produces repetitive sameness and boredom. Grid development must include a description of how and when the structure (or "normal" placement) will be violated. The rules of violation focus creativity and make grid-based design look fresh. The most important rule of violation is to have an element break the grid when it deserves to stand out. In a context of sameness, that lone element becomes very visible (above right).

In addition to organizing complex information on a particular page or spread, grids unite the cover and interior pages and relate one issue to the next. Grids also organize an entire company's visual requirements. They build family resemblance among on-screen applications, brochures, data sheets, and advertising.

"Simplicity of form is never a poverty, it is a great virtue."
Jan Tschichold (1902–1974), typographer and designer

To which photo does this caption belong? This lack of organization is poor craftsmanship.

Arbitrary or uneven spacing makes the reader guess about relationships that should be clear

Centered captions are less clearly attached to their photos than flush left captions

Spacing between captions and photos is not equal in this example

Flush left captions align with their respective photos.

Captions may run as deep as necessary because they have enough relating attributes.

Equalize spacing between photos and captions.

Captions should never run the same width as their photos. It is too obvious a relationship!

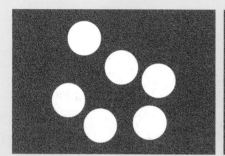

An ideal six-point space bonds this caption to its image. A narrower separation makes the caption look like it is crowding the image. Wider distances make captions look unconnected.

A wide twelve-point space is as large the separation between an image and a caption ought to be. Any wider and the distance destroys the caption-image relationship.

A too-narrow three-point space separates but makes the caption look like it is crowding the image.

The space between elements acts as mortar (which is a mixture of lime with cement, sand, and water, used to fill the gaps between stones and bricks and bind them together): craftsmanship in bricklaying is determined by the quality of the mortaring. Similarly, designer's craft is measured by our handling of space that binds design elements together.

Space connects when it is proportionally less than the surrounding space, that is, when it is handled like mortar between bricks, as in this poster for a United Nations conference.

Space connects elements two ways in this poster: the interior spaces, or counterforms, in the letters are emphasized, and three letters in "BENIDORM" are dropped down one line.

Look carefully until you see that the colors and mixed baselines are intentionally misleading. The only thing that matters here is letter-to-letter proximity: the top line reads "Jazz in Willisau."

The sets of six dots (left) are identical: our *perception* of them changes because of the altered spaces between them.

Captions are more or less connected by the distance that separates them from their attendant artwork. A half pica is an ideal default distance: not too near to look like it is crowding and not too far to look like it is unconnected.

8 Connecting elements and pages

Space is never complete and finite. It is in motion, connected to the next space and the next. – Marcel Breuer (1902-1981)

The mason's craft is defined by applying mortar evenly between stones or bricks (opposite, top). Masons don't make the bricks; rather, *they manage the space between the bricks*. The typographer's craft is similarly defined by applying space between letters, words, and areas of type. White space can be used like mortar between bricks to cement elements together. White space connects when used in consistent, measured amounts in a design. As an abstract illustration, a group of six dots can be made to mean something by changing only the *space* between the dots (opposite, second row).

Wide spaces separate and narrow spaces connect. That is, elements can be separated by distance or related by nearness. The closer elements are, the more related they seem to be. The first set of black rectangles at left are seen as a group of three plus one. Overlapping elements shows maximum relationship. The four rectangles are now seen as a single multi-sided shape.

It is easy to make copy look crowded inside a box, which is why we see this ugly effect so often. As with every other design relationship, *proportion* is vital. The appearance of sufficient space between box and text is dependent on the type size and linespacing used in the copy. In this example, the linespacing is greater than the spacing between the type and the box. This emphasizes the relationship between type and box rather than the correct relationship of type to itself.

For greatest legibility, the relationship of type to itself must be emphasized over the relationship of type to its surrounding box. Note that the linespacing used in this paragraph is less than or perhaps equal to the space separating the type from the box. White space is used as a connector of type to itself and as a separator of type from its surroundings.

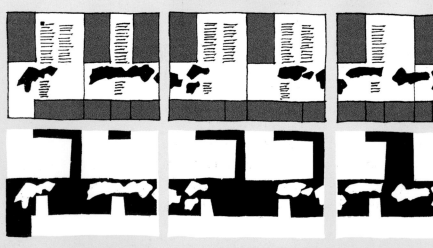

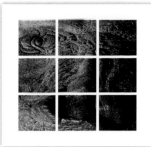

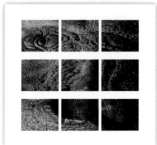

Using space to emphasize direction Equal spacing creates directional gridlock because neither direction dominates. Each of the nine rectangles appears equally near to one another.

Wider horizontal spaces create rows because the thicker horizontal spaces dominate and separate, while the narrower spaces connect through *proximity*, or relative nearness.

Wider vertical spaces create columns because the vertical spaces dominate and separate. Vertical columns appear as the result of relative nearness.

Space separates groups of elements in this Swedish magazine's department page, despite the excitement (or visual cacophony) of type weights and colors.

Visual flow is shown in this handsome four-spread story from *Audubon* magazine.

There is a risk to defining areas by using boxes. While boxes effectively enclose space, they tend to *over*separate, harming the unity of the page. Instead of boxes, use wider alleys between elements (above). Space that is carefully measured reveals intentional separation of content, and intentionality is one key to great design.

Rather than using boxes, the addition of a rule, or line, near the beginning of an item is sufficient to make it stand out. If boxes absolutely must be used, leave between six and twelve points of space between the text and the box. Placing a box too close to text creates a tension and reading discomfort that looks like crowding and makes reading unappealing.

"Rhythm is in time what symmetry is in space."
Matila Ghyka (1881–1965), *The Geometry of Art and Life*

Space connects pages

A multiple-page document, whether a magazine story or a technical user manual, is made of many individual pieces. They must be unified into a clear, ordered statement that looks deliberate and purposefully presented. They must catch and hold the reader's attention.

Repetition and rhythm are shown in these six-page diagrams in which white space is as consistently formed as any other element. Careful determination of the materials at hand develops such a pattern.

White space connects pages when the spaces remain the same. In magazine design, repetition and rhythm of spaces and elements help the reader recognize flow from spread to spread and from issue to issue. Repeated department pages, which define the visual personality of a magazine, should be unified by distinctive head and outer

①

Voltaire
Common sense
is not so common

②

Voltaire
Common sense
is not so common

③

**Vol-
taire**
Common sense
is not so common

④

Voltaire
Common sense
is not so common

All applications for admissions must begin at the undergraduate level with the Office of Admissions and Records. This includes both new freshman students as well as
transfer students.

At the undergraduate level, the School of Art recog-
nizes that competence in the visual arts as well as intellectual capacity are necessary qualities in students who plan
to prepare for a career in one of the art fields. Therefore, the
right is reserved to require evidence of achievement in art
and related areas from all students endeavoring to enroll
for the first time as majors in the School of Art. Early admission is recommended. Students meeting the general requirements for transfer admission must submit a portfolio for
review by a faculty committee. Students who have transfer
credits in art must complete a minimum number of hours in
residence. The Director of the School of Art may impose
additional requirements considered reasonable and
necessary. Transfer credits are evaluated consistent with the
University policy, although each student will be evaluated
individually in terms of his or her ability to perform within the
program. A transfer applicant's strengths and deficiencies
will be considered and his or her transfer credits will reflect
that consideration.

Each new freshman and transfer student must complete or have the equivalent of a core program common to
all art majors. This program includes beginning design,
color, drawing, painting and three dimensional work. In
addition to this common curriculum in studio work, students
may elect to take the required Art History sequence and are
expected to take academic courses as well. Additional
information regarding specific requirements of the various
majors and degree programs is available in divisional
catalogs which may be obtained by writing directly to the

Introduction The School of Art at KC ranks in the midwest. It
consists of almost 1,300 undergraduate fully accredited by the
National Association of Schools of separate buildings, two of
which are on the central campus, the School is the sole
occupant of three and showcase of this section is to briefly
discuss the organization, adisc School of Art. Further sections
of this catalog will more fully cover the major. Any questions
concerning issues not fully cover of Art, Kent State University,
Kent, OH 44242.

The School is organized with rels. These divisions include:
1) art education, 2) art history, 3) crafts constitutes complete
majors in enameling, glass, ceram design, industrial design,
and the area of illustration. It shou lca combined Design and
Crafts undergraduate major. The Drawing, and cinematog-
raphy. Each Division has an elected Cox, the School has an
Assistant Director, Graduate Coordinatorrogram. All these
positions occupant of three and shares the fourth with two

jest, most comprehensive academic units in the midwest. It
consists a degree candidates. It is fully accredited by the
National School is located in four separate buildings.

Each Division has an electoralogs, the School is the sole
occupant ofrtments. The purpose of this section is to briefly
discuss the requirements in the School of Art. Further sections
of this catalog details relating to the major. Any questions
concernings the Director, School of Art, Kent State University,
and the area of illustration. It should combined Design and
area of illustration.3 graduate levels. These divisions include:
catalog writeue. The Division of Crafts constitutes complete
majors in enesign includes graphic design, industrial design,
and the area.dents to complete a combiner.

Crafts undercludes printing, drawing, and cinematog-
raphy. Eacministrative capacity. Further, the School has an
Assistant Detoss of the Blossom-Kent Art Program. All these
positions capacity.

Space as a directional force (L-R): ❶ Space exerts pressure from below, emphasizing verticality; ❷ type aligned at the right edge of the page creates horizontal direction; ❸ white space in the foreground indicates diagonal direction; and ❹ traditional optically centered position (just above geometric center) of the page produces perfect equilibrium.

Space connects pages, as in this spread from a sports marketing brochure. The red background of the right hand page is interpreted and applied as smaller red boxes on the left hand page. Note, too, the consistent pattern of black intro copy and white text, which adds to the spread's unity.

Space connects spreads, particularly in magazine feature stories which require distinctive layout to break the format of regularly occurring department pages.

The grid-determined empty areas of this layout help emphasize a strong horizontality through the story.

Use space in thick slabs to direct eyeflow. Big elements (above), like big animals (below), need big space.

margin sinkage so their recurrence creates a familiar and identifiable pattern. A feature story, which by definition is special material, must *appear* to be special throughout its length, including "continued on" pages. Its design, therefore, cannot be the same as either departments or other feature stories. Inventing a different formula for handling space is one way to unify pages in a feature story.

Elements and surrounding spaces must be identically placed. Create a pattern of occupied and unoccupied spaces by distilling commonalities among the materials at hand. To ensure unity, design pages in spreads or, even better, as complete stories, as they will be viewed and perceived by the reader. Make their repetition and rhythm unavoidable.

Repetition is not dull. Variety for its own sake, on the other hand, disintegrates unity. The most visible elements to treat consistently are borders and white space, typefaces, illustration and photo sizes and styles, the logo, and color.

"One reads from the top left to the bottom right and must design accordingly." Walter Dexel (1890–1973), designer and typographer

JACKSON POLLOCK

THE NEW FACE OF TRADE UNIONISM

A COLD CALL *from* MIGHTY MOUSE

In 1974, Ron Alghini was transferred from New York to manage a small Jefferies branch in Chicago. That same year, Frank Baxter was hired as an institutional salesman. The plan was to train him in Los Angeles and eventually

l'Argent
parlons -en

Les conseils financiers de la Caisse d'Epargne d'Alsace

POINT DE MIRE
Une réserve d'argent toujours disponible

Comment financer vos projets : vous partez à la neige, mais votre équipement de ski est à changer. Votre lave-linge vous a lâché, il faut le remplacer sans tarder. Votre enfant fait ses premiers pas, un caméscope permettrait d'immortaliser ces précieux instants...

Avec la Carte Satellis Aurore de la Caisse d'Epargne, vous disposez d'une réserve d'argent permanente,

la Carte Satellis Aurore est acceptée dans des commerces en Belgique, en Italie et en Espagne. Satellis Aurore, c'est également la possibilité d'alimenter votre compte chèque, dans la limite de votre réserve disponible, en téléphonant à **Allô Financement** et sous 48 h, vous recevez un virement du montant demandé sur votre compte chèque Caisse d'Epargne. Certains mois, vous souhaitez disposer de plus de

Nathan Carter and the Morgan State University Choir

Brooklyn Philharmonic Orchestra

From Gospel to Gershwin

Conducted by Gunther Schuller

White space leads the reader through the competing elements of a design, much like a walking path leads through a garden. If separation can be achieved with a spatial adjustment alone, it is likely to be a more elegant solution than through the addition of lines or unnecessary type and color contrasts. The strong horizontality of this typographic example – and the three clearly defined sizes of display type – make it appealingly easy to navigate. The garden path (a *space between* the shrubs) similarly makes negotiating the groundcover both easy and pleasant.

This photography annual compresses images into hairline-thick strokes on the cover. The only recognizable image is printed on the perimeter of each page, which becomes more visible when the pages are fanned out. The flap type is set vertically, connecting it with the cover art.

The prevailing direction created by other elements is the starting point for shaping white space, as shown by these four headlines. Controlling space between words and lines of type creates direction, which can be manipulated to craft a dynamic design. Specific *nonalignment* can be used in this regard: contrast a single element outside the prevailing alignment to give it visibility (*Jackson Pollock* and *The New Face of Trade Unionism*).

Space emphasizes direction

Readers look first in the upper left corner. Does this mean designers must design for an upper left starting point? No, but as Walter Dexel, German artist and Bauhaus-era proponent of simplified typography, says, designs that stray from the expected norm must do so knowingly. Designers must make accommodations for diverging from the expected, like beginning a message in the upper left corner. Guiding the reader in nontraditional directions requires greater accord between all elements. For example, make hierarchy extremely clear so a focal point in, say, the bottom of the page, stands out visibly.

Messages are delivered over time, whether it is the few seconds it takes to scan a page or spread, or the few more seconds it takes it takes to flip through a multipage story. Time implies space and motion, from one element to the next and from one spread to the next. Motion requires direction. Direction is used to unify and guide attention to key information. Dynamic design needs emphasis in a prevailing direction, whether vertical, horizontal, or diagonal. Equalizing directional force produces a motionless design that evokes a classical or traditional look. Motionless design is, of course, a legitimate choice under the proper circumstances, but in general does not serve the reader's need for dynamic

"Ça leur plaira bien un jour."
(They'll learn to like it someday.)
Ludwig van Beethoven
(1770-1827), composer

10 tips om rip och fotosättare

Här är råden som betyder skillnaden mellan bra och dålig investering av fotosättare och rippar. Tio handfasta tips som leder dig till den maskin som passar bäst för din speciella produktion. **AV HANS KLAHR**

⊙ Det som i första hand avgör vilken fotosättare man skall använda är typen av produktion. Vilka tryckpressar skall och vilka olika format behöver skriva ut? Det är inte varje fotosättningsutrustning taget, det är vanligare från företag med d da fallen behövs k

1 Trygg produ
till att man gital utskjutni pel Aldus Pres full dator. Är innehåller de återges korrekt digital utskjutn vänta på att ett u

$$\frac{a}{a+a} \quad 3$$

de till. A
vissa finns int
måtgången är s
bredd så att den p

a
3 Internal Drum
några år seda
kallas Internal
trumma som fil
terande laser
ligger stil

lämnar materialet har varierande kunskaper. En fotosättare kommer då inte till lika stor nytta eftersom filmåtgången skulle bli omfattande.

2 Olika filmformat i samma fotosättare. Även om man har en fotosättare som klarar filmtillverkare och fotosättare de är anpassade till. Alla filmbredder är inte vanliga och vissa finns inte att få tag på i Sverige. Om filmåtgången är stor kan man specialbeställa en bredd så att den passar produktionen.

3 Internal Drum eller planfotosättare? För några år sedan kom en fotosättare som kallas Internal Drum. Den har en stabil trumma som filmen placeras i, varpå den roterande lasern belyser materialet direkt. Det ligger stilla under exponeringen och nog-

---

13 mars - 10 juin 1996

Un trésor gothique : la châsse de Nivelles

Musée national du Moyen Age - Thermes de Cluny

6, place Paul Painlevé
75005 Paris
Tél (1) 43 25 62 00
Métro : Cluny/La Sorbonne
Visites-conférences :
(1) 43 25 61 91

Ouvert tous les jours, sauf le mardi, de 9h15 à 17h45.

Billet d'entrée de l'exposition donnant accès aux collections permanentes : 36 f, tarif réduit et dimanche : 26 f.

En mai 1940, la monumentale collégiale de Nivelles (au sud de Bruxelles) et la célèbre châsse d'argent de sainte Gertrude qu'elle abrite, sont très gravement endommagées par les bombes. Plus d'un demi-siècle plus tard, ce chef-d'œuvre d'orfèvrerie est en partie ressuscité grâce aux reliefs, statuettes et morceaux d'architecture subsistants. Présentés autour d'un moulage en plâtre de la châsse et selon un dispositif redonnant à voir l'œuvre dans une perspective éclatée, ils sont l'occasion unique pour le public de découvrir ce trésor du gothique rayonnant.

Nivelles, châsse de sainte Gertrude, Ange du couronnement du tombeau © Rheinisches Bildarchiv, Cologne

31 mars - 10 juin 1996

L'Amérique furtivement. Photographies d'Henri Cartier-Bresson

Musée de la Coopération franco-américaine, château de Blérancourt

02300 Blérancourt
tél : (16) 23 39 60 16
Accès SNCF, gare du Nord ;
par la route à 110 km
de Paris entre Compiègne
et Soissons.
Visites-conférences :
(16) 23 39 69 86

Ouvert tous les jours, sauf le mardi, de 10h 30 à 12h 30 et de 14h à 17h 30 (fermeture des caisses à 16h45).

Billet d'entrée de l'exposition donnant accès aux collections permanentes : 23 f, tarif réduit et dimanche : 18 f.

© Henri Cartier-Bresson Magnum Photos, Uvalde. Lunch Wagon, Etats-Unis, 1946.

Cofondateur en 1947 à New York de l'agence Magnum Photos, Henri Cartier-Bresson nous

Ce travail effectué sur commande ou par plaisir nous permet de découvrir ou de redécouvrir

---

IL MOVIMENTO TURISTICO IN ITALIA

Fonte UIC	Entrate valutarie	Uscite	Saldo
1° trim. 52	4,554	3,197	1,357
2° trim. 52	6,852	4,221	2,631
3° trim. 52	7,877	7,362	515
Totale	**19,289**	**14,780**	**4,503**
1° trim. 51	4,495	2,953	1,542
2° trim. 51	5,829	2,451	3,378
3° trim. 51	6,817	4,803	2,014
Totale	**17,141**	**10,207**	**6,934**

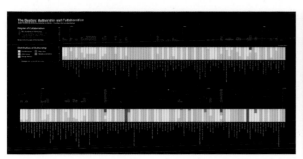

Information mapping is used to describe the Beatles' songwriting collaboration from 1963 to 1970. Colors show the band's gradual fracturing. Red tabs, which signify jointly written

songs, decrease in late 1967. The second diagram compares the Beatles' main activities from 1963 to 1966. Consistencies in scheduling from year

to year are revealed: the blue areas show movie filming in March and April of 1964 and 1965, for example. These diagrams, by Michael Deal, are at ChartingTheBeatles.com.

Using a photo of lightning, the cause of many power surges, this chart diagrams the business costs of not protecting computer equipment in a full-page business-to-business ad.

To isolate one part of a design from another yet still retain their appearance as a single entity, create a standardized space within the story, say, half a linespace, and double it to a full line space between the story and its illustration. Mathematical ratios like 2-to-1 and 3-to-1 ensure a built in harmony among parts.

Consolidate bits of white space and put them in chunks at the bottoms – or tops – of columns (facing page, bottom left). This makes the editing process easier and gives an informal chattiness to text columns.

Careful balance of horizontal and vertical pathways is essential in making a table legible (facing page, bottom right). Both reading directions are intended and necessary.

expression. Diagonal emphasis has been misunderstood as the most dynamic arrangement. In practice, it is often used when a designer lacks a better idea. Diagonal emphasis should be used with caution because its startling effect is extremely self-conscious and its use can actually detract from the message.

Use white space to echo the prevailing direction of design elements. Headlines correctly broken for sense make their own shapes that should be exploited.

Information mapping and wayfinding

Information mapping is patterning or tabulation of data so it signals relevance and connections that are best illustrated, not merely described verbally. By showing connections, information mapping makes data easier to glance through and to access. Research – and common sense – shows that readers like finding information easily and they like documents that simplify the process of finding things. Information mapping requires that content be prepared in segmented, hierarchical structure and the structure be given simplified form.

Information mapping is a user-focused process of handling and presenting content shaped by users' needs and the purpose of the information. It has three steps: analysis, organization, and presentation. The three steps extract the core message and make it evident to the user,

"Order ... is a function of the horizontal and vertical reference lines on a page and the frequency with which the corners of the items fall on these lines."
Gui Bonsiepe (1934–),
A Method of Quantifying Order in Typographic Design

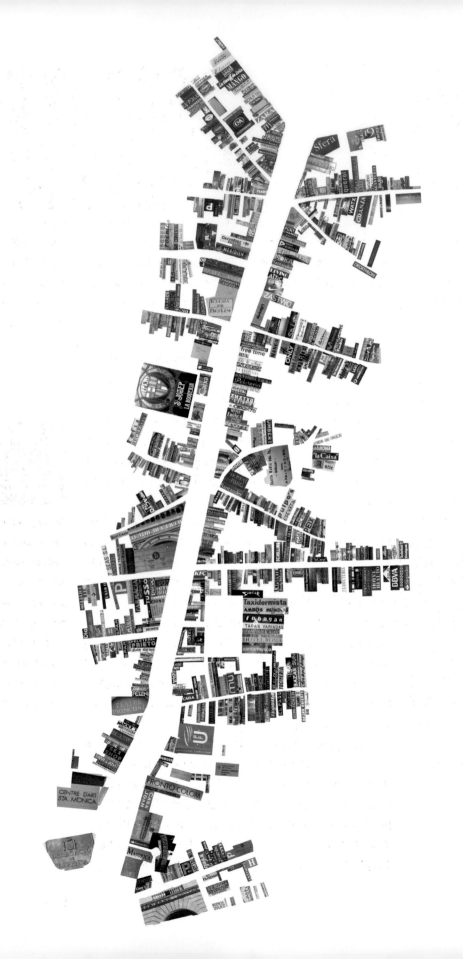

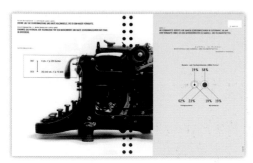

Information mapping explains complex data visually. This spread from an electronics retailer's annual report explains how typewriters made

little money for the inventor in 1867 (he sold four units) but lots of money for subsequent sellers (340,000 in 1924).

Color-coded wayfinding, as in this temporary system for a show at a Spanish convention center, is limited to a few colors which can be readily recognized and remembered.

Wayfinding can be useful even from 30,000 feet, a problem this 100' tall airport "environmental communications system" resolves. From the ground, it is also a memorable experience.

Information mapping is illustrated in this visual description of a Spanish main street and its twenty-three street crossings based on use density and people flow.

Wayfinding is used in signage and as department heading signals in multi-page documents.

which results in an easy-to-scan format that increases readability (attracts casual and uncommitted viewers), highlights details, and enhances comprehension.

Information mapping is a subset of graphic design, as well as information visualization, information architecture and design, data analysis, user experience design, graphic user interface design, and knowledge management systems.

Wayfinding has been compared to information mapping but in three dimensions, for example, in sign systems. Though the designed results may be quite different between the two disciplines, they share a common purpose of making information user friendly and adding comfort to complex messages and environments. Wayfinding is particularly important to designers as a signalling tool on Web sites and in lengthy, mixed-content paginated documents like magazines, where design in three dimensions becomes evident as pages are turned or clicked through.

Though it is a term coined in 1960 by an urban planner in reference to environmental planning, wayfinding's meaning was expanded in the 1980s to include architectural signage. Its meaning has grown further to encompass any navigation tool that furthers acclimatization in a complex environment. In short, wayfinding helps people orient themselves to their surroundings.

"The way we make sense out of data is to compare and contrast, to understand differences. Using the analogy of a map, a map isn't the territory, it's the difference – be it in altitude, vegetation, population, or terrain."
Gregory Bateson (1904–1980), *Steps to an Ecology of the Mind*

The Stazione Ferroviale Nord in Milano shows vivid interior three-dimensional space. This fourteen-inch sculptural model

for a ten-foot, life-size installation defines both confined interior and unconfined exterior space.

Sculptural dimensionality is shown in this Korean War memorial in New York City in which the figure has been cut out of the block.

Three-dimensional space in print can be realized with pop-up books, some of the most sophisticated of which, like this one on Formula One racing, are designed by Ron Van der Meer.

The Lauterbrunnen valley in the Swiss Alps is one of the most dramatic inhabited landscapes in the world.

Henry Moore's 1935 *Reclining Figure* shows space fully infiltrating the form, particularly where the ribcage is expected to be. The effect is accentuated by the pronounced grain of the elm wood used in this thirty-five-inch-long sculpture.

Three-dimensional space

People live in a three-dimensional space, an atmospheric volume above the land surface ... The experience of being in fine three-dimensional volumes is one of the great experiences of life. – Garret Eckbo, landscape architect (1910-2000)

Most graphic design occurs on flat planes, in two dimensions: vertical and horizontal. But we see the world in three dimensions, with the addition of depth. How does design change when the third dimension is added?

Carl Dair, in his excellent mid-1960s booklet series for Westvaco Paper, wrote, "All artists and designers are confronted with the same problem: here is a space, how do I divide it, enclose it, define it, intrude forms into it, so that the space becomes alive with meaning and function? ... The blank space is a challenge to the graphic designer, demanding that he utilize it for the most effective presentation of visual-verbal forms in order to communicate clearly to the reader. To the architect, the task is to enclose a space ... and to divide it for human activity. The sculptor working on a block of stone or wood

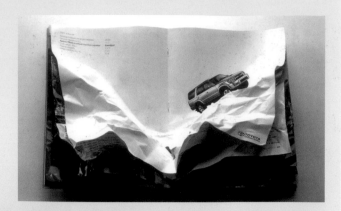

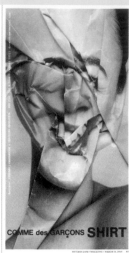

INNER CITY INFILL

Inner City Infill
A Housing Design Competition
for Harlem

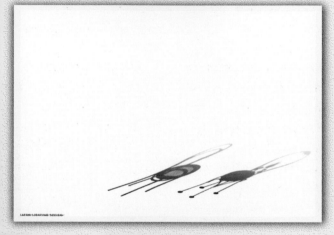

bulthaup

Overlapping three figures creates a single gyrating dancer on this poster for a nightclub, known for the cancan, as it updated itself with the Charleston in 1928.

Overlapping elements creates an intimate relationship that can be enhanced. Activate negative space by overlapping figures and switching their black and white polarity (and remove perimeter lines to allow surrounding space into the imagery). Or wrap one part into or through another, as in the leopard's tail through the "o," which increases the Finnish illustration's implied dimensionality. Or use overlapping planes to imply a folded piece of paper, as in Leo Lionni's full-page ad for a paper company.

Imply three-dimensional space by rephotographing a printed and damaged piece of paper. Here, paper is an illustrative symbol, in this case a mountain. Greater logical license is allowed for fashion ads: why is this lovely woman's face crumpled? Perhaps for no other reason than to make you look.

Depth is implied on a two-dimensional poster by Michael Bierut. Shadow is used to suggest the third dimension. Shadow is also used without the object that casts it in a poster for a Japanese interior lighting designer.

Gravity is suspended in a light-hearted Korean ad. Actual three-dimensional space is used on the fronts of escalator steps. And a printed knife with two die cuts curls the sliced sheet.

liberates the imprisoned form by letting space into it." Sculptor Henry Moore said, "A hole made through a piece of stone is a revelation. The hole connects one side to the other, making it immediately more three-dimensional. A hole can itself have as much shape-meaning as a solid mass."

Depth in design is real. It is real as we turn pages. It is real as we photograph objects. And it is real as we try to show one element in front of another. Depth is a powerful tool to attract readers and it's an opportunity for designers to explore new limits.

Two- and three-dimensional space

We live in a three-dimensional world that has height, width, and depth. The printed page, however, is flat. It has only height and width. Depth must be added through illusion. Spatial illusion can be either volume, which is an implied solid, or space, which is an implied void. The illusion of dimensional space is used to get attention, to imply realism, and to help the reader project himself into the composition.

There are a few ways to create an approximation of three-dimensional space in two dimensions:

■ *Overlap elements:* Placing an object in front of another and obscuring the back one recreates reality most effectively. Be careful not to make type unreadable when plac-

"Good design isn't just good looks. People don't buy æsthetics, they buy emotions. They want an experience: what it does for them, how it behaves, how it works for them. And most importantly, how it makes them feel."

Robert Brunner, *Ammunition*

This headline reads, "This is not enough space." The top half of the page is left mostly blank (defining "space"), and the life-size shoe, being too big to fit the page, still must bleed.

Motion can be translated into two dimensions by using bleed, which implies "This is so real, it exists beyond the picture's edges."

Motion can be implied by slicing a photo into strips and moving them somewhat randomly; using speed lines and selective repetition, as in this

poster by Armin Hofmann; and by taking a photo with a shutter speed that is slow enough to capture more than a motion-freezing instant of time.

Scale and visual hierarchy suggest size and relative nearness to the viewer.

Perspective: Herb Lubalin's mark for a construction company is an isometric visualization (from the Greek, *isometria*, meaning "having equal measurement").

Atmospheric perspective is grayer and less distinct as space recedes, showing air's actual thickness.

Masaccio's *Trinità* in Firenze's Santa Maria Novella is considered the first painting to use perspective to create a sense of volume.

ing it behind another object. Ambiguous space is created when one or more of the elements are transparent. This sense of "floating in front" is especially remarkable when printing an element in spot varnish. Drop shadows are an effective but overused way of overlapping to create depth.

■ *Imply motion by blurring elements:* This can be done in the original photography, by manipulation in Photoshop, by slicing an image into pieces, or by using startling repetition of some elements, explored by Armin Hofmann in the late 1950s and early 1960s.

■ *Use scale and visual hierarchy:* Transpose the expected sizes of elements for startling new relationships. Use foreground/background contrast to imply greater depth.

■ *Use perspective:* Perspective is a technique for depicting volumes and spatial relationships on a flat surface. Shown are a dimensional logo in isometric perspective; "atmospheric perspective," in which distant objects appear grayer and less distinct (Photoshop filters exaggerate this effect); and Masaccio's *The Holy Trinity,* c1427, the earliest true perspective painting.

Layers and transparency

The key to emulating three-dimensional reality in two dimensions is to interpret the way real things interact in real space. Real objects overlap, partly hiding the objects

"People are readers, listeners, and viewers simultaneously, participating in an exchange."
Steve McCaffrey (1947-), poet

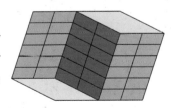

Perspective can be manipulated to create ambiguous depth, as in this reversible figure (try looking at it "from above" and "from below").

five graphic designers,
five world capitals,
five points of view:
a symposium sponsored
by the new york
chapter of the american
institute of graphic
arts in association with
the alliance graphique
internationale.

saturday, may 22
10:30am to 3:30pm
the great hall
cooper union
7 east seventh street
new york city

admission by advance
reservation
(includes lunch)
$25.00 AIGA/NY chapter
members
$35.00 general public

at the door
(if available)
$35.00 AIGA/NY
chapter members
$45.00 general public
free to cooper union
students with valid id and
advance reservations
members' fee available
to CU faculty with
advance reservations

space is limited. reservations are on a first come,
first served basis. events
have been sold out in the
past. we suggest you make
reservations early.

cooper union

global-
ism(s)

an international designers' saturday

may 22

ken cato **australia**

shigeo fukuda **japan**

werner jeker **switzerland**

pierre mendell **germany**

bruno oldani **norway**

introduced by michael bierut

introduced by massimo vignelli

introduced by stefan sagmeister

werner jeker lives and
works in lausanne, switzerland since 1974 he has
been head of the depart-
ment of graphic design at
the lausanne school of
applied art. in 1984 he
founded the collaborative
studio "les ateliers du
nord" with industrial
designers antoine cohen
and claude brossard and
graphic designer fairouz
joublie. he is best known for
the swiss public for his
design of that country's
currency system.
michael bierut is
a partner in pentagram,
new york.

ken cato is principal of
cato design inc which was
established in 1970 and is
based in melbourne, aus-
tralia. with offices also in
sydney, tokyo, singapore,
hong kong, auckland and
los angeles, cato design is
one of the largest in the
southern hemisphere.
he is a founder and former
chairman of the
australian writers and art
directors association.
b. martin pedersen is
publisher of graphis.

shigeo fukuda is a native
of tokyo. his pictures have
won prizes at international
graphic design exhibitions
in warsaw, brno, lahti,
nimes, and moscow. in
1987 he was elected to the
hall of fame of the new
york art directors club. last
year he was invited to
design the official poster
for the 2nd united
nations conference in
rio de janeiro.
seymour chwast is principal of the pushpin group.

pierre mendell studied
with armin hofmann in
basel. he established his
studio, mendell & oberer,
in munich with partner
klaus oberer in 1961. exhibitions of the firm's award-
winning work in poster,
packaging and corporate
identity design have been
held at die neue sammlung
in munich and the design
center in stuttgart.
massimo vignelli is
massimo vignelli.

bruno oldani established
his design studio in oslo in
1965. since then he has
received widespread
acclaim for his work in illustration, book covers, corporate images, package
design, magazine and
newspaper design, sign
and information systems,
television graphics, exhibition design, industrial
design, interior design,
audiovisual programs and
photography.
staff geissbuhler
is a partner in
chermayeff & geismar.

all of the participants in
global(ism) are members
of the alliance graphique
internationale (agi), an
international organisation
of designers founded in
1950. the membership of
agi now numbers nearly
240 men and women who
live and work in 25 coun-
tries around the world. this
event was organised in
conjunction with agi's 1993
congress, which will be
held this spring in mon-
tauk, long island.

10:30am to 3:30pm

the new york chapter of
the american institute of
graphic arts (aiga/ny), with
more than 1,700 members,
supports the principals,
goals and objectives of the
national organization
(aiga), founded in july, 1983.
the chapter serves professionals in graphic design
and related fields in the
greater metropolitan area
of new york, new jersey,
connecticut and long
island. aiga/ny offers programs that seek to chal-
lenge, educate and
encourage the exchange
of ideas and information
related to graphic design
among its members, activities evolve around the
needs of a changing,
dynamic profession.

reservation form

The logo for this Manhattan hotel was developed in part because of the limitations of the camera used to photograph the enormous neon sign on the building's roof. It was not possible to capture the entire sign without a distortion-causing extreme wide angle lens (or to fall off the twelfth floor as we stepped back and back and back once more), so the decision was made to take left side and right side captures separately and stitch them together into a single image (left). Because the photos couldn't be aligned perfectly, other opportunities presented themselves. Resolution was tried, but the final positive and negative versions are above at far right.

The airplane is printed on the *back* of this "globalism(s)" poster by Pentagram, which takes advantage of the transparency of the poster's paper. In addition, this poster succeeds at exploiting "two-level readership," in which primary information is offered for more distant absorption, then detailed secondary information is provided for closer reading.

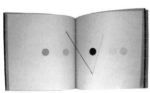

Bruno Munari's *Libro Illeggibile N.Y. 1* was designed so "visual discourse, rather than a text composed of words, carries the thread of the story."

in back. Real objects can be transparent or translucent, letting details show through. Observe reality clearly and then translate what you see into flat planes.

A publication is both two- and three-dimensional

Pick up a magazine or book and thumb through the pages. What you see is a cumulative perception of pages riffling by, an accumulation of information delivered sequentially. Each page and spread is flat, but pages have two sides and some small amount of thickness. These are attributes which may be exploited.

Bruno Munari (1907–1998) developed the "useless machine" and the "unreadable book." Shown at left are spreads from his 1967 book, *Libro Illeggibile N.Y. 1*. The "story line" is literally a piece of red string that punctures some pages and runs through die cuts in others. He forces awareness of reading a three-dimensional book.

Three-dimensional space, or depth, in graphic design should take into account the process of reading. Posters, for example, are designed for two-level readership: they make a primary effect at long distance and, having lured the reader closer, have secondary, close-up information.

Three-dimensional space can be emphasized by looking creatively at the substrate, at the paper itself. Semitransparent paper suggests unusual front and back

Paper's thickness is revealed in this letterform study whose outer counterform can be found on the following verso. To see it fully, hold this page up to the light.

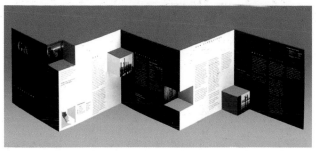

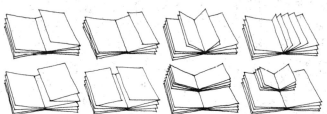

Die-cutting and scoring transforms this flat sheet of paper into a three-dimensional design with alternating black

and white panels and reverse folded cutouts adding very intentional play of light on the paper.

Page size contrast can show off a special event, a special section or process, a magazine-within-a-magazine, a special advertising section, or a very large event. Creative use of pa-

per causes the user to notice the publication as an object, not just an invisible information delivery system, which increases the publication's perceived value.

Texture is a tactile experience: the surface must be *felt* to be fully appreciated. These Swedish paving stones can certainly be felt, but a photo of them must convey the tactile impression in only two dimensions: height and width. By adjusting the image to maximum contrast, the inherent *pattern* in a texture overwhelms its tactility. *So a pattern results when tactility is reduced.*

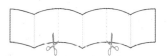

"Horizontal design" can be enhanced by ignoring natural spread limitations. Design a multiple-page story in a continuous horizontal space and crop it every seventeen inches. A six-page story, for example, would be developed in a single 51" (8½"x 6 pages) x 11" horizontal rectangle.

opportunities. Die-cutting makes paper's thickness and opacity visible and usable. Cutting some pages shorter or longer also emphasizes the dimensionality of paper. Telling a story panel by panel as a brochure is unfolded, for example, makes good use of paper's three-dimensional qualities.

Though a magazine or book is seen by readers one spread at a time, multiple-page stories are best planned in a single horizontal strip. This ensures design continuity from spread to spread (see also chapter 7). Because you only see one spread on screen at a time, computer makeup does not encourage the technique of "horizontal design." This failing is mitigated a little by the computer's support of design consistency through the use of guides, master pages, and typographic styles. It remains up to the designer, however, to create and use these tools that ensure consistency in a repetitive pattern.

Texture and pattern

Texture is tactile – it is three-dimensional and must be felt. Pattern is a repeated motif. A photo of a texture is no longer three-dimensional, so it isn't true texture any more. Capturing three-dimensional texture in two dimensions makes it flat and increases the chance that it will be perceived as a pattern. Increasing contrast (facing page) will often help describe the original dimensionality.

"Thus let it be the golden rule that everything be demonstrated to all the senses ... the visible to sight, the audible to hearing ... and if something can be perceived by several senses, let it be demonstrated to several senses." Jan Amos Comenius (1592-1670), "The Father of Modern Education"

"*Unless typography
is being used as central
to the communication,
as the pivotal illustration,
what makes the communication
work is always the content.*"
Saul Bass (1920–1996)

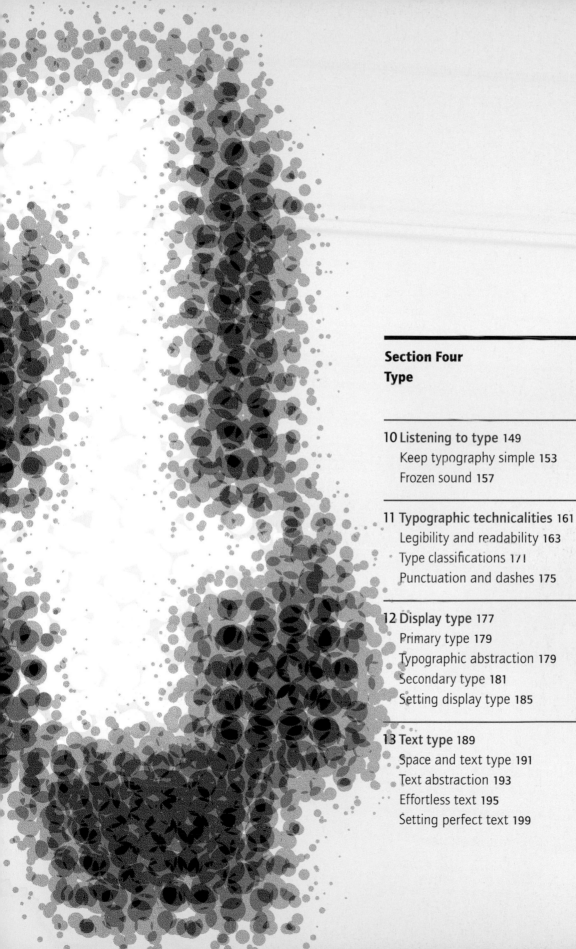

Pluck less often

Hair follicles around the lips and chin grow when they receive too much hormone. Vaniqa slows hair growth.

Vaniqa™ slows facial hair growth so you can significantly reduce your current maintenance program.

Unwanted Facial Hair is a condition that develops in women with the onset of menopause or an increase in body weight. Hair follicles around the lips and chin grow when they receive too much androgen, a naturally-occurring hormone. • Vaniqa™, a trans-parent cream, blocks androgen from hair follicles, so hair grows more slowly. You won't have to pluck, shave, bleach, wax, or zap as often. • Visit our Web site or ask your doctor about **VANIQA™**

Eflornithine HCl 13%

Bristol-Myers Squibb Company
www.bristolmyerssquibb.com

이제 21세기의 언어로 말하자
이제 21세기의 언어로 말하자
이제 21세기의 언어로 말하자
이제 21세기의 언어로 말하자

It is not enough to have "nothing wrong" with a design. There must be something recognizably "right" to be considered good design. What makes a design ugly, like the example above left, is the random combination of pieces, chosen on whim. The arbitrary font choices and uncertain positioning make designs complex and sloppy. Simpler letter forms with design consistencies, used in a way that is in some way sensible, make designs handsome and descriptive.

Every typeface has a "visual voice," an equivalency to the spoken word. These are the same characters in four Korean alphabets.

Typographic elements, like headline and text, are distinct visual voices. They are equivalent to the different voices one might use to indicate characters in a story that is read aloud. The information hierarchy is revealed in an ad in descending order of importance. Notice the circuitous path the reader has to follow in this design before getting to the text. This may deter casual browsers.

Typography creates clear differences in content, valuable even in small, subtle doses. Note the contrast between text and caption in the example on the right, and the subsequent stronger relationship between the caption and the picture, which deserves to be exploited.

10 Listening to type

Typographic arrangement should achieve for the reader what voice tone conveys for the listener. – El Lissitzky (1893-1941)

What do we mean by "listening to type"? Imagine listening to a book recorded on tape. The reader's voice changes with the story, helping the listener hear various characters and emotions. A story told on paper should do the same thing. The "characters" typographers work with are categories of type: headlines, subheads, captions, text, and so forth. These typographic characters are our players and must be matched for both individual clarity and overall unity.

Typography is, according to the dictionary, "the art or process of printing with type." The root words that make up *typography* are *typo* (type) and *graphy* (drawing), so it literally means *drawing with type*. My definition is: *applying type in an expressive way to reveal the content clearly and memorably with the least resistance from the reader.*

Typography involves far more than working with the abstract black shapes. In practice, typographic

Keep typography simple 153
Expressive type requires relative quietness in its surroundings to be heard.

Frozen sound 157
Our alphabet is made of glyphs that represent sounds, so writing can and should be considered "graphic speaking."

Abdrucke von grösster Schärfe und Farbkraft

Pelikan

KOHLENPAPIER

Günther Wagner

Typographic rules, like the development of word spacing, have evolved over centuries. These samples, which precede the development of word spac-

ing, date from 196 BC (left) and AD c500 (center). Typographic rules, like the adherence to word spacing and default line

breaks, may be manipulated to create startling results, as in this broadside found at an art school (right).

Breaking design rules makes a design more visible. This 1995 Neville Brody panel from *Fuse* magazine reads "Superstition" in one of Brody's many idiosyncratic typefaces.

El Lissitzky's ad for carbon paper uses typestyles to illustrate meaning (left). The four typographic elements are each treated differently, but the alignments, spacing, and artwork act as unifiers to counteract these differences.

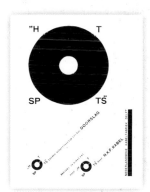

Piet Zwart's typography (above) shows complex relationships using simple letterforms. An architect until age thirty-six, when he turned to typography, Zwart approached letterforms unrestrained by design convention.

decisions are – or should be – 90 percent about *the manipulation of the space around the letterforms.* Indeed, poor typography results from misunderstanding the importance of the "not-letterforms" and concentrating only on the letters themselves. "Not-letterforms," or the space surrounding letters, is seen between characters, words, lines, and between blocks and columns of type. It is the contrast of the letterform to its surrounding space that makes type either less or more legible. Legibility is central to typography because type is, after all, meant to be read.

Consistent spacing makes reading easier because the reader is unaware of inconsistencies in rhythm, which is to reading what static is to the radio. The measure of a good typeface is whether every letter combination is spaced for optical equivalency so no dark spots appear where letters are too close. Even spacing produces even typographic "color," or gray tone.

Typographers use elements and traditions inherited through generations of writing, printing, and reading. Many typographic rules were adopted from handwriting as printable type forms were developed in the 1400s and 1500s. Historically, typography was handled by the printer who cut his own typefaces, designed the page, and reproduced the design on paper. In the twentieth century, typography and printing separated. Around

"The quality of ... typography is dependent on the relationship between the printed and unprinted parts. It is a sign of professional immaturity to ignore the decisive contribution of the unprinted area." Emil Ruder (1914–1970)

asics.com

(SOUND MIND) × (SOUND BODY) ×
120 DECIBELS = INNER PEACE

Shoes made for the sport of living. The new **Stormer.**™

sound mind, sound body

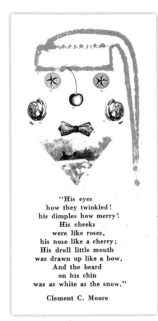

"His eyes
how they twinkled!
his dimples how merry!
His cheeks
were like roses,
his nose like a cherry;
His droll little mouth
was drawn up like a bow,
And the beard
on his chin
was as white as the snow."

Clement C. Moore

Type and illustration echo each other in a one-to-one translation. This is a literal illustration of nouns using found pieces.

The flexibility of letterforms as distinct and worthwhile shapes unto themselves was developed in the first half of the twentieth century, as shown in this magazine cover.

Typographic pyrotechnics (left) contrast with clear simplicity (center) and a balance between eye-catching novelty and elegant clarity (right).

Unlike typography, musical notational styles (below) generally don't add to or detract from the musical message. This is a Bach Prelude written by the composer.

(SOUND MIND)x(SOUND BODY)x
120 DECIBELS = INNER PEACE

Attitude in advertising is often best described using hand lettering (facing page). The headline set in an ordinary typeface (above) makes the message much more rigid, not at all the feeling the ad is trying to evoke as it holds a mirror up to its intended audience.

1950, typographers and typesetters became outside vendors who set type to the specifications of the designer or art director, which evolved into a new responsibility. Computers, forcing a new working methodology, have nearly obliterated the typography specialist since all type decisions are made within a page design program. Designers are widely expected to be masters of an art form that takes many years to learn.

Choosing a typeface that matches the content is important. Words are symbols of emotions and ideas that manipulate the reader. But choosing the right typeface is not as important as using a more neutral typeface well. Dutch designer Piet Zwart (1885–1977) said, "Pretentious [letterforms] oppose the utilitarian task of typography. The more uninteresting a letter is in itself the more useful it is in typography." The danger is that typography will begin and end with choosing the typeface rather than be used to reveal the content. And that is not typography, but fashion.

Keep typography simple

The essence of typography is clarity. R. Hunter Middleton said, "Typography is the voice of the printed page. But typography is meaningless until seen by the human eye, translated into sound by the human brain, heard by the human ear, comprehended as thought and stored as

ESPERIENZA

*Del sollevamento de' fluidi nel vano de' cannellini sotti-
lissimi dentr' al voto.*

*Opinione d'al-
cuni, che il sol-
levarsi quasi
tutti i liquori
ne' cänelli stret-
tissimi di vano
sia effetto del-
la natural
pressione dell'
aria.*
*Come segua,
secondo loro,
tal solleva-
mento.*

TRAGLI altri effetti della pressione dell' aria è stato da alcuni annoverato anche quello del sollevarsi, che fanno quasi tutti i fluidi dentro a' cannelli strettissimi, che in essi s'immergono. Dubitano questi, che quel sottilissimo cilindro d' aria, che giù pel cannello preme, verbigrazia, in sull'acqua, operi più debolmente la sua pressione, per lo contrasto, che gli fa nel discendere il gran toccamento, ch' egli à colla superficie interna dell'angustissimo vaso. Dove per lo contrario, a giudizio loro, quell'aria, che liberamen-

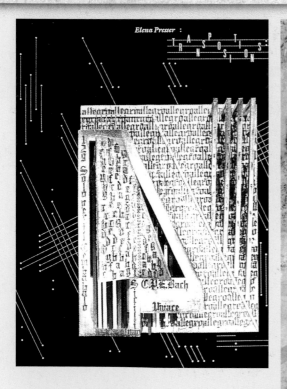

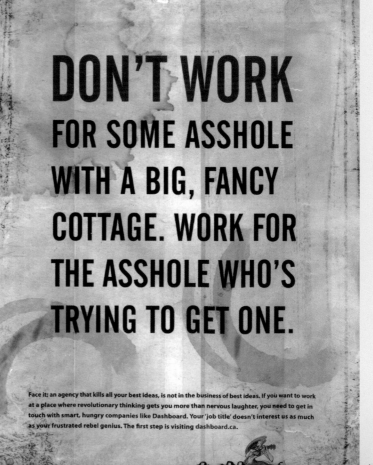

Abstract word and letter shapes can be manipulated to express meaning as shown in this poster for Herman Miller (above left) and spread ad for Nike. These

design solutions are born of the attitude that type can be damaged in service to the message.

Type, like the spoken voice, can be powerfully bold or elegantly understated. It can warn by shouting or gracefully inform. It can be stuffy or informal, universal or parochial,

traditional or state of the art, highly complex or primitive. Type's intrigue is often best expressed in combination, as shown in this department page from *Esquire* magazine.

Flavors of type, c1691, Filippo Cecchi, Florence: contrasts of size, capitalization, letterspacing, and column width show lively differences. A single type family unites these four voices, balancing their variety with one strong consistency.

"I try to bring type to the maximum level of its expressive potential," says William Longhauser of his poster, far left. "It is essential that [type] can be read, but I play with it until it expresses the content of the message. It may take longer to recognize the word "Transpositions," but the experience of deciphering the meaning is more memorable. In a sense, I am forcing participation."

Typographic tone of voice is shown in this no-nonsense use of workaday Trade Gothic.

memory." Canadian teacher and author Carl Dair wrote, "Between the two extremes of unrelieved monotony and typographical pyrotechnics there is an area where the typographic designer can contribute to the pleasure of reading and the understanding of what is being read."

Complexity will not get a message across because, though it may be interesting to look at, the message won't be legible. Simplicity alone will not get a message across because, though it may be easy to read, its importance won't be recognized. Only simplicity combined with expressiveness will make the message both legible and interesting.

Establish a tone, a typographic attitude in the display type, where flirtations with reduced legibility are best tolerated by readers. But unless the reader grasps something of value, his conversion from a looker to a reader will not occur. Put interesting information where it can be found. Break the type into palatable chunks and recognize that readers enter stories through picture captions.

The key to creating expressive typography is to predigest the copy and show off its meaning and its importance to the reader. This can't be separated from the editing process. Read the story, know the subject, ask the client or editor what the thrust ought to be, then make that point crystal clear through design choices.

"I want to use type to enhance the meaning of the words, not contradict, ignore, obscure, or interrupt what's being said. My goal is to inject decisiveness; to show that these words know what they are saying."
Susan Casey (1962–)

LIGHT
NIN
GHTNIN

LIGH
GHT

WETTBEWERB
FUER DIE
AUSSTELLUNG
DAS NEUE HEIM
1928

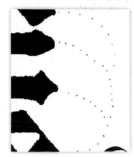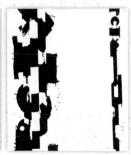

Abstract studies in typographic contrast (facing page and above) express voices to introduce the idea of type as frozen sound. The exercise requires the use of materials from a limited set of typographic samples and limits some design choices to force creativity with shape and form. Neither legibility nor making sense are desirable in this exercise. Each designer is using exactly the same ingredients, so simply choosing more eye catching material is taken away. Multiple critiques help designers recognize the need to *add* *creativity* for their work to be noticeable. That is true "value added" design, and the essence of what designers must bring to their assignments.

Contrast type style, size, weight, position, color, or treatment to show hierarchy and give enough information for the reader to decide to become involved with the text, where the story really is. Type strategy includes crafting a size and weight sequence for the headlines, subheads, captions, and text so each is distinctive and all work as one to make an appealing design.

For a design to work effectively, the type must be an integral part of the composition. If the type is altered or removed, the piece should fall apart. It doesn't matter if it's a poster, a cover design, an advertisement, or a corporate identity.

Frozen sound

Jerry Lewis, in a *Vanity Fair* interview about his increasingly controversial muscular dystrophy fundraising telethon, said, "I must be doing something right; I've raised one billion, three hundred million dollars. These nineteen people don't want me to do that. They want me to stop now? Fuck them ... Do it in caps. FUCK THEM." Mr. Lewis understands the translation of oral sound into typeset form. He understands that verbal emphasis becomes visual emphasis, most usually by contrast of size. This is the essence of typography: translating the equivalencies of spoken language into printable form.

Treating typography as frozen sound begins with being sensitive to what Gene Federico, a master of advertising design, calls "sound tones." Federico says, "You must choose a typeface with a sound that isn't against the idea and image you are trying to convey, unless, of course, you are introducing an irritating sound, an irritating typeface for a specific reason." English designer Neville Brody says, "Let's say a French person comes

"Typography is simply the voice, for the head is the destination."
Rick Valicenti (1951–)

Concerto No.2 Piano Symphony No.5 The Vienna Philharmonic Daniel Barenboim, Conductor and Piano Orchestra Hall, Chicago Saturday October 19 1988 8:00pm

In. The. Past. 99. Dollars. Got. You. Speech. Recognition. Software. That. Works. Like. This.

Starting today 99 dollars buys you speech recognition software that works like this.

Oh ruh-vwarr — Baskerville Old Face

Oh ruh-vwarr — Bernhard Antique Bold Condensed

Oh ruh-vwarr — Aritus Regular

Oh ruh-vwarr — Meta Normal

Oh ruh-vwarr — Basketcase

Oh ruh-vwarr — Goudy Text

Oh ruh-vwarr — Sketchy

Oh ruh-vwarr — ITC Veljovic

Oh ruh-vwarr — Harting

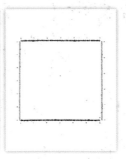

Rhythm requires breaking repetition unexpectedly, which creates visual surprise and a focal point.

Experimental typographic studies express multiple voices and hierarchy using only the contrast of relative position.

Part of this exercise is helping designers discover the edges of legibility, so they may chose to flirt with it in subsequent designs. Without that barrier

being broken in a laboratory environment, the rote adherence to legibility is a hindrance to expressive typography.

Studies in typographic contrast express typographic "voices." Students are provided with the same type and must explore design ideas like *rhythm* and *organic/geometric contrast.*

Punctuation, capitalization, and extra word spacing make this headline (far left, bottom) a typographic illustration.

Setting the same text in different typefaces changes the message.

Fine
dining, it
ain't

Fine dining,
it ain't

Breaking for sense makes display type understandable by grouping words into logical phrases.

up to you and starts talking. The first thing you notice is that he's speaking French – not the words that he's said. Just set a piece of text, first in Baskerville, then in several different faces and observe exactly how the message changes. The choice of typeface is critical to the emotional response to the words" (facing page, bottom right).

Also important is developing sensitivity to rhythm. A speaker who drones at a single speed is causing his listeners extra work to dig out the good content. By comparison, a speaker who alters her rhythm of delivery, by pausing before beginning a new idea, for example, makes the content clearer by grouping information into sensible clusters. Such pauses in rhythm are expressed typographically by altering a single element unexpectedly (above, left) and by breaking the ends of lines of display type at logical places, rather than whenever a line happens to be filled with letterforms (left), as is common and generally appropriate with text settings. If the line of display type is broken arbitrarily or in the wrong place, reading and comprehension is slowed down. If natural line breaks don't work well visually, editing the copy, adjusting the layout, or changing typefaces may be necessary.

"The use of words – their sounds, their meanings, and their letterforms – has been an intriguing aspect of design since the invention of the alphabet. A picture may be worth a thousand words, but as one wit pointed out: It takes words to say that."
Allen Hurlburt (1911-1983)

VERENOVOGELIDVSCANISCVMMONTIBVMOR
LIQVITVRETZEPHYROPVTRISSEGLAEBARESOLVI
DAMNONVERVM·EGONISNVLERMIHITRADIDITAEGON
MENINFELIXOSEMPEROVISPECVSIPSENIAERAM

Cor gran facilita : ma gran lauoro
Qui numero aureo : e tutti i segni fuoro
Descripti dil gran polo da ogni lai :

Vertere Mæcenas, ulmisq; adiun gere uites,

Si est ce que je n'eusse pas encore maintenãt ozé
entreprendre, luy dedier la traduction, & im-

ex Cardinale, mense Maio, anni 1572. põtifex Ma-
ximus denũciatur, paucisq; diebus pòst pro more

Opinione d'al-
cuni,che il sol
levarsi quasi
tutti i liquori
ne'cãnelli stret
tissimi di vano

TRAGLI altri effetti della pressione dell'aria è
stato da alcuni annoverato anche quello del
sollevarsi, che fanno quasi tutti i fluidi dentro a'can-

Huc, pater o Lenæe; (tuis hic omnia plena
5 Muneribus: tibi pampineo gravidus autumno

Ligatures are overlapped kerning pairs, as shown in the A⁄ (AV), Ɛ (TE), Ð (DE), and Ɲ (NE) pairings on a Quito stone plaque. Such expressive lettering is today produced by either the wholly ignorant or the highly educated. Everyone in between is trying to "get it right" by following typographic conventions.

The proportional changes necessary to render three type weights are shown in this composite study of light, regular, and bold versions of roman and italic members of a type family.

11 Typographic technicalities

> *The practice of typography is one that requires both an intuitive grasp of form and considerable study to achieve mastery. Typography gradually reveals its expressive potential.* – Milton Glaser (1929-)

Today's use of type is based on thirty-five centuries of typographic evolution, on countless improvements based on our need to record ideas in writing. Developments in the speed, accuracy, and precision in both the marks we make and the way we reproduce them – in the substrate (paper), printing presses, and even the inks – are driven by technological improvements.

The history of the written word is the history of the changing needs and opportunities of human society. Designers who are not fully informed about the traditions and subtleties of type use are mere typesetters. And typesetting is not typography. Readers are well served when the type they are being offered is at once expressive and transparent in its content delivery. That balance is hard to achieve and requires the careful, measured revelation of levels of meaning.

Legibility and readability 163
Making type attractive to passersby and easy to understand once you've stopped them.

Type classifications 171
A simple system to recognize typefaces and appreciate their differences.

Punctuation and dashes 175
Adding road signs to reading in order to control and guide comprehension.

The future city
transcends the
city hall,
Urban academy
takes place
indoors. The
street,
once absent, fall
quiet, but now
all the voice
becomes a touch.

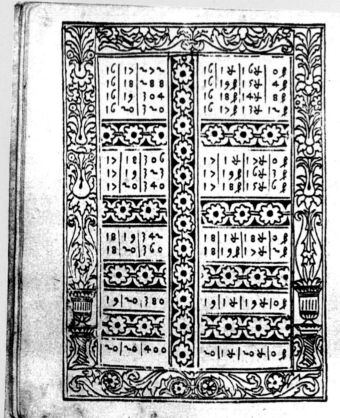

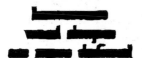

Lowercase
word shapes
are more defined

ALL CAPS
LOOKS LIKE
BRICKS

This paragraph shows lining figures inappropriately set amid lowercase Truesdell, designed by F.W. Goudy in 1931. This version was digitized in 1993 from letterpress proofs of 16-point fonts. Truesdell was Goudy's forty-seventh typeface design. LINING FIGURES, LIKE 1931 & 1993, SHOULD BE USED WITH ALL-CAPS AND IN CHARTS. AS

This paragraph shows old style figures properly set amid lowercase Truesdell, designed by F.W. Goudy in 1931. This version was digitized in 1993 from letterpress proofs of 16-point fonts. Truesdell was Goudy's forty-seventh typeface design. Old style figures, like 1931 & 1993, blend in with lowercase type They stand out in an all-caps setting by look-

We read by subconsciously recognizing word shapes. So the more distinctive the word shape, the easier reading becomes. Lowercase words are easier to scan than all caps because they have more distinctive word shapes. That's why setting type in all caps should be limited to a few words, as in a headline.

Numerals unintentionally stand out in text (left) because they are set in *lining figures*, which look like capital letters. *Old style figures* look like lowercase characters and blend into text. Use lining figures amidst all caps like headlines charts, and use old style figures amidst lowercase or running text.

Legibility is a measure of how easily we can decipher the letterforms as we read (far left). Neville Brody pushes the edges of legibility in this work which reads, "The future city transcends..." Readability is a measure of how strongly a design attracts and holds a reader. This poster is much easier to notice than it is to read.

The shapes of numerals have evolved just as letterforms have. These numerals, from a c1460 Renaissance book made for merchants' day-to-day use (the relative hastiness of the manufacture – the lack of page alignment – reveals this), look a little different than today's characters. The book shows basic mathematics: multiplication tables on the left and exchange rates for Florentine coins on the right.

Legibility and readability

There are some characteristics that make type more legible and readable. Legibility, which is closely related to the design of the letterforms themselves, is the ease with which type can be understood under normal reading conditions. Readability is the quality of attracting and holding a reader's interest. It is the result of how the designer makes type comfortable to read. High readability – making something noticeable and interesting – often produces low legibility, that is, the piece becomes hard to read. So be aware of letting art obscure content rather than reveal it.

The following six aspects of typography affect its readability, or ability to attract readers: the inherent legibility of the typeface, type size, letterspacing, word spacing, linespacing, and format.

■ **The inherent legibility of the typeface** If the reader becomes aware of the letterforms, the typeface is a bad choice because it detracts from the smooth transmission of the message within. Legibility is most affected when what we are accustomed to is challenged. ☐ All-caps are harder to read than lowercase: the white space around lowercase words makes more distinctive shapes than all caps, which look like nearly identical rectangular bricks. All-caps settings should be kept to no more than two lines deep. The mind perceives three of anything as be-

1234567890
Lining figures

1234567890
Old style figures

"Typography which appeals to the eye embodies the same set of principles of design that goes into any work of art."
Carl Dair (1912–1967)

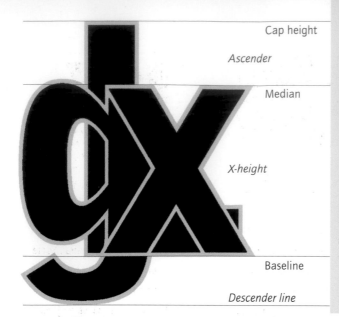

Cap height

Ascender

Median

X-height

Baseline

Descender line

ABSTRACTED

KitHinrichs:"Typographyisoneofthemostpowerfulemotionaltools availabltodesigners.Itcommunicatesmuchmorethanjustthewritten word.Whenusedeffectively,itcangivereadersa sense of the mood and pacing of a story, convey whether the content is serious or light, instructive or entertaining. Type can

LEGIBLE

Kit Hinrichs: "Typography is one of the most powerful emotional tools available to designers. It communicates much more than just the written word. When used effectively, it can give readers a sense of the mood and pacing of a story, convey whether the content is serious or light, instructive or entertaining. Type can

AUTARKY

AUTARKY

This is 8-point Frutiger set with 2 points of additional linespacing. Because it has a comparatively large x-height, it looks as big as the 10-point Perpetua below..The same two fonts are contrasted at 24 points to show detail. This is 8-on-10 Frutiger set across 13 picas

This is 10-point Perpetua set with 2 points of additional linespacing. Because it has a comparatively small x-height, it looks as big as the 8-point Frutiger above. The same two fonts are contrasted at 24 points to show de-

Frutiger Perpetua

This column is 13 picas wide and, in order to achieve an average character-per-line count of thirty-nine to fifty-two characters, the necessary type size in this font is 10 point.

This column is 18.5 picas wide and, in order to achieve an average character-per-line of thirty-nine to fifty-two characters, the necessary type size in this font is 15 point.

we yo Av Aw Ay Ta Te
To Tr Tu Tw Ty Ya Yo Wa
We Wo AC AT AV AW
AY FA LT LV LW LY OA
OV OW OY PA TA TO
VA VO WA WO YA YO

Reversing type calls for special handling. White letters look slightly smaller, so boost the point size a bit. Space around letters tends to fill in, so open the letterspacing when revers

ing type. The bottom example on the right is a script face whose tails should abut the leading edge of the next character, so the open setting makes it look "wrong."

"Counters," short for "counter spaces," are left white in the hand lettered display type of this ad, giving the already character-filled type treatment a quirky uniqueness.

Letterspacing There are three basic letter shapes: rectangular, round, and angular. Some combinations don't match up for optically even space distribution. These must be *kerned*.

"Not-letterforms," or the spaces surrounding letters, exist between characters and words. It is the contrast of the letterform to its surrounding space that makes type legible.

The best way to ensure spacing accuracy is to create display type in Illustrator and convert to paths. Position characters and adjust spaces individually as discreet shapes, not as letters in words.

Type size The x-height affects our perception of type's size and legibility. An ideal column width or line length contains about an alphabet and a half (thirty-nine) to two alphabets (fifty-two) characters per line. Type size must thus increase as line length increases.

ing many, so three or more lines of all-caps text repels readers. □ Old style figures look like lowercase letters and are used when numerals are set in text type. Lining figures, which look like capital letters, should be used in charts and in all-caps settings. □ Sans serif in text may be harder to read than serif. Serifs aid horizontal eye movement, so add extra line spacing to sans serif settings. □ Italics are harder to read than roman. Most italics are lighter than their roman counterparts and contrast less with the white paper. And readers are not used to reading italics. Use italics briefly and for emphasis. □ Shaded, outline, and inline faces are difficult to read and should be used only for display purposes. □ Any legible typeface becomes useless in, say, six-point italics reversed out of 40 percent gray.

■ **Type size** Ten-point type is thought of as the smallest legible type, but some eight-point looks as large as some ten-point type because of relative x-height, the part of the lowercase letterform that exists between the baseline and the median. Type size should be proportional to line length: the longer the line, the larger the type must be.

■ **Letterspacing** Letterspacing should be consistent. This is particularly important at display sizes where exact spacing is most noticeable. Spacing should be in proportion to the letterforms: wide letters need more letterspace than narrower letters; small letters need more letterspace

"The symbols of our lettering system are too familiar to provoke us into reflections on their basic construction."
Armin Hofmann (1920–)

Wordspacingdevelopedduring Medievaltimeswhenscribesaddedvaryingamountsofspaceto perfectlyfilloutlinesofhandwrittentext. Writtenperfectionwasthoughttomirror God'sownperfection. Thescribesalsoinventedcontractions,whichallowedlongwordstobemadetofitintoavailablespace.

Too little word spacing

Gutenberg continued the practice of justifying type as much for aesthetic as practical reasons. His moveable type needed to be "locked" in position before printing, and each line had to be the same length to accept being locked up.

Too much word spacing

Gutenberg cut pieces of wood that could be inserted between words to achieve the smooth right edges his machine required. Today's digital typesetting can adjust spacing with unprecedented precision, but putting the right amount of word space in a block of text or display type still requires a designer with knowledge, vision, and experience. Word spacing

Ideal (invisible) word spacing

Setting justified type across a line length that is too narrow causes uneven word spaces which become noticeable to readers. Meticulous attention must

Setting justified type across a line length that is sufficiently wide produces even word spaces. Meticulous attention must be given to hyphenation in all justified settings. Conversely, a flush left setting always produces even word spacing be

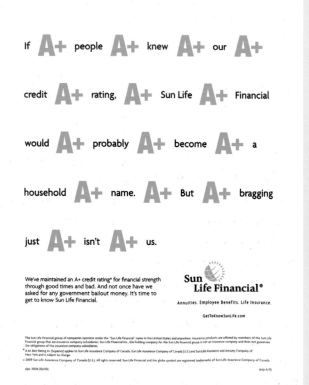

If A+ people A+ knew A+ our A+ credit A+ rating, A+ Sun Life A+ Financial would A+ probably A+ become A+ a household A+ name. A+ But A+ bragging just A+ isn't A+ us.

We've maintained an A+ credit rating* for financial strength through good times and bad. And not once have we asked for any government bailout money. It's time to get to know Sun Life Financial.

Sun Life Financial®

Annuities. Employee Benefits. Life Insurance.

GetToKnowSunLife.com

The quality of a cathedral's construction (shown in this 1465 Jean Fouquet illumination) was judged by the use of mortar between the stones. Letter*spacing* similarly indicates type quality.

Word spacing that is greater than line spacing becomes unavoidably visible because the eye connects to the nearest neighbor, which is vertical.

Word spacing in condensed letterforms must be tighter than normal to preserve the integrity of each line.

Letterspacing may make this newspaper ad (announcing an upcoming redesign or "facelift") harder to read. But it contributes the only personality to an otherwise ordinary design.

Word spacing Invisibility is the optimal amount of spacing between words. It should just separate one word from another. More than that breaks up the horizontal flow of reading.

Two modern samples of word spacing used intentionally.

Enraged cow injures farmer with machete

Enraged cow injures farmer with machete

Enraged cow injures farmer with machete

Hyphenation in display type is poor practice (unless the idea of "breaking" is itself the point of the headline). Otherwise, break a headline into segments that are natural phrases, as shown in the third example.

than larger letters; caps need more than lowercase letters. "Tracking" alters letterspacing paragraph by paragraph. "Kerning" alters letterspacing between specific character pairs. "Ligatures" are conjoined letter pairs.

■ **Word spacing:** Cathedral construction was judged by quality and consistency of the mortar as much as by the stonework itself. Similarly, typographers' work is judged by the spaces between letters and words. Word spacing should be *invisible*, just enough to separate word thoughts while maintaining the integrity of the line, and not so much that the reader perceives the presence of spaces and individual words (like this). Justified type gets its even right edge by forcing space throughout the line. Short lines of justified type have the least consistent word spacing because they have the fewest word spaces available to be distributed. The flush left/ragged right paragraph style has consistent word spacing and provides an equivalent visual rhythm, regardless of line length. □ Hyphenation in justified text allows more consistent word spacing, but hyphenation should never be used in display type, where breaking for sense is more important than breaking to fill a line.

■ **Linespacing:** Maximum legibility calls for text to be set no wider than forty to fifty characters per line. Longer measures must have added linespacing so the reader has an effortless return path to the left edge of the column

"Don't confuse legibility with communication."
David Carson (1952–)

graph indents should be set in proportion to the type size being used.

Larger type needs a deeper indent. Smaller type can function with a less obvious signal of, say, about a pica.

Adding space between paragraphs can be overdone. In this example, a full line space is too much added space (above). It fights the flow of ideas in a column.

Half a line space is usually a good distance to separate ideas and still maintain unity, as shown above.

It is redundant to *both* skip space between paragraphs *and* indent the first line, as such redundancy reveals the designer to not have thought about

the *purpose* of paragraphing.

A hanging indent pushes the first line out to the left and ensures that conscious, purposeful white space is built into the page.

Another signal is to indent whole paragraphs in an alternating rhythm. This works especially well with justified copy, where the right edge's smoothness contrasts with the left edge's fluctuations.

The point is to make each successive idea appear at once discrete, yet belonging with what precedes and follows in a cohesive, unselfconscious way.

Drop paragraphs begin each new paragraph directly below the previous

period. This can be achieved using tabs.

THE DARKNESS OF a bold lead-in is an excellent cue that a new idea is beginning. It may have space above the paragraph added, but it doesn't *need* it.

Initial caps should echo the distinctive display type used for a story. They may either stick up into emptiness – a "raised initial" – or hang down into the text, as shown here. This is called a "drop cap" and is another signal to indent whole paragraphs in an alternating rhythm. This works especially well with a purposeful flow of ideas where the right edge is an excellent cue that a new idea is built and follows in an obvious signal of ideas

COUNTING CROWES

BROODING BAD BOY AND BRILLIANT ACTOR. HELL-RAISER AND HEARTTHROB. PLAYER AND POET. THE MANY-SIDED STAR OF A BEAUTIFUL MIND GIVES US A PIECE OF HIS OWN. BY BENJAMIN SVETKEY

>> IN 'A BEAUTIFUL MIND', RUSSELL CROWE PLAYS A MATHEMATICAL GENIUS WHO FINDS COVERT MESSAGES HIDDEN IN THE TEXT OF OTHERWISE INNOCUOUS MAGAZINE >>

Note that the word spaces are larger than the line spaces and that your eyes prefer moving vertically rather than horizontally. Blur your eyes and you will see wiggly "rivers of white." TIP: Never use "Auto" as a line spacing attribute because it avoids making a specific decision about how much space should exist between lines. This must be a *choice* based on increasing type's legibility.

Note that the word spaces are now smaller than the line spaces and that your eyes prefer moving horizontally rather than vertically. Much of typography is making such subtle changes in the specifications and fine tuning the relationship of letters to the space surrounding them. This is

Linespacing cannot be smaller than word spacing, or the eye travels downward rather than across lines of type. Default spacing attributes will keep you out of embarrassing mis-

takes, but they cannot produce superior spacing, which is the domain of the graphic designer. Defaults should always be overridden with more thoughtful spacing characteristics.

Format Justifying text across a too-narrow measure will produce uneven word spacing (*left*). Flush left/ragged right always has even word spacing (*right*).

Format Type set in a funny shape forces the viewer to get past the visual trickery to pry out the message within – and they probably won't bother.

Format Traditional paragraphing signals are indentation and skipping space between paragraphs. Less conventional paragraphing signals include the hanging indent, the whole-paragraph indent, drop paragraphs, bold lead-ins, and initial caps.

"Minus-leading" is typesetting so the baseline-to-baseline distance is less than the size of type being used. It is usually seen in all caps settings like this, since there are no descenders to overlap into the tops of the next line of characters. Word spacing, which is always seen in relation to line spacing, has been tightened to avoid reading downwards. Here, word spacing and line spacing are about equivalent.

for the next line. Two narrower columns are often better than one wide column. (Notice how claustrophobic this decreasing linespacing makes you feel? Experiment to find the optimal linespacing for comfortable reading. Every typeface and column width combination has its own needs.) Linespacing must be greater than word spacing, or the eye flows down a stack of words rather than horizontally across a line.

■ **Format:** Readers recognize several key visual signals. *Position on the page* signals importance. The top of the page usually holds the best stuff because the top is where our eyes go naturally. The bottom of the page is less valuable real estate, so it may have the less important material. □ *White space* signals relative belongingness between elements. Elements that are close together appear to belong together and elements that are further apart appear to be less related. □ *Paragraphing* announces the beginning of a new idea. Any signal of a new beginning will work, though the most common are indention or skipping space between paragraphs. This is a fruitful area for discovery and reinterpretation and reiteration of existing design attributes, making the overall design more unified. □ *Punctuation* signals the pauses and stops that occur in copy. There are a few rules that punctuation must follow, the important ones having to do with connecting and separating clauses. □ *Type set in a funny shape* draws attention to itself rather than to its content, which is counterproductive.

"Perfect typography is certainly the most elusive of all arts. Out of stiff, unconnected little parts a whole must be shaped which is alive and convincing as a whole."
Jan Tschichold, *Clay in a Potter's Hand*

ABCDEFGHIJKabcdefghijklmnop

ABCDEFGHIJKabcdefghijklmnopq

ABCDEFGHIJKabcdefghijklmnop

ABCDEFGHIJKabcdefghijklmn

ABCDEFGHIJKabcdefghijklmn

ABCDEFGHIJKabcdefghijklmn

ABCDEFGHIJKabcdefghijklm

ABCDEFGHIJKabcdefghijklmnopq

ABCDEFGHIJKabcdefghijklm

ABCDEFGHIJKabcdefghijkl

ABCDEFGHIJKabcdefghijklm

ABCDEFGHIJKabcdefghijklmn

ABCDEFGHIJKabcdefghijklmnopq

ABCDEFGHIJKabcdefghijklmnop

ABCDEFGHIJKabcdefghijklmnop

ABCDEFGHIJKabcdefghijklmnopq

ABCDEFGHIJKabcdefghijklmnop

ABCDEFGHIJKabcdefghijklmnop

ABCDEFGHIJKabcdefghijklmnopqrs

ABCDEFGHIJKabcdefghijklmnop

ABCDEFGHIJKabcdefghijklmnopqrst

❶ SERIF TYPES
Oldstyle
Centaur
Garamond 3
Truesdell

Transitional
Baskerville
Bell
Caslon

Modern
Bodoni
Ellington
Fairfield

Slab Serif
Clarendon
LinoLetter
PMN Cæcilia

❷ SANS SERIF TYPES
Grotesque and Neo-Grotesque
Akzidenz Grotesk
Franklin Gothic
Univers

Geometric
Futura
Avant Garde Gothic
Neuzit Grotesk

Humanist
Officina Sans
Thesis (The Sans)
Delicious

totius generis o1
iuftitiá quá non
Moyſes naſcitu
atteſtatur. Credi
Quare multaru
ipſo benedicéda
aperte prædictu

1440
Die in ð werlt geſchaffi ſint Czu gꝛꝛ
ửn werủ audh zu nicht Als man we
1465
ucro enã legatos Erithreos a ſenatu eẽ miſſos
mẽna Romã deportarenẽ.et ea conſules Cur
1467
ſectantes illuſtrant. Legiſt Sulpitiủ
nimú plurimủ honoriſ & utilitatiſ act
1470
brꝛorủ appellatus eſt:apud qu
ulla mentio erat . Quare nec iu

Early serifs shown in Pompeiian brushstrokes and Nicolas Jenson's 1470 *Eusebius* typeface (shown actual size, about sixteen point). Jenson, a French-

man who moved to Venice, developed typefaces based on local northeast Italian writing, which was much lighter than the blackletter used north of the Alps.

Possibly the world's first sans serif letters are on a fifth-century BC Greek headstone. Though these stroke ends are very gently swelled, this is a residual effect of stone carving.

Earliest development of types shows movement from blackletter (1440 Gutenberg) to roman (1465 and 1467 Sweyenheym and Pannartz, and 1470 Jenson).

1501 First italic type: Aldus Manutius
deſipere fateatur. ſed ſicut a
alijs tollitur omnibus . Nihi
1527 Ludovico degli Arrighi
N ulla uia eſt. tamen ire iu
I nuiaque audaci propero t
1575 First oblique capitals
Fert Fatum parteis in-r
Prælia, debellatum Or
1545 Claude Garamont
Chriſtianiß. Regis prum
tum editis ſuis in ſacras li
1660 Christopher van Dyck
Ædem, is admonen
Amſtelodamo,non mod

Italic type was based on regional handwriting. First made in 1501 by Aldus Manutius, he called it *corsivo* and, because he made only lowercase letters, he used them with existing roman capitals. The French crafted slanted capitals to be used with italic lowercase types a few years later.

Type classifications

Letterforms have been evolving for about 3,500 years; type has been evolving for about 450. Writing has passed through periods of slow changes and great growth. There are many ways to classify styles of type. I prefer a relatively simple system of eight classifications. Of these, serif and sans serif are the most important because they are the most often used. My digital font collection has three catalogs filled with serif typefaces, two showing sans serifs, two of scripts and handlettered types, five with display faces, and four showing picture fonts.

❶ **Serif** Has cross-lines at the ends of strokes, which date from stone carving during the Roman period. Serif types are subcategorized into four divisions (each of which can be further reduced, though my desire is to keep it relatively simple here): *Oldstyle*, the first roman typefaces, based on the writing of Italian scribes in the late 1400s; *Transitional*, from the 1700s, which combine characteristics of both Oldstyle and Modern; *Modern*, from the late 1700s, which have the greatest contrast between thicks and thins; and *Slab Serif*, from the 1800s, which have thick serifs to darken the letters and increase visibility for the new business of advertising.

❷ **Sans serif** Type "without serifs" introduced in 1817, embraced by the design avant garde in the early 1900s. Sans serif types are subcategorized into three divisions:

Aldus Manutius, the Latinized version of his given name, *Aldo Manuzio*, introduced several typographic characters and converted local handwriting into what came to be known as *italic* type. This is a replica of Manutius' print shop in Venice, where he elevated typographic form and printing technique to new and more elegant levels.

ABCDEFGHIJ*Kabcdefghijklmnopqrstuvw*
ABCDEFGHIJKabcdefghijklmnopqrstu

ABCDEFGHIJKLMNOPQRSTUV
ABCDEFGHIJKabcdefghijklmn

ABCDEFGHIJKabcdefghijklmnopqrs
ABCDEFGHIJKabcdefghijklmnop

ABCDEFGHIJKabcdefghijl
ABCDEFGHIJKabcdefghijk

Ampersand, 1470
Nicolas Jenson, Venice

Ampersand, 1532
Antonio Blado, Rome

Ampersand, 1549
Robert Estienne, Paris

Ampersand, 1556
Gabriel Giolito, Ferrara

Comma, 1495
Aldus Manutius, Venice

Question mark, 1501
Aldus Manutius, Venice

Exclamation, 1791
Giambattista Bodoni, Parma

Quotations, 1826
Edward Walker, England

ABCDEFGHIJKLMNOPQRSTUVWXYZ
Capitals

Lowercase
abcdefghijklmnopqrstuvwxyz

Lining figures   Old style figures
0123456789   0123456789

Small caps
ABCDEFGHIJKLMNOPQRSTUVWXYZ

Superscript and Subscript figures   Punctuation   Ligatures & Diphthongs
0123456789 X 0123456789   .,:;-¿?!/""""|·'[{()}]   ff fi fl ffl æ Æ Œ

Fractions   Accented characters   Reference & Miscellaneous marks
¼ ½ ⅛ ¾ ⅝ ⅔   åçéîñøüÅÇÉ   ©®™&$¢£†‡§¶

William Caxton made this ad in 1478 to show off his new typeface, *Sarum Ordinal*. Based on northern European blackletter – Caxton had just learned his trade in Belgium – he soon developed his own character sets, which came to be known as *Old English*. As England's first printer, Caxton was instrumental in standardizing English spelling and usage.

A font is made of many more characters than the twenty-six characters in the Latin alphabet: both capitals and lowercase letters, plus one or more sets of numerals, small-caps, punctuation and assorted glyphs. The simplest display face might have as few as fifty characters while the most complete text face might have as many as two hundred characters.

The ampersand is an evolution of *et*, Latin for "and." Drawn in many variations, it is one of the oldest abbreviations.

The question mark is a "Q-o" (or ℺), an abbreviation of *quaestio*, Latin for "what" or "I seek." The exclamation point is a Latin "I-o," equivalent to "wow."

Grotesque and *Neo-Grotesque*, based on earliest designs from the 1800s, so called because early type without serifs was considered ugly; *Geometric*, influenced by the Bauhaus and featuring circular bowls and consistent character weight; and *Humanist*, which looks organic and somewhat hand-drawn with greater stroke contrast.

❸ Script and hand-lettered Closest approximation of hand-lettering; range from formal to casual.

❹ Glyphic Based on letters carved in stone. Usually all-caps because minuscules did not exist in the days of actual stone carved letterforms.

❺ Blackletter Also called *Gothic* and *Old English*. Northern European flat-pen handscripts at the time of Gutenberg's movable type, c1450.

❻ Monospaced Types in which each letter occupies the same space, regardless of their proportional width, a remnant of typewriters. These are still valuable as figures in tables and charts where vertical character alignment is useful.

❼ Display A vast category that includes types that don't fit into other categories (and even some that do). By definition, these typefaces would be significantly less legible at text sizes and should not be used for extended reading.

❽ Symbol and ornaments Simple illustrations of representational and decorative ideas.

"A typeface is an alphabet in a straitjacket."
Alan Fletcher (1931–2006)

414-horsepower V-8

0-60 in 4.8 seconds

Redline 8400 rpm

Quote, sedan, unquote.

Introducing the all-new 2008 BMW M3. Just when you think you've seen it all, another BMW M3 is unveiled. This time it takes the shape of a sedan that delivers an unexpected rush of 414 horses while redlining at a hair-raising 8400 rpm. Every inch meticulously redefined, there is simply no more fat left to trim from this first-ever production V-8 M3 Sedan. **Amazement. Crafted at BMW M.** **/M**

Ho lasciato il bambino solo un momento in cucina – e l'ho ritrovato infarinato — da capo a piedi. Mi ri|

Hyphens and dashes come in three widths. Each has its own role, but it is up to the designer to choose which character will be used. A vertical hyphen has been proposed as a way to solve the need to hang a horizontal hyphen. A *hyphen* is a short horizontal bar used to indicate breaks in words at the ends of lines. An en-dash is slightly longer and used as a separator in elective situations, as between multiple compound words, and between numbers. An em-dash is the longest – I believe too long, because it becomes too noticeable in a text setting – and is used for sudden breaks in dialogue.

Never use primes in text (top). Reduce the size of punctuation and the space after commas and periods *particularly in display type* for optical evenness.

A verbal interpretation of the "air quote," those annoying finger gestures people use to step outside what they are actually saying, is used to novel effect in this car, uh, *sedan*, ad.

Punctuation and dashes

Punctuation developed as a way for scribes to indicate reading speed for out loud delivery of religious services. There were no standards for the use of punctuation until the invention of printing. In general, dots indicated word separations and were replaced by spaces by about AD 600. The dot, when aligned at cap height, was then used to indicate a stop, like a modern *period*, and when aligned at the baseline, to indicate a pause, like a modern *comma*. Aldus Manutius, one of the first printers in Italy, introduced the *semicolon, question mark,* and the slanted, condensed humanist letterforms, which came to be known as *italics*.

«*Quote marks* were introduced in Paris in 1557 as a pair of sideways Vs.» English printers eventually replaced those with inverted commas ("6s") at the opening and apostrophes ("9s"), which had been invented in the 1600s, at the end of a quote. Smart quotes like these are used in text while prime (') and double prime (") symbols – also called the vertical apostrophe – are used in numerals.

French spacing is the insertion of two word spaces after a period to highlight a new sentence. French spacing was used in monospaced typewritten copy through the twentieth century to help make sentence beginnings more visible. It is not necessary – and actually bad form – in proportionally spaced digital typesetting.

ype is the glue holds a publintent together. s the constant read to spread issue to issue, t are the vital ype is the glue t holds a publintent together. s the constant read to spread l issue to issue, t are the vital

Hung punctuation, the placement of punctuation marks in the margin beyond the flush edge of a column, was first use in type by Gutenberg, though it is today an automatic process in InDesign. Hang punctuation by placing it in the margin to create an *optically even* column edge.

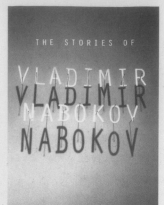

❶

❷

❸

Display type is often the biggest type, and as such, it can be treated as pure form, as can the spaces between its characters.

Letterforms and imagery become one, abstracting both in the process. This technique is successful if the imagery is directly related to the message.

Detail of the top half of a running clothing ad has primary type rendered as a shoelace – a noticeable and relevant treatment for this message.

Display type's purpose is to attract attention, and this two-letter illustration certainly does it with style, as it precisely describes the "g" and "o" letters from Visa's typeface.

Display type stops browsers and it should lead directly to secondary type.

Display type is not *necessarily* large: its true intention is to be seen first (*Tchaikovsky*). Its visibility is dependent on the surrounding type, so the focal point is the element *with the greatest contrast with its surroundings* (Vivaldi). Huge letterforms cropped by the edges of the page in the first study are a powerful attractant.

Three headline styles exhibit ❶ Contrast of alignment and position: the headline is visible by separating it from the text; ❷ Contrasting type styles: the headline is visible by setting it in a different typeface; and ❸ Type and image integration: the headline is visible by blending the type and image into one.

12 Display type

The correctly set word is the starting point of all typography. The letters themselves we have to accept: they are shaped by the type designer. – Jan Tschichold (1902-1974)

There are two kinds of type: display and text. Text is where the story is. Display is there to describe content and lure readers through a sequence of typographic impressions so they can make an informed decision about committing to the first paragraph of text. At that point, the story is on its own and, aside from ensuring legibility in the text by crafting optimal characters per line, harmonizing letter-, word-, and linespacing, and choosing an adequate type size, the designer's job of revealing content is largely done.

There are various opportunities for the designer to describe content and lure browsers. Primary type is usually a headline. Secondary type, intended to be read after the headline and before the text, includes subheads and decks, captions, department headings, breakouts, and pull quotes.

Readers are accustomed to looking at big type first,

Primary type 179
Type meant to be seen first doesn't have to be the biggest type.

Typographic abstraction 179
Balance eye-catching singularity with reasonable legibility.

Secondary type 181
The payoff for abstracted primary type is relatively clear backup type that explains and leads to the text, where the story is.

Setting display type 185
Display type is not merely "large text." Spacing is far more visible in large type, so it needs more attention.

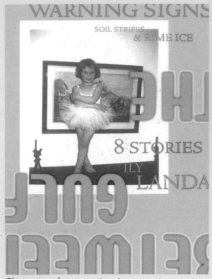

Character shape contrast

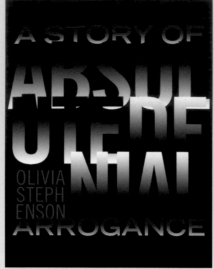

Character width contrast

Color contrast

Density contrast

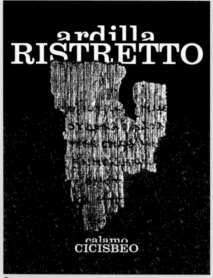

Format contrast

Position contrast

Size contrast

Stress contrast

Weight contrast

Abstracting type includes rebalancing the figure/ground relationship by making the ground more important. Here is an example that repeats parts of a single typeform c.

Tops of letters are easier to read than bottoms and lower-case are easier to read than caps because word shapes are varied.

Sometimes abstracting a word by leaving letters out entirely is the best way to get an idea across.

Display type based on position, not just bigger size. Unity with matched size of text. Symmetry is stable, and may reveal something about chair's stability?

The nine typographic abstractions Typographic abstraction can be expressed in infinite ways, but it always exploits just nine type contrasts. It is nearly impossible to express only a single contrast by itself, so intentionally pairing them will lead to multiple alternatives.

Character shape Serif vs sans serif

Character width Expanded vs condensed

Color Dark vs light

Density Tight vs loose; Positive vs negative; Solid vs outline

Format Caps vs lowercase

Position Vertical vs horizontal; Top vs bottom; Front vs back

Size Small vs large

Stress Vertical vs oblique

Weight Heavy vs light

but "display" is not necessarily large type. Nor is "text" necessarily small type. The real definitions are *intentional*: "display" is the type intended to stop the browser and to be read first; "text" is the destination to which the reader is drawn.

Primary type

Headlines and the structure of a page create the personality of printed material. Primary type is used to draw attention to itself, to stop the browser and to lead to a specific piece of secondary type. The secondary type's purpose, in turn, is to lead to the text. The text is always the final destination.

Headline treatments fall into three categories: alignment and position, contrasting type styles, and the integration of type and imagery. Regardless of design treatment, a great headline is provocatively written and makes an immediate point.

Typographic abstraction

There are places where playfulness with legibility is inappropriate. Text, for example, is simply too small to absorb abstraction without substantially losing legibility. But display type is tailor-made for unusual treatments that flirt with illegibility. Display type is meant to attract attention and it is usually big, so letterforms can be

"Sometimes you have to compromise legibility to achieve impact."
Herb Lubalin (1918–1981)

NEW ORLEANS FEBRUARY 14TH-15TH

PROBABLY
THE ONLY TIME

YOU'LL LONG FOR

Bigger

THIGHS

IT'S NOT A CULT

POPEYES CAJUN CHICKEN FESTIVAL

BUT IT'S CLOSE

FRANKLIN GOTHIC CONDENSED

BEADED	OCEAN	SLASH
CHAIR	PIXEL	SPACE
CRUMPLE	PLASTIC	STITCH
GRID	SCREW	TREE

Space between letters can be used to enhance identity. It is shown here in three quantities: completely removed, normal, and very open. The BLEU ex-

ample, a 1921 magazine logo, trades individual character recognition for overall unity as a shape.

Typographic expression and playfulness is best done with relatively plain typefaces. Simple letterforms are editable while keeping their recognizable shapes. For this reason,

sans serif faces are more useful than serif, and roman is more useful than italic. These are variations on Franklin Gothic produced by students as fully functional display fonts.

Damaged letterforms suit some messages perfectly, as in this example for a Cajun chicken festival. One of a series of equally scratchy, down-home designs, these letters look authentically hurting. Beware of using premade "damaged type" fonts in which the imperfect letters are repeated, giving away the canned, premade, fake nature of the damage. Any designer unable or unwilling to craft a custom damaged treatment for a client should have to perform community service.

read even if they are "damaged." There are an infinite number of ways to "harm" letter and word forms, and they are all combinations of the nine typographic contrasts. Type abstraction simply pushes a normal contrast to an extreme. For example, making type "big" isn't enough. *Making type so big that the edges are indistinct* works because it forces an interaction of figure/ground.

Some typefaces are inherently abstract and hard to read. With these, ordinary typesetting is all that's needed to create an attention getting abstracted message.

spabefgomty SPABEFGOMTY Spabefgomty SPABEFGOMTY Spabefgomty SPABEFGOMTY

A typeface's character may be corroborative (**Nuclear**), contradictory (Nuclear), or neutral (**Nuclear**) to the meaning of its message. Use typography that is laden with character sparingly, only in the primary and secondary type where its attention-getting strength is at least as important as its legibility.

"I believe there is one perfect use for every typeface ever drawn, no matter how hideous."
Fred Woodward (1953–)

Secondary type

If the headline is the lure, the subhead is the readers' payoff. Here is the opportunity to hook the reader by explaining the headline. The headline leads to one or more secondary messages, first a subhead or deck, but possibly a caption, breakout, or pull quote. The mes-

Deaf college opens doors to hearing

Local school dropouts cut in half

by Karla Kohn

Deaf college opens doors to hearing

Local school dropouts cut in half

by Karla Kohn

Deaf college opens doors to hearing

Local school dropouts cut in half

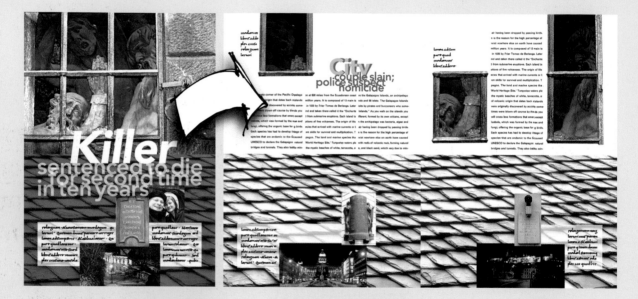

Killer
sentenced to die for second time in ten years

City
couple slain; police suspect homicide

DRUNK GETS
9 MONTHS IN
in escapes to
VIOLIN CASE
Suchdol hideout

STOLEN PAINTING FOUND BY TREE

RED TAPE
HOLDS UP
NEW BRIDGE
for Karlov Most
urgently needed

DRUNK GETS
9 MONTHS IN
VIOLIN CASE

STOLEN PAINTING FOUND BY TREE

RED TAPE
HOLDS UP
NEW BRIDGE

Story by Klaus Körki
Photos by Milan Kincl

"Mala Strana couple slain"
Police suspect homicide

Subheads are secondary type that explain headlines. A *deck* is a subhead immediately beneath the headline. A

floating subhead is secondary type placed away from the headline. A *breaker head* is placed in the text column and regularly hints at the worthwhile goodies within.

Captions are display type: they are read before the text and should provide information about the story. These captions are labels that tell us how to interpret the image.

Subheads are secondary type that explain or support the headline. Sometimes, they can be taglines at the end of text, as shown here.

Secondary type exists hierarchically between the primary type and the tertiary type. This Nike spread ad has a few pieces of secondary type, contributing to its screechy visual tone.

Breakouts and pull quotes are *brief* extracts from the text that are handled like verbal illustrations. Provocatively edited, their purpose is to make browsers stop and *consider* reading the story. Breakouts and pull quotes can visually connect pages of a long story by repeating a variation of the type treatment of the opener's headline.

Captions explain photos. Because they are read before the text, they must be thought of as display type and be fascinating enough to persuade potential readers to enter the text.

sages in the headline and subhead should be two parts of a complete thought, provocatively showing why the story is important to the reader. Readers should, after a total of three or four information "hits," have been given enough information about the story to make an informed decision about whether or not to get into the text. Actually becoming committed to the text can happen only after they have begun reading it.

Secondary type should be smaller – or less noticeable – than the headline, but more prominent than text. A balance must be struck between contrasts and unity among the three levels of type. Variations of one typeface in the primary and secondary type contrast well against a highly legible text face.

Selecting the right typeface is a significant decision, but how you use a typeface is at least as important as what typeface is used. Imagine if your work were given an award for design excellence: would the typeface designer get the credit or would you be recognized for having used type well?

A friend redesigned a magazine in the days of hot metal type (this was in the 1960s), when a font was truly a single typeface in one size and weight. The client had purchased only two fonts: twelve-point Franklin Gothic Regular and Bold. The magazine could only use those two fonts, yet had to do all that a magazine's ty-

Spabefgomty Franklin Gothic
Spabefgom Monotype Grotesque
Spabefgomt Meta
Spabefgomty News Gothic
Spabefgomty Quay
Spabefgom Clarendon
Spabefgomt Loire
Spabefgomty Menhart Manuscript
Spabefgomty Nicolas Jenson SG
Spabefgomty Californian

Ten favorite typefaces.

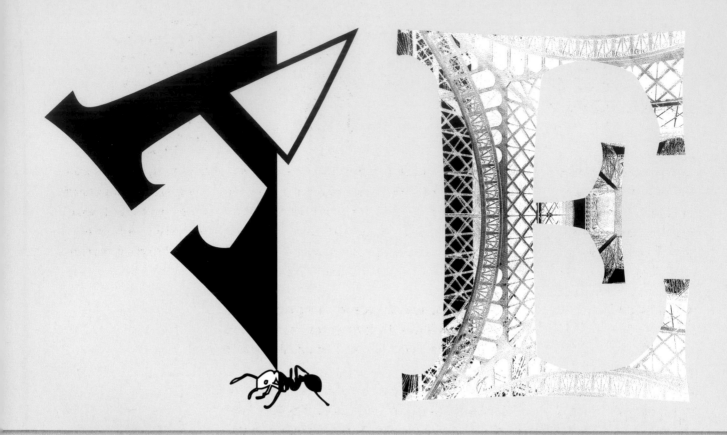

Avenir 95 Black	Loire Sombre		
Avenir 85 Heavy	*Loire Sombre Italique*		
Avenir 65 Medium	Loire Regular		
Avenir 55 Roman	*Loire Italique*		
Avenir 55 Oblique	Loire Pale		
Avenir 45 Book	*Loire Pale Italique*		
Avenir 35 Light			

In general – and to make contrasts look intentional – use no more than two typeface families in a design, and don't use more than two weights of each face. If you add italic versions of the regular weights you have six typographic "voices," equivalent to hearing six people reading aloud, which should be enough to convey any message.

This theater poster announces the season's lineup, so each play title is handled as secondary type, between the theater's name/season year and the directors' names/performance dates.

Secondary type provides structure as a five-line musical staff to a presentation of clusters of letters in this German poster for a concert of Mozart's music.

Letterforms are both vessels of communication (as part of an alphabet) and beautiful forms. These studies, using characters from Martin Wilke's 1988 *Wilke*, blend letterforms with illustrative content, creating new hybrid art and type messages.

pography must express. The redesign, using only position and emptiness to make display type visible, succeeded because of the extremely limited typographic contrast.

Setting display type

Display type shows off mis-spaced characters more than text simply because of its larger size, where character-to-character relationships are particularly visible.

Letters are strung together into words. The space between individual letters goes unnoticed when the type is smaller than about eighteen points. The optimum letterspacing is "invisible," that is, it is unself-conscious. The reader should not be aware that letterspacing exists when it is done well.

Words are grouped into lines of type. Word spacing is the glue that holds lines of type together. The secret to good word spacing is also invisibility. The reader should not be aware of the type that is being read but should be concentrating on its meaning. Display word spacing is often too large because it is set with built-in text algorithms. In general, display type's global word spacing can be reduced to 50 to 80 percent of normal.

The secret to developing an eye for perfect, invisible type spacing is to assume that your spacing is either too open or too tight. If it can be only one of those choices – never just right – adjust it until it truly looks just right.

"The expression in a (typographic) design is what is most important, not the typeface that is used."
Wolfgang Weingart (1941–)

Seventy percent	Seventy percent
Eighty percent	Eighty percent
Ninety percent	Ninety percent
One hundred percent	One hundred percent
One hundred ten percent	One hundred ten percent
One hundred twenty percent	One hundred twenty percent
One hundred thirty percent	One hundred thirty percent

Torskü Torskü Torskü

TRACKING "NORMAL"
NO KERNING

TRACKING "TIGHT"
NO KERNING

-3 -4 0 -2 -3

TRACKING "NORMAL"
WITH KERNING

 SMALL CAPS
TRUE SMALL CAPS ARE FOUND
IN "SC" FONTS

 SMALL CAPS
TRUE SMALL CAPS ARE FOUND
IN "SC" FONTS

 SMALL CAPS
FALSE SMALL CAPS ARE REDUCED
IN SIZE AND LOOK TOO LIGHT

 SMALL CAPS
FALSE SMALL CAPS ARE REDUCED
IN SIZE AND LOOK TOO LIGHT

Man minus ear waives hearing

Man minus ear waives hearing

Man minus ear waives hearing

Steals clock, faces time

Steals clock, faces time

STEALS CLOCK, FACES TIME

STEALS CLOCK, FACES TIME

"Quote"
23'9"

	= !
shift	= ll
option /	= `
option shift /	= '
option /	= ``
option shift /	= ''

More opportunities than streptococcus in a room full of 5 year-olds.

MedCAREERS
www.medcareers.com

UTAH ARTS FESTIVAL
CHARACTER

Real quote marks look like "66" and "99." The inch (") and foot (') marks are incorrectly used as ambidextrous quote marks, a leftover from typewriters' need for few keys. The default in most programs is set to use "smart quotes," so you must consciously deselect this to get proper prime symbols in numbers. Shown here are the keystrokes used on a Mac for these six glyphs.

Display type can have "poor" spacing attributes if it is the very thing that defines the type. This headline for an employment ad was typeset on a prescription label printer.

Display type requires especially careful spacing. The best way to achieve optically consistent spacing is to treat each individual letter as a form: convert it to paths and adjust manually.

Digitally compressing or expanding type creates anomalies. Visible distortion becomes apparent in most typefaces at about ±5 percent of normal set width.

Kerning is the optical spacing of letterform pairs, which is far more important than global tracking at display sizes.

Small caps match the weight of full-size caps. False small caps, which are merely reduced in size, look too light because they are *proportionally* smaller.

Breaking for sense puts meaning above form and should be seriously considered in display headings.

Linespacing should be tightened in headlines to make the chunk of type darker.

Headlines are made of clusters of phrases and should be "broken for sense" into these clusters, regardless of the shape this forces on the headline (facing page, fourth row). To find the natural breaks, read a headline out loud. Try not to break a headline to follow a design; rather, break a headline so that it makes the most sense to the reader. Hyphenating type communicates that shape is more important than meaning. Display type should never be hyphenated, unless its meaning is to illustrate "disconnection."

The effectiveness of display typography is principally dependent on the management of the white space between and around the letterforms, not only on the letterforms themselves. Because display type is brief (to snag the reader's attention), letterspacing, word spacing, and line breaks become more important.

Increase contrast and visibility of headlines by making them darker on the page. Reduce white space in and around characters in letterspacing and linespacing (facing page, bottom). All-cap headlines in particular should have linespacing removed because there are no descenders to "fill in" the space between lines. In upper- and lowercase settings, don't let ascenders and descenders touch, or they'll create an unintentional stigma on the page.

"Typography exists to honor content."
Robert Bringhurst
(1946–)

of freſh graſs. In a ſhort time, accordin[g]
[h]is wiſh, the warm weather, and the freſh g[rass]
[c]ame on; but brought with them ſo much
[a]nd buſineſs, that he was ſoon as weary of
[s]pring as before of the winter; and he now
[b]ame impatient for the approach of ſumm[er]

[s]lediſſe. Alterũ eim quum per aſpera ſcander[e]
[ha]c ita expiraſſe. Alterum quum eques per litt[us]
[l]apſum una cum equo fuiſſe aquis demerſu[m]
[e] morbo conſumptum: alii quũ templũ Inabis[...]
[s] fuiſſe tradiderũt. Nemo profecto hæc caſu n[...]
[s] Omnes enim hos tres eiſdem temporibus pr[...]
[i]lus ſuppliciis ã lex uolebat iure punitos no[...]

COLLAPSE
UPPER CASE
LOWER CASE

COLLAPSE FONT WAS DESIGNED IN 1995, ESPECIALLY
FOR A BROCHURE FOR THE ACADEMY OF FINE ARTS AND
DESIGN IN BRATISLAVA, SLOVAKIA. IT IS A SINGLE USE
TYPEFACE; I HAVE NOT USED IT SINCE THEN, AND PROBABLY
I WILL NEVER USE IT AGAIN. AS THE NAME OF THE FONT
MAY SAY, COLLAPSE IS HIGHLY AFFECTED BY A NEW WAY OF
DESIGNING-COMPUTER GRAPHIC, AND BY THE COMPUTER
ERRORS THAT ARE CONNECTED WITH IT. THIS SEEMED TO BE
A SATISFACTORY REASON FOR ME TO DESIGN A NEW FONT.
BECAUSE OF A CHARACTER OF THE TASK (STUDENTS' EXHIBITION)
THE TYPEFACE WAS AIMED TO BE "NONTRADITIONAL".
ANOTHER REASON FOR THE CREATION OF THIS TYPEFACE
WAS THE LACK OF MONEY; WE COULD NOT AFFORD TO BUY A
FONT, AND TO MAKE ONE UP AS A SCHOOL PROJECT DOES NOT COST
ANYTHING.
IN ORDER TO GIVE THE FACE A RANDOM LOOK, EVERY
LETTER HAS TWO DIFFERENT VERSIONS, SO THE FONT EXISTS
IN TWO DIFFERENT SETS-UPPER AND LOWER CASE.

LECTURE ON NOTHING/121

Textus to text: *Textus* is a late Middle English term from the Latin for *woven fabric*, the closest thing to which the recent invention of movable type could be compared. Here are samples from Eric Gill, 1931; Aldus Manutius, 1505; and St. John Hornby, 1902.

Weight, stress, and density determine type's texture, as illustrated by this student exercise.

Type's space is imaginatively used in *Silence*, a collaboration by composer John Cage and typographer Raymond Grimaila.

Variable character spacing affects the text's right edge in this study by Peter Bil'ak.

Word spaces were nearly non-existent in Nicolas Jenson's 1470 *Eusebius*. They had widened by 1761 in John Baskerville's *Aesop's Fables*. The samples are upside-down to show the spacing.

Linespacing indicates either horizontal or vertical reading in Japanese, which provides varied typographic texture.

Paragraph widths have been sized to align and flirt with the tightly cropped imagery in this example. Combined with

alternating weights, this is an unusual alternative to simple paragraph indentions.

Text columns nearly abut, but their baselines are staggered to indicate line ends, an echo of the subtle shifts in the display type.

13 Text type

N o matter how fine are the types we select, our work's appearance depends on good composition: the combination of type into words, the arrangement of words into lines, and the assemblage of lines to make pages. – D.B. Updike (1860-1941)

The term text comes from *textus*, Latin for the texture of woven fabric. There are two interpretations of this etymology: that text blends ideas and words into a single message as threads are woven into cloth; and that text areas have a visual pattern that suggests fabric. With regard to the latter, just as cloth's texture varies with the weight and material of the threads being used, type's texture depends on the letterforms' weight, angle of stress, and density.

Though there is a good deal of overlap in the way text and display type are handled, their purposes are different, which affects the details of text's setting. Display type's purpose is to be noticed, to convey meaning, and to motivate the reader to the next "type opportunity." But the ultimate destination of all display type is the text, where the full story and, in ads, the sales pitch is.

Space and text type 191
Managing the "spaces between" is crucial in text settings.

Text abstraction 193
Abstracting text is different from abstracting display: balancing legibility is a far greater concern.

Effortless text 195
Effortful text is repellent and will cause readers to drop out: you will not likely get a bonus for doing *that*.

Setting perfect text 199
Craft is essential in text settings: it is where your typographic knowledge is most revealed.

Acegmorty

10-point Scala Regular

Acegmorty

36-point Scala Regular reduced

Acegmorty spabef gomty

10-point Scala Regular

Acegmorty spabef gomty

24-point Scala Regular reduced

Acegmorty

36-point Scala Regular

Acegmorty

10-point Scala Regular enlarged

Acegmorty spabef gomty

24-point Scala Regular

Acegmorty spabef gomty

10-point Scala Regular enlarged

An education isn't how much you have committed to memory, or even how much you know. It's being able to differentiate between what you do know and what you don't. *Anatole France* I cannot give you the formula for success, but I can give you the formula for failure, which is: try to please everybody. *Herbert Bayard Swope* The right to be heard does not automatically include the right to be taken seriously. *Hubert Humphrey* Being frustrated is disagreeable, but the real disasters of life begin when you get what you want. *Irving Kristol* Tact is the knack

10/10 Scala Regular *with Italic*

An education isn't how much you have committed to memory, or even how much you know. It's being able to differentiate between what you do know and what you don't. *Anatole France* I cannot give you the formula for success, but I can give you the formula for failure, which is: try to please everybody. *Herbert Bayard Swope* The right to be heard does not automatically include the right

10/15 Scala Regular *with Italic*

An education isn't how much you have committed to memory, or even how much you know. It's being able to differentiate between what you do know and what you don't. *Anatole France*

I cannot give you the formula for success, but I can give you the formula for failure, which is: try to please everybody. *Herbert Bayard Swope*

10/15 Scala Regular *with Italic, 0p6 indent, which is too small for this linespacing to be visible*

An education isn't how much you have committed to memory, or even how much you know. It's being able to differentiate between what you do know and what you don't. *Anatole France*

I cannot give you the formula for success, but I can give you the formula for failure, which is: try to please everybody. *Herbert Bayard Swope*

10/15 Scala Regular *with Italic, 1p3 indent to match text's baseline-to-baseline distance*

An education isn't how much you have committed to memory, or even how much you know. It's being able to differentiate between what you do know and what you don't. *Anatole France* I cannot give you the formula for success, but I can give you the formula for failure, which is: try to please everybody. *Herbert Bayard Swope*

An education isn't how much you have committed to memory, or even how much you know. It's being able to differentiate between what you do know and what you don't. *Anatole France* I cannot give you the formula for success, but I can give you the for-mula for failure, which is: try to please everybody. *Herbert Bayard Swope*

An education isn't how much you have committed to memory, or even how much you know. It's being able to differentiate between what you do know and what you don't. *Anatole France* I cannot give you the formula for success, but I can give you the for-mula for failure, which is: try to please everybody. *Herbert Bayard Swope*

A women's magazine uses classic newspaper column structure and typography – and spins traditional 1960s breakfast reading material – in an editorial promotion.

A stock photography company shows, rather than tells, "a picture is worth a thousand words" by abstracting the image with empty text columns.

Removing line spacing creates overlapped lines of text, which reveals a texture or pattern of text-size type that, while intentionally illegible, evokes a feeling of city buildings. This bank's sales message, which is a bit disguised though entirely legible, is in the paragraph immediately beneath the space between "in a word" and the "ING" of the logo.

Text's letterspacing needs to be more open than display type's so each letter can be more distinctly seen. Text's word spacing must proportionally follow.

Have more linespacing than word spacing to force the eye *across* lines of type. Optimal line length is about fifty-five characters per line (as shown in this example). If longer than that, add more linespacing.

Indents should be the same distance as the baseline-to-baseline distance of the text. On the left, it is only six points deep. On the right it is 1p3, or fifteen points.

Column spaces should be significantly larger than word spaces to avoid confusion and readers' "jumping the gutter."

Space and text type

The goal of superior text typesetting is even "type color." This is achieved by balancing, on the one hand, individual letters and groups of letters as words and, on the other hand, words and unified lines of type. Too much spacing weakens words and lines. Too little spacing sacrifices letters and words.

■ **Between characters:** Optimal text character spacing must be more open than display type's to compensate for its small point size. Space between a specific pair of characters is *kerned*. Space between all characters in a paragraph is *tracked*.

■ **Between words:** Optimal word spacing is inconspicuous and barely separates word-thoughts. It never breaks a line of type into chunks. Word spacing is seen in proportion to letterspacing: tight letterspacing goes with tight word spacing and loose with loose.

■ **Between lines:** Optimal linespacing must be greater than word spacing so the eye travels horizontally. The space should be sufficient so descenders and ascenders don't overlap, but not so great that it breaks up the integrity of the column.

■ **Between paragraphs:** A paragraph contains a single idea. Each paragraph must be perceived both as an entity and as part of a string of ideas. Separate paragraphs with an indent, a hanging indent, or addi-

"The greatest literary masterpiece is no more than an alphabet in disorder."
Jean Cocteau (1889–1963), writer and artist

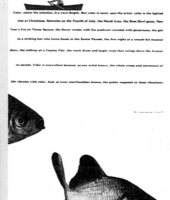

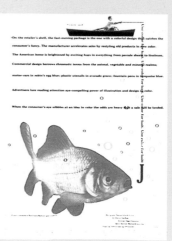

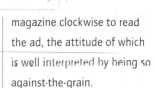

Type as imagery: Herb Lubalin's 1958 ad for *Holiday* magazine that lists clothing advertisers. The hanger does all the work to make us see type as imagery.

The standard column structure is adhered to, but the shape of the column bottoms is cropped to accommodate a very unusual ad shape in this *New York Times* spread.

Decreasing type size is the second most remarkable feature of text in this spread ad. It is necessary to turn the whole

magazine clockwise to read the ad, the attitude of which is well interpreted by being so against-the-grain.

Text as hair and dress: 1962 Vogue ad by Malcolm Mansfield; a 1959 shoe ad by Reba Sochis. The more pronounced the shape, the more attention is put on the treatment and the less on the content.

Text as racetrack, rain, seawater, and emotion: Bradbury Thompson's Westvaco *Inspirations* paper promotions included *Run your eyes around these pages* and *Color/Fishing* from 1949. A more recent car ad shows text as rain. Otto Storch's 1960 spread for *McCall's* magazine shows playful text use.

*Paragraph indents are a remnant of incunabula printing in which space was left for a rubricated (handpainted) initial. After a while, the space alone indicated another beginning.

tional space between paragraphs. ¶ Paragraphing may also be achieved through use of a dingbat, allowing continuous text. The first paragraph of text should never be indented: it spoils the clean left corner and it is a redundant signal – the typographic contrast between deck and text indicates a new idea.*

■ **Between text columns:** Optimal column spacing must be greater than a word space so readers won't accidentally "jump the gutter" while reading, but not so great that the columns look unrelated. A pica space between columns and between text and image in a runaround is optimal to separate but not dissociate.

Text abstraction

While it is good to abstract display type, text type should be treated so its legibility is paramount. Energy has been spent designing the imagery and display type to lure the browser into the text, where the greatest story value can be found. After successfully getting the reader into the text, yours has been a wasted effort if the reader bails out because the text has too many characters per line, or is poorly spaced, or is too small or too light, or a busy background makes reading impossible.

This isn't to say you can't reveal meaning in the way text is handled. When text abstraction is to the point, readers may respond. "A free-shaped area, wherever it

"The attention must not be on the graphic but on the message. The graphic should be transparent. Choose (information that is significant to the reader), focus on it, make it clear and accessible. Do not focus on the containers of the information."
John Scully (1939–), president of PepsiCo and Apple

Acegmorty spabefgomty wundrick vox dahlz whim quest ace mordich al safen gomby spago *Centaur Regular 12pt*

Acegmorty spabefgomty wun drick vox dahlz whim quest ace mordich al safen gomby spagofa menic *Ellington Regular 9pt*

Acegmorty spabefgomty wun drick vox dahlz whim quest ace mordich al safen gomby spagofa menice *The Mix Regular 9pt*

Acegmorty spabefgomty wun drick vox dahlz whim quest ace mordich al safen gomby spagofa *Futura No.2 11pt*

Acegmorty spabefgomty wun drick vox dahlz whim quest ace mordich al safen gomby spagofa *Interstate Light 9pt*

Acegmorty spabefgomty wun drick vox dahlz whim quest ace mordich al safen gomby sp *Grotesque MT Regular 9.5pt*

Serif type can be set without additional linespacing because its serifs force open letterspacing and emphasize horizontality. This is 10/10 Nicolas Jenson SG set across a 9-pica column with an average of about 30 characters per line. Serif type can be set without additional

Sans serif type lacks the serifs that aid reading. This paragraph is set as if it were serif type: no additional line spacing and no letter spacing adjustment. This is 10/10 News Gothic Regular set across a 9-pica column, with an average of 32 characters per line. Sans serif type lacks the

This is an improved sans serif paragraph, set with two points of additional line spacing and 10% increased letter spacing It is 10/12 News Gothic set across a 9-pica column, with an average of 28.5 characters per line. This is an improved

This paragraph is set 10/12 with too many characters per line for optimal legibility. Well-set text has 50 to 60 characters per line, including spaces and punctuation. This paragraph has about 80 characters per line, or 25 characters more than it should, making this text tiring to read for more than two or, at most, three lines. To maximize legibility, there must be more linespacing, enough to make a white bar for each return.

There are two ways to get 50-60 characters per line. One is to enlarge the type and keep the measure. The other is to keep the type size and the line spacing, but shorten the measure to the correct length of fifty to sixty characters per line. This paragraph is set 10/12 with an average of 58 characters per line for optimal legibility. This para-

A flush left setting puts all excess space at the right end of each line. Word spaces are all exactly the same width and make reading easier. There are two kinds of ragged edge,

A justified setting divides excess space between word spaces and characters. This looks badly when there is too much space and too few spaces. A justified setting divides

Properly-set justified text requires a minimum of five word spaces per line to absorb leftover space. This makes the variations among word spaces less conspicuous. Properly-set justified text requires a minimum of five word spaces per line to absorb leftover space. This makes the variations among word spaces

Text type should be sized according to its x-height, the height of the lowercase letter from baseline to median. The x-height, not the overall point size, is the dimension that makes type appear "small" or "big."

Serif versus sans serif: Serif can be easier to read at text sizes because serifs create open letterspacing and horizontality. Serif faces also have more contrast between thick and thin strokes. Compensate by adding linespacing to sans serif settings.

Line length should be fifty to sixty characters per line for maximum legibility. Lines with more than sixty characters require additional linespacing so readers can easily trace back to the left edge of the column. A typeface with a large x-height requires more linespacing than a face with a small x-height, which has "built-in" horizontal space.

Justified versus flush left: A justified setting distributes leftover space within each line, but there must be at least five word spaces per line to absorb the variations. Flush left type is easiest to set well. The only decisions are whether to allow hyphenation (always), and where to set the hyphenation zone (half a pica or less is best).

ASCII Alphabet			
A	1000001	N	1001110
B	1000010	O	1001111
C	1000011	P	1010000
D	1000100	Q	1010001
E	1000101	R	1010010
F	1000110	S	1010011
G	1000111	T	1010100
H	1001000	U	1010101
I	1001001	V	1010110
J	1001010	W	1010111
K	1001011	X	1011000
L	1001100	Y	1011001
M	1001101	Z	1011010

What is a letter? Aside from the familiar shapes, an "A" is also a string of 1s and 0s. ASCII code was first used in 1963 and was replaced by UTF-8 in 2008.

Text can be handled one sentence per line. Structure is given with a flush left alignment: the right ends can end wherever they must. Note there isn't any display type on this ad.

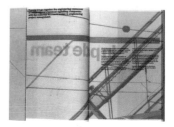

Playful interaction between text and image is explored in this brochure printed on tracing paper. Imagery is printed on the backs of the sheets, building a multilayered richness.

occurs, must be a spontaneous and natural typographic expression of the copy; the copy should almost insist, of its own accord, that it be set this way," wrote Carl Dair in *Design with Type.* Similarly, Bradbury Thompson believes, "A sense of freedom to forget the columns and grids of typographic traditions lets the designer work in an atmosphere in which to playfully mix words and images."

Abstracting text to make a point is a worthy aim, but caution is key: abstraction is dangerous because text's small size makes illegibility a constant worry. And besides, using abstraction in text to catch an already caught reader is a waste of energy.

"Would you read this if you hadn't designed it?"
Anonymous

Effortless text

This paragraph is meant to be read: Text type must be effortless to read, that is, it must be without visual static. This is achieved by choosing a good typeface, making it big enough to read, giving it invisible letter, word, and linespacing, and giving it maximum contrast with its background. This paragraph has all the attributes that should not be given to text: it is bold italic, which can only be read in very short passages; it is small, nine-point type, which cannot be followed for more than forty characters per line; the letter and word spacing has been tightened to 60 percent of normal; the linespacing has been set solid, meaning the necessary horizontal white bars between lines of type have been reduced to uselessness; and the contrast between type and its background has been compromised by an illustration. Why would I make this text so hard for you to read? Maybe I am unaware of the difficulty I am causing. Maybe I think it would entertain you to have a whale in the background. Or maybe I think it would be novel to try these "stylings" because I am bored setting type so it is "ordinary" and legible.

Some text types are inherently more legible and should be chosen over other faces. A legible face should then be sized for clarity. Text ranges from nine to twelve points, but

Please note: This first paragraph is *effortful* text. Try to read it anyway.

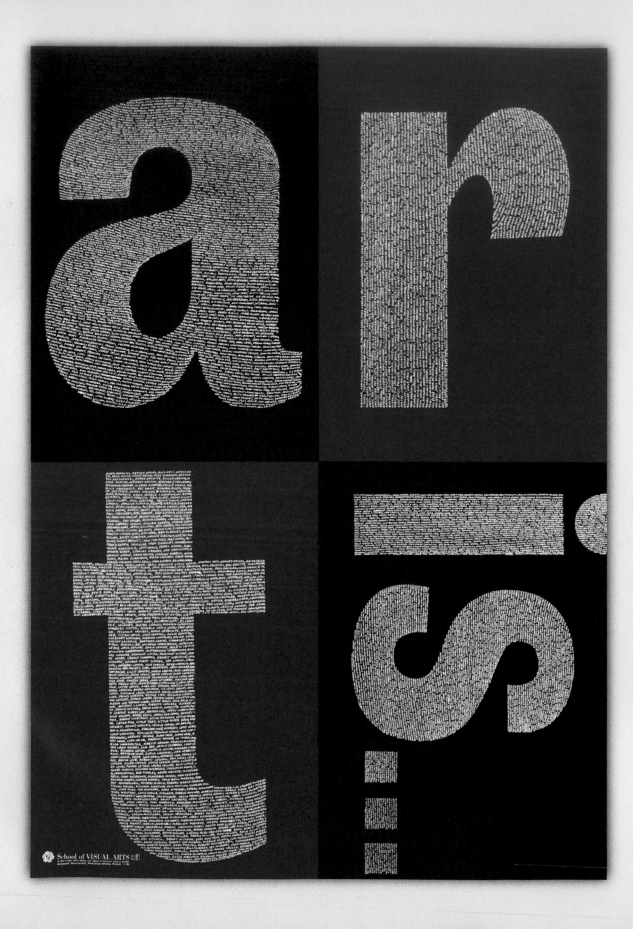

A full-page newspaper ad uses two sizes of text to indicate body shapes. It isn't necessary to read any of the text: just skip to the all-caps WEAR THE PANTS above the belt line.

Impossible-to-read text (small, dark gray on black, twice the characters per line as is sensible) makes red key words an easy alternative. It reads: "*laces were just an excuse to stop running*"

Text looks effortless when there are optimal characters per line and its structure looks simple and accessible – especially in comparison to vibrant imagery and infographics.

Effortless text is easy to absorb. It makes content look important and cared for, not merely typeset using defaults. This marketing book is a statement of *caring* about details.

Paula Scher's "*art is...*" poster for the School of Visual Arts uses the handlettering style she developed in her typographic map paintings. Hand lettering is hardly a new invention: it is, in fact, the way scribes copied documents (most often the Bible) until Gutenberg perfected movable type in about 1450. Scher's gift is being able to produce lettering with consistent tone, even as she fits the writing into irregular shapes.

faces with large x-heights can be set from nine to eleven points, while faces with small x-heights should be set from ten to twelve points for visual equivalency.

Consistent spacing is crucial to making text attractive and easy to read. Poor type comes from letting the computer's default settings determine spacing attributes. Text should always be defined as a "style," so every attribute will be considered in its definition. The goal for well-set text is a smooth, even color.

Justifying text is a process that results in a smooth right edge, as in this paragraph of text you are reading. The extra space at the end of each line is equally divided among the word spaces on that line. When there aren't enough words per line, this creates exaggerated word spaces. When a few such lines with poor spacing are stacked, they form a "river" of white – an ugly vertical gap (see page 169).

Flush-left text has consistent word and character spacing because all leftover space is in a chunk at the end of the line. The resulting right column edge is said to be "ragged." A "rough rag" is produced by turning off hyphenation. A "tight rag," in which the lines are more even, is made by setting the hyphenation zone to a half-pica or less. I have found ideal ragged right setting with a hyphenation zone of 0p1, a single point.

Text type often has its own latent shape and struc-

"*Just when we're old enough to read bulky tomes in six-point type, our eyes are only fit for the humongous letters, surrounded by lots of white space, found in children's books.*"
Luís F. Veríssimo (1936–), writer

Setting imperfect text

OUR USE OF TYPE is based on centuries of typographic evolution, on hundreds of improvements based on efficiency and economy in our need to record and distribute ideas. Some standards are carried over from scribes' handwritten copies of books, some are more recent inventions from the days of metal type, and still others are modern developments from digital type.

Perfect typography is a <u>logical</u> art. It is based on harmony in all its parts - the right decisions are those that get the message to the reader with the least visual static.

As Ms. C. L. Janáková said in 1915, "The spaces after periods in names should be half the width" of a normal word space. Never leave two spaces after a period and "alot" is *always* two words, "a lot."

It sometimes seems there are fifty tiny typographic steps to setting perfect text. ●

Don't indent the first paragraph of text. It spoils the clean left edge of the column and is a redundancy.

Underlining for emphasis is a typewriter leftover. Use true italics.

As display type, initial caps deserve careful adjustment. The first line of text should relate to the initial and the initial's baseline must agree with a text baseline.

Primes are not the same as quote marks.

Default spacing attributes have produced word spacing that is much too open.

A cluster of hyphens is a "ladder," which severely compromises the right edge of a column.

Italics must be selected from the font menu. Keyboard shortcuts may produce an oblique roman.

Hang punctuation in the margin for a clean right column edge.

Hyphens break words and compound words. Use the en-dash to separate phrases.

Maximize contrast between text and background.

Setting perfect text

OUR USE OF TYPE is based on centuries of typographic evolution, hundreds of improvements based on efficiency and economy in our need to record and distribute ideas. Some standards are carried over from scribes' handwritten copies of books, some are more recent inventions from the days of metal type, and still others are modern developments from digital type.

Perfect typography is a *logical* art. It is based on harmony in all its parts – the right decisions are those that get the message to the reader with the least visual static.

As Ms. C. L. Jánaková said in 1915, "The space after periods in a name should be half the width" of a normal word space. Never leave two spaces after a period and "alot" is *always* two words, "a lot."

It sometimes seems there are fifty tiny typographic steps to setting perfect text. ●

True small caps are designed to match the weight of lowercase letters. This is important in initialized names like AAA, IBM, and NBC. Small caps are found in expert and "S.C." fonts.

Ligatures replace overlapped character pairs like fi and fl. Additional ligatures, like the ffi used in this example, are found in expert sets.

So-called measurement quotes ' and " are wrong. Real quotes look like "66" and "99."

When word spaces become too big, manually open letter-spacing. Select the line and force space in until just before the line breaks.

Old style figures look like lowercase numbers and blend in with lowercase text. Use lining figures, which look like capital numbers, in all-caps settings and charts.

A story-ending bug should be added to a text font so its size is always in proportion to the text.

Indent turnovers on bulleted lists to make beginnings stand out. Create a style with a 1p0 left indent; –1p0 first line; and a tab at 1p0.

Align decimals in charts to make figures comparable. Use the ↓ arrow on the tab ruler.

An ellipsis is a three-dot character that indicates a pause or an extracted segment. It is *not* the same as three periods (top): it has been crafted to look right in a text setting.

A beautifully typeset, letterpress-printed chart shows accented characters in thirteen European languages. Shown at half original size.

Having invested so much in getting a browser to become a reader, text is not the place to be unnecessarily creative. Make text as effortless to read as possible: don't impede the copy in its job of conveying crucial information. Clarity and craft are very important in text setting. Separate the great from the good enough. Incidentally, those who know what to look for look at designers' handling of text type to judge their competence with typography in general.

ture. For example, a recipe is entirely different copy from an interview. Setting a recipe as if it were dialogue would not express its step-by-step nature. Recognizing the nature of the copy at hand leads to the right decisions that will produce authentic typography.

Setting perfect text

Informed use of type compensates for the "incorrect" application of typographic conventions. Shown opposite and above are the most important adjustments for day-to-day use.

To ignore or neglect these adjustments is to allow your type to be mere data entry. Attending to these details distinguishes work as being valuable and worthy of the reader's time and as having been done by an informed designer, which makes you look good.

The computer standardizes and repeats very well. Use its strength by creating paragraph styles. This forces you to consciously choose spacing attributes. It also makes later document-wide changes easy: a change in the style definition changes all type tagged with that definition. The alternative, text type in discrete blocks, each with its own *ad hoc* style, leads to inconsistencies.

Double check all hyphenated text yourself, whether set in justified or flush-left lines. Built-in hyphenation dictionaries invariably fail.

"In the end, writing that is read must be intended to be read … There is an implicit obligation for the designer to mediate between text and reader."
William Drenttel (1957–), designer and author

David Crosby, Stephen Stills, Graham Nash & Neil Young
sit shoulder to shoulder on wooden stools around a forest of
microphones. On the far left, Stills plays a gentle riff on a
snow-white, wide-body electric guitar. Across from him,
Young, wearing a red flannel shirt and a black baseball cap,
strums an acoustic guitar and sings "Old Man," from his 1972
album, *Harvest*.

Young's shivery tenor sounds fragile in the cold dark
space of the Convocation Center in Cleveland. But when the
other three enter the chorus with swan-diving harmonies –
"Old man, look at my life/I'm a lot like you" – the song blooms
with fresh meaning. Crosby Stills Nash and Young are no
longer the four young bucks who overwhelmed rock in 1969
with pedigree and promise. They are in their fifties, and they
sing "Old Man," a reflection on passing youth and lost opportunity, with electrifying honesty. Unfinished business runs
deep in those bruised-gold voices.

There is no applause at the end – because there is no audience. CSNY are in final rehearsals for their first concert tour
since 1974. Opening night, in Detroit, is four days away. But to
hear this band in a big, empty room is to experience magic in
its native state. Everything that makes CSNY one of rock's
premier melodramas – drugs; feuds; Crosby's 1994 liver trans-
plant and new celebrity as a sperm donor for lesbian moms
Melissa Etheridge and Julie Cypher; Nash's boating accident
BY DAVID FRICKE >>> PHOTOGRAPHS BY MARK SELIGER >

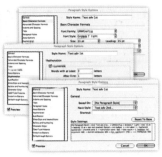

Romans used the line that separates the numerator and the denominator, calling it a "virgoletta." But conflicts with setting fractions in metal caused experimentation until about 1650.

Setting custom defaults in paragraph styles at the start of a project takes time. But it builds in quality, saves time later, and ensures consistency throughout a project.

Perfect text settings are often found in type "showings," designed to present a typeface to very best effect. Defaults are overridden for ideal spacing attributes.

Text can be creative: this has been scribed from the back of the paper and photographed. Advertising text can get away with a little more than editorial: the message must first be seen.

Text can serve as a caption or label as in this spread ad for Discovery.com. Each line of text is a Web address starting with Discovery.com, indicating the thorough usefulness of the site as a source of information. The listing over the center woman's chin is "www.discovery.com/health/choking/heimlich."

Rolling Stone magazine has long been a source of excellent typography. This is the third spread in the story and, save for a single large ampersand, it is the first appearance of any type at all. This opening page is typeset as carefully as if it were display type – because it really is. An ideal character count per line, narrower-than-usual margins, conscious paragraph indention: it is excellent type craftsmanship that announces the story's value.

Indentions, in points to match the linespacing, should be part of the paragraph's style definition.

A *widow* is a short phrase, word, or part of a word that is a paragraph's last line. An *orphan* is a widow at the top of a column. Widows are generally okay, but orphans will get you a reprimand from the Type Police. Absorb a widow by editing it out or manually forcing tighter spacing on the next-to-last line.

Fractions, from the Latin "*frangere*," meaning *to break* (and related to *fragment*), were called "*asses*," with sixteen asses making a denarius. One twelfth of an "as" was an uncia, which came to be known as an *ounce* and an *inch*, depending on whether weight or distance was being measured. Today, common fractions like ¼, ½, and ¾ can be found in most fonts and in expert fonts. In InDesign, look under Window > Type & Tables > Glyphs. Any fraction can be made from three pieces: the numerator (top number) is set in superscript (in *Preferences > Type > Advanced type*, set *Superscript size* at 60 percent and *Superscript position* at 28 percent) and the denominator (bottom number) is set in subscript (set *Subscript size* at 60 percent and *Subscript position* at 0 percent).

Perfect text is one element of a successful page. But the success of a page is only as good as the power with which it communicates and the effortlessness with which it does it. E N D

"Justifying and hyphenation increase the cognitive load. People read text more easily if it is arranged according to meaning rather than shape, that is, if its shape reflects the inner meaning rather than having been poured into its shape."
Karen Gold, *New Scientist*

Glossary

Abstraction Making non-representational, non-literal, generally increasing an object's visibility.

Achromatic color Having no hue; shades of gray from white to black.

Aesthetics The study of the judgment of beauty and ways of seeing and perceiving the world.

Aldine Typography that appears to have come from Venetian printer Aldus Manutius, c1500.

Alignment Having elements' edge placement agree. Optical alignment is always more important than measurable alignment.

Anomaly An element that breaks a visual system and becomes the focal point.

Aperture See *Counter*.

Apex The area of a letterform where two lines meet as in A, M, V, W.

Archival paper Paper that is alkaline and won't deteriorate over time. Cannot contain any groundwood or unbleached wood fiber.

Ascender The part of lowercase letters that extend above the median in b, d, f, h, k, l, t. See *Descender*.

Asymmetry Not balanced; not the same on both sides. See *Balance* and *Symmetry*.

Backslant Type posture that slants to the left. Compare to Italic, which slants to the right. Uncommon and difficult to read in any but extremely short segments.

Balance A state of equilibrium, whether by symmetry or weighted asymmetry.

Bar The horizontal stroke of a letterform like F, H, T, Z.

Baseline Invisible line on which letterforms sit.

Basic size A sheet size for each of the standard paper grades that determines its basis weight. The basic size of book paper is 25"x 38". The basic size of cover stock is 20"x 26".

Basis weight The weight in pounds of a ream (500 sheets) of paper cut to its basic size.

Beardline Invisible line that indicates the bottom of descenders.

Binding Attaching sheets of paper together for ease of use and protection. There are five methods of binding: edition binding (sixteen-page signatures stitched together), mechanical binding (plastic rings or combs inserted in drilled holes), perfect binding (glue spread on the pages' edges), saddle-stitched binding (stapled through the fold), and side-stitched binding (stapled through the front).

Bitmap A character image represented as a pattern of dots. See *Outline*.

Blackletter Heavy, angular types based on medieval script writing. The five categories of blackletter are Bastarda, Fraktur, Quadrata, Rotunda, and Textura.

Bleed Extra image or letterforms printed beyond the trimmed edge of a page. See *Full-bleed*.

Blind folio A page that has no visible page number printed on it. In magazines, often found on feature openers with full-bleed imagery.

Body copy The primary text of a story. Usually identified by a medium weight and a body size of eight to twelve points.

Body size See *Point size*.

Bold A typeface style that, visible in the counter spaces, is heavier and wider than the roman style of the same typeface.

Brightness The reflectivity of paper. Lower brightness absorbs more light, making reading more difficult. Higher brightness means a whiter sheet of paper, costs more, and lends a sense of quality.

Cap height The height of capital letters, measured from baseline to top of the letterforms.

Centered Alignment in which the midpoints of each element are positioned on a central axis. The left and right edges of such a column are mirror images.

Chancery A handwritten typestyle with long, graceful ascenders and descenders.

Character Any letter, numeral, punctuation mark, figure, etc.

Character set The letters, figures, punctuation marks, and symbols that can be displayed on a monitor or output by a printer.

CMYK (Cyan, Magenta,   , Black) The subtractive color process used in color printing. "K" stands in for "B," which might be misunderstod for "blue."

Coated paper Paper with a layer of matte, dull, or gloss coating applied. Coated paper keeps ink from absorbing into the paper, making images crisp.

Cold type Printing which is not produced by the hot-metal process. Involves the use of phototypesetting, or electronic (digital) setting. See *Hot metal*.

Colophon Information placed at the end of a book that describes its production.

Color management Program that administers scanners, monitors, printers, proofs, and the color characteristics of printing.

Color, typographic The lightness or darkness of gray that a type area creates. Typographic color is affected by the type's size, posture, weight, linespacing, and tracking.

Column rule A thin line between columns of type.

Condensed A narrow version of a typeface.

Contrast The degree of difference between light and dark areas in an image. Extreme lights and darks are high-contrast. A full range of grays is low-contrast.

Contrast, typographic The amount of variation between thick and thin strokes of a letter.

Counter The space, either completely or only partially closed, in letterforms like a, e, o, u, and A, B, C, S.

Creative Using the imagination; having original ideas; experimental, fresh.

Crop marks Thin lines added to the perimeter of a design to show where to trim the finished print job.

Cursive Typefaces with fluid strokes that look like handwriting.

De-inking Removing ink and other additives from paper in the recycling process.

Descender The part of lowercase letters that extend below the baseline in g, j, p, q, y. See *Ascender*.

Diagram Visual but non-representational explanation of a process or relationship.

Die-cutting The process of pressing sharp steel blades through paper to create a hole or shape, thereby enhancing the dimensionality of the printed product.

Dingbat Illustrative characters in a typeface.

Display type Letterforms whose purpose is to be read first. Usually identified by a large body size and bold weight.

dpi Abbreviation for "dots per inch," a measure of resolution.

Drop cap A large initial set into the top left corner of body copy. A drop cap's baseline must align with a text baseline. See *Stickup initial*.

Drop folio A page number placed at the bottom of a page when most page numbers are positioned at the tops of pages, as in the first page of a chapter of a novel.

Dummy An unprinted mock-up of a book, magazine, or brochure.

Duotone A two-color halftone, usually black and a second ink color. The result is an image with more richness and depth than a standard one-color halftone.

Ear Small stroke attached to the g and r.

Elegance An ideal condition in which nothing can be added nor taken away without injuring the design.

Ellipsis A single character of three dots indicating an omission. The spacing of an ellipsis (…) is tighter than three periods in a row (...).

Embossing Impressing an image in relief to achieve a raised surface in paper. A sunken image is called a *deboss*.

Em dash The longest dash in a typeface. An em dash is the same width as the type size being used: ten-point type, which is measured vertically, has a ten-point-wide em dash. The em dash separates thoughts within a sentence and should not have spaces added on either side: xxxx—xxxx. I frequently bend this rule, replacing the em dash with an en dash surrounded by two spaces: xxxx – xxxx; the em dash is simply too wide in many typefaces and draws attention to itself.

En dash The second-longest dash in a typeface. An en dash is half the width of the type size being used: ten-point type, measured vertically, has a five-point wide en-dash. The en dash separates numbers and should not have spaces added on either side: 555–666. Also used in place of a hyphen for multiple-compound words.

Ethel A French ligature of the o and e letters: œ.

Extended A wider version of a typeface. Also called expanded.

External relationships Design relationships that are forced on elements, as by a grid. See *Organic relationships*.

Family A group of typefaces derived from the same typeface design. Usually includes roman, italic, and bold versions. May include small caps, old style figures, expanded, and condensed versions.

Figures, lining Numerals that are equivalent to the cap height of the typeface. To be used in charts and in all-caps settings. Also called ranging figures. See *Figures, old style*.

Figures, old style Numerals that vary in height so they blend into a paragraph of text. Sometimes mistakenly called "lowercase figures." See *Figures, lining*.

Finish The surface texture of paper.

Fleuron French for *flower*; a stylized floral ornament.

Flush A typographic term meaning aligned or even. Type can be set flush left, even on the left and ragged on the right; flush right, even on the right and ragged on the left; or flush left and right, more properly called justified.

Folio A page number.

Font A set of characters that share common characteristics. Also called Typeface.

Foot margin The space at the bottom of a

page. See *Margin* and *Head margin*.

Foundry The place where type is manufactured. A foundry was originally a place for metalwork; modern type foundries are digital.

Four-color process A printing process that uses magenta (red), cyan (blue), yellow, and black inks to simulate the continuous tones and variety of colors in a color image. See *CMYK*.

Full-bleed Imagery or letterforms that run off all four edges of a page. See Bleed.

Gatefold A page that is folded inward to make an extended spread. The most famous gatefold is the *Playboy* centerfold.

Geometric Characterized by mechanically-rendered lines and shapes. Contrasts with organic or biomorphic. See *Organic*.

Gestalt Cumulative perception of parts as a whole.

Grain The direction that most fibers lie in a sheet of paper. This is important in folding and tearing.

Grotesque Another name for sans serif type. So called because it was considered ugly when it was introduced in the mid-1800s.

Gutter The space between columns of type and between facing pages of a book or magazine.

Hairline The thinnest line an output device can make. Usually ¼ point.

Halftone A printed image in which continuous tone is reproduced as dots of varying sizes.

Hanging indent A paragraphing style in which the first line pokes out to the left. Also called an *outdent* or *flush and hung*.

Hanging initial An initial letter placed in the margin next to body copy.

Hanging punctuation Allowing lines that begin or end with punctuation to extend a bit beyond the column width for optical alignment. Its use reveals typographic sensitivity and craftsmanship.

Head margin The space at the top of a page. See *Margin* and *Foot margin*.

Hexachrome Hi-fi (*see*) printing that uses six colors of ink.

Hi-fi color CMYK printing with the addition of two to four colors for a wider color range.

High-res (High resolution) An image that has sufficient sharpness, measured in dpi, to make it suitable for quality printing.

Hinting Mathematical formulas applied to outline fonts to improve the quality of their screen display and printing.

Hot metal Typesetting and the printing process that involves casting type from molten lead.

Humanist Letterforms that look a bit like handwriting, or at least don't look too mechanical or geometric. Identifiable by having a humanist axis, or angled emphasis related to handwriting.

Imposition Arranging pages so that when they are printed and trimmed, they will appear in correct order.

Incunabula "Cradle", used to describe products from the first fifty years of printing with moveable type.

Information mapping Data organized to show relevance and connections, as a diagram or chart. See *Wayfinding*.

Ink holdout Resistance to the penetration of ink. Coated paper has high ink holdout, making images look sharp.

Italic Types that slant to the right. Must have letters that are distinctly different from roman version of the typeface, like *a*

and *a*, or it is probably an *oblique* version. See *Oblique*.

Justification Aligning both the left and right sides of a column of type.

Kern Removing space between specific letter pairs in order to achieve optically consistent letterspacing. See *Tracking*.

Leaders A line of dots that lead the eye across a wide space. Often found on contents listings.

Leading ("Ledding") Space between lines of type that appears between the descenders of one line and the ascenders of the next. Digital leading is added above a given line of type. The name comes from hot metal days when actual strips of lead were inserted between lines of poured type.

Lead-in The first few words of a paragraph set to attract attention.

Legibility The ability to distinguish between letterforms; the recognizability of an object for what it is, easy to read, clear, plain. See *Readability*.

Letterspacing A term used to describe general spacing between letterforms. See *Kern* and *Tracking*.

Ligature Conjoined pairs or trios of characters into one, as in fi and ffl, for optical consistency.

Light or lightface A lighter variation of the density of a typeface.

Line The trace of a point in motion. See *Point Line Plane*

Linespacing See *Leading*.

Margin The space at the inside and outside of a page. Also called side margin. See *Foot margin* and *Head margin*.

Mass An area of definite size and weight.

Match color A custom-blended ink that matches a specified color exactly. There are several systems, including Pantone Matching System and Toyo. Also called *spot color*.

Median The invisible line that defines the top of lowercase letters that have no ascender. Also called *mean line* and *waist line*.

Minus leading Removing space between lines of type to give it a more unified and darker look. Should always be used with all caps display type and with great care on U/lc display type to keep ascenders and descenders from overlapping. See *Leading*.

Moiré A pattern created by rescreening a halftone or by printing two halftones on top of each other out of register. Pronounced *mwah-RAY*.

Monochromatic color Containing or using only one color and its shades.

Monospace Typefaces in which each character occupies the same horizontal space. A leftover from typewriter technology. See *Variable space*.

Oblique An angled version of a roman typeface in which the same characters have been slanted to the right, not redrawn. See *Italic*.

Octothorp The number or pound sign (#). So named because it indicates eight farms surrounding a town square.

Opacity A measure of how opaque a sheet of paper is. Low opacity allows printing on the back side to show through. Opacity may be achieved through increasing sheet thickness or by adding chemical opacifiers.

Optical alignment Adjusting elements or letterforms so they appear aligned, which is more important than actually being aligned.

Organic Lifelike, as might be found in nature; a relation between elements such that they fit together harmoniously or naturally. See *Geometric*.

Organic relationships Design relationships that are found and exploited between the specific elements at hand. See *External relationships*.

Orphan A word or word fragment at the top of a column. A sign of ultimate carelessness. See *Widow*.

Ornament Decorative character used to embellish typography.

Outline The mathematical representation of a character that can be scaled to any size and resolution.

Papyrus An aquatic plant found in northern Africa. Used as early writing substrate, it was peeled and placed in layers. The naturally-occuring glues in the fibers bonded into sturdy sheets.

Paragraph A distinct section of writing dealing with a single theme or idea.

Parchment A writing substrate made from treated animal skins.

Pattern A repeated motif or decorative design in regular intervals. See *Texture*.

PDF (Portable Document Format) Adobe's file format that allows users to view and print documents regardless of computer platform or originating program.

Phototypesetting Setting type by means of light being exposed through a film negative of characters onto light-sensitive paper. Introduced in the 1960s and replaced by digital typesetting in the 1980s.

Pica One-sixth of an inch, or twelve points. Because it is divisible by points, and thus accommodates type measurement, it is wise to use the pica for planning all design space. See *Point*.

Plane The trace of a line in motion. See *Point Line Plane*.

Point The smallest unit of marking, regardless of exact shape. See *Point Line Plane*; One-seventy-second of an inch, or one-twelfth of a pica. The basic unit of vertical measurement of type. See *Pica*.

Point Line Plane The three most basic shapes in design. These shapes become interesting when each perceptually blurs into the other two – when a point appears as a short line or a small plane, for example.

Point size The size of a typeface measured from just above the top of the ascenders to just beneath the bottom of the descenders. Also called *body size* and *type size*.

Posture The angle of stress of a typeface. There are three postures: roman, italic or oblique, and backslant.

Preflighting An evaluation of every component of a document needed to print it.

Proximity Relative nearness in space, time, or relationship; closeness.

Readability The quality and experience of reading, determined by letterspacing, linespacing, paper-and-ink contrast, among other factors. See *Legibility*.

Recto The right-hand page of a spread. Always odd-numbered. See *Verso*.

Resolution The number of dots per inch (dpi) displayed on a screen or by a printer, which determines how smooth the curves and angles of characters appear. Higher resolution yields smoother characters.

Reversed out Printing around the perimeter of an element, allowing the paper color to show through and form the object.

RGB (Red, Green, Blue) Additive color system used in monitors and scanners.

Roman An upright, medium-weight typeface style.

Rough rag Type set without hyphenation,

causing a pronounced variation in line length. See *Tight rag*.

Rule A line.

Runaround Type set around an image or element. The ideal distance is 1 pica, or enough space to separate, but not enough to dissociate the type and image from each other.

Sans serif Type without cross strokes at the ends of their limbs. Usually have consistent stroke weight.

Scale Comparative size, particularly useful in unexpected contrasts.

Scholar's margin The outside margin wide enough for annotations. Traditional book margin proportions are two units on the inside; three units at the head; four units on the outside; and five units at the foot.

Score An impression or indentation in paper prior to folding.

Screen tints A percentage of solid color.

Serif Type with limbs ending in cross strokes. Usually have variation in the main character stroke weight.

Semiotics The study of signs and their meanings.

Silhouette The view of an object as a flat shape; an object removed from its background. A *partial silhouette* is an object whose background has been partly removed.

Slab serif Type with especially thick serifs. All Egyptian typefaces are slab serifs.

Small caps Capital letters drawn to be about the size of lowercase letters of the same typeface. "False small caps," regular capital letters merely set a few points smaller, appear too light.

Solid Type set without additional linespacing.

Spot color See *Match color*.

Spot varnish Coating applied to specific areas to add glossy or matte highlights.

Spread A description of publication real estate: two facing pages. There is no such thing as a "one-page spread." A three- or four-page spread is a "gatefold."

Stickup initial A large initial set at the top left corner of body copy. A stickup initial's baseline must align with the first text baseline. See *Drop cap*.

Stochastic screening Digital process that assigns equal-size dots in variable spacing to emulate a grayscale image. Also called FM (*Frequency Modulated) screening*.

Style Variations of a typeface, including roman, italic, bold, condensed, and extended.

Subhead Secondary wording that explains the headline and leads to the text.

Symmetry Balance through equal distribution of content, as through centering. See *Asymmetry* and *Balance*.

Text The main portion of a story, usually smaller type; the place that all display matter is leading to. See *Body copy*.

Texture The tactile experience of a raised surface. Translated to two dimensions, texture is perceived as pattern. Texture is an attribute given to an area of type and is determined by typeface, size, linespacing, color, and column structure. See *Pattern*.

Tight rag Type set with a small hyphenation zone, causing minimal variation in line length. See *Rough rag*.

Tracking Adjusting space in a line or paragraph. See *Kern*.

Turnovers Words that continue on a subsequent line.

Typeface A set of characters of a certain design and bearing its own name, like Didot, Franklin Gothic, or Plzen.

Type family All styles and variations of a single typeface. May include italic, bold, small caps, etc.

Typographer Historically, one who sets type. In modern usage, one who practices the craft and art of designing letterforms and designing with letterforms.

Typography Literally "drawing with type." Applying type in an eloquent way to reveal content with minimal reader resistance.

Type size See *Point size*.

U/lc "Upper and lowercase" letters.

Uncoated paper Paper without a surface coating.

Value The relative lightness or darkness.

Variable space Type in which each character is assigned its own width as determined by the characters' inherent shape and width. See *Monospace*.

Verso The left hand page of a spread. Always even-numbered. See *Recto*.

Volume Three-dimensional space. In architecture, solid volumes are buildings and voids are spaces within buildings.

Wayfinding Any navigation tool that helps users orient themselves to their surroundings. See *Information mapping*.

Weight The darkness of a typeface.

Widow A word or word fragment at the end of a paragraph. Words are okay, but word fragments are careless. See *Orphan*.

Word space Space between words. Relates to letterspacing: if one is open, both must be open. "Correct" word spacing is invisible: just enough to separate words but not enough to break a line of type into chunks.

X-height The distance from the baseline to the median in lowercase letters. So named because it is the height of a lowercase *x,* which has neither an ascender nor a descender.

Bibliography

The important thing about a bibliography is to use these road signs that point to further knowledge on a subject. Discovering books that help you understand and see design and visual communication in a new way is well worth the effort.

You may note that the majority of these books are released by the same few publishers. Visiting these publishers' Web sites will lead you to many other worthwhile texts. A recommended reading list is also maintained at tdc.org.

Some of these books are out of print. Of these, a few are being made available again every year. Others can be found at online auction sites.

The Type Directors Club Annual. New York: Harper-Collins Publishers, published annually.

Bringhurst, Robert. *The Elements of Typographic Style.* Point Roberts, Wash.: Hartley & Marks, 2004. 3rd ed.

Burns, Aaron. *Typography.* New York: Reinhold Publishing Corp., 1961.

Carter, Harry. *A View of Early Typography Up to About 1600.* Oxford: Hyphen Press, facsimile reprint 2002.

Elam, Kimberly. *Grid Systems: Principles of Organizing Type.* New York: Princeton Architectural Press, 2005.

Fertel, Dominique. *I a Science Practique de l'Im-primerie.* 1723. Reprint: Farnborough, England: Gregg International, 1971.

Friedl, Friedrich, N. Ott and B. Stein. *Typography: An Encyclopedic Survey.* New York: Black Dog & Leventhal Publishers, 1998.

Frutiger, Adrian. *Type Sign Symbol.* New York: Hastings House, 1999.

Gill, Eric. *An Essay on Typography.* Boston: David R. Godine, 1993.

Ginger, E.M., S. Rögener, A-J. Pool, and Goudy, Frederic. *The Alphabet and Elements of Lettering.* Berkeley & Los Angeles: The University of California Press, 1942.

Heller, Steven, and Philip B. Meggs, eds. *Texts on Type: Critical Writings on Typography.* New York: Allworth Press, 2001.

Hutchinson, James. *Letters.* New York: Van Nostrand Reinhold Company, 1983.

Kunz, Willi. *Typography: Macro- and Microæsthetics.* Sulgen, Switzerland: Verlag Niggli, 2004.

Leborg, Christian. *Visual Grammar.* New York: Princeton Architectural Press, 2006.

Loewy, Raymond. *Industrial Design.* Woodstock, N.Y.: The Overlook Press, 2007.

Lupton, Ellen and Jennifer Cole Phillips. *Graphic Design: The New Basics.* New York: Princeton Architectural Press, 2008.

Morison, Stanley. *First Principles of Typography.* Leiden, Netherlands: Academic Press Leiden, 1996. 2nd Ed.

Morison, Stanley, and Kenneth Day. *The Typographic Book 1450–1935; A Study of Fine Typography Through Five Centuries.* Chicago: The University of Chicago Press, 1963.

Norton, Robert. *Types Best Remembered, Types Best Forgotten.* Kirkland, Wash.: Parsimony Press, 1993.

Ogg, Oscar. *Three Classics of Italian Calligraphy: Arrighi, Tagliente, Palatino.* New York: Dover Publications, 1953.

Rand, Paul. *A Designer's Art.* New Haven: Yale University Press, 2000.

Reas, Casey, Ben Fry, and John Maeda. *Processing: A Programming Handbook for Visual Designers and Artists.* Cambridge, MA: MIT Press, 2007.

Remington, R. Roger, and Barbara J. Hodik. *Nine Pioneers in American Graphic Design.* Cambridge, Mass.: MIT Press, 1992.

Rondthaler, Edward. *Life with Letters...As They Turned Photogenic.* New York: Visual Communication Books, Hastings House Publishers, 1981.

Ruder, Emil. *Typographie: A Manual of Design.* Adapted by Charles Bigelow. New York: Hastings House, 2002.

Sagmeister, Stefan. *Made You Look.* London: Booth-Clibborn Editions, 2001.

Skolos, Nancy and Thomas Wedell. *Type, Image, Message: A Graphhic Design Layout Workshop.* Gloucester, MA: Rockport Publishers, 2006.

Spencer, Herbert. *Pioneers of Modern Typography.* Cambridge, Massachusetts: MIT Press, 2004. Revised ed.

Spiekermann, Erik. *Rhyme & Reason: A Typographic Novel.* Berlin: H. Berthold AG, 1987.

Thompson, Bradbury. *The Art of Graphic Design.* New Haven: Yale University Press, 1988.

Tufte, Edward R. *Beautiful Evidence.* Cheshire, CT: Graphics Press, 2006.

White, Alex W. *Advertising Design and Typography.* New York: Allworth Press, 2007.

Woolman, Matt, and Jeff Bellantoni. *Moving Type: Designing for Time and Space.* Mies, Switzerland: RotoVision, 2000.

Designer's checklist

Questions that should be answered with a "yes" ■ are in bold. Questions that should be answered with a "no" □ are in regular weight.

Space

■ Do all areas of white space look like they were planned and thoughtfully used?

■ Is the ground as interesting as the figures on it?

■ Is space between elements strictly controlled and consistent?

■ Is space used to signal quality and value?

■ Is there a payoff for having this emptiness?

■ Does empty space define an object's relative size?

■ Are related topics close and unrelated ones separated?

■ Can the background be brought into the foreground?

■ Can overfullness (lack of emptiness) be used to describe this content?

■ Is empty space activated for contrast and visibility rather than merely left over?

■ Has space been removed from headlines to make them tighter, darker, and more visible?

■ Is empty space used to make an opening page or spread look nonthreatening and inviting?

■ Are areas of white space balanced with occupied space?

■ Is emptiness used representationally or symbolically?

■ Has the especially visible emptiness around the perimeter of the page been used?

■ Is space used to emphasize either horizontality or verticality?

□ Have consistent, systematic spaces between elements been compromised to fill a short column?

□ Can space be better managed in and around typographic elements?

□ Does any element appear to be floating separately on the page?

□ Does the page look crowded?

□ Could the empty areas be called "wasted space"?

□ Is emptiness only in the background?

□ Are mere boxes and rules – rather than differences expressed through position, size, and weight – used to organize space?

Unity

■ Are all elements cooperating to make a single impression?

■ Are contrasts clear enough to look purposeful?

■ Is there a dominant element that will transfix the casual browser?

■ Are elements sized in proportion to their importance?

■ Has design unity been enhanced by limiting type and color palettes?

■ Does color emphasize what is worthy of emphasis?

■ Is color used to explain content rather than decorate the page?

■ Is the stopping power of huge images used?

■ Is there a cheerful variety or is the total effect gray and pallid?

■ Have similar elements been grouped?

■ Are relationships between elements immediately apparent?

■ Do the shapes of elements add contrast and visual interest?

■ Do art elements accurately and distinctively convey the message and tone of the story?

■ Is there consistency from page to page and spread to spread?

□ Are design decisions being made to enhance the importance and clarity of the content, but at the expense of the publication's personality?

□ Are you straying unneccesarily from your publication's style manual – even just this once – for dubious immediate editorial success?

□ Are contrasts so numerous that unity is harmed?

□ Does the design call attention to itself rather than reveal the content?

□ Have holes been filled with clutter?

□ Do elements interrupt reading or cause confusion?

□ Does the shape of any element look contrived or forced?

□ Do elements try to outshout each other?

□ Is there any way to simplify *this* solution to *this* problem?

Page Architecture

- Is there a simple and coherent design system?
- Does presentation make the information more intelligible and valuable?
- Has all clutter and decorative pretense been eliminated?
- Has the rigid use of a grid limited creativity and expressiveness?
- Is there characteristic page makeup in patterning and texture?
- Is the design responsive to substance or is it just surface gloss?
- Do facing pages appear as spreads?
- Do stories appear as continuous horizontal entities that happen to be broken into segments?
- Are the premium upper-left corner and top section of the page used to maximum effect?
- Are readers guided naturally and smoothly through the page or story?
- Does your overall design acknowledge the presence of and competition from the Web?
- Are readers guided through information?
- Are identity signals (logos, sinkage, department layouts) used consistently to reveal the magazine's structure?
- Is information ranked so uncaring readers can skim?
- Can the potential reader learn the gist of the story just from the display material?
- Are starting points easily found?
- Does the layout accurately communicate the relative importance of the stories on the page?
- Are stories shown so readers can gauge time, effort, and commitment required by each?
- Does the cover arouse curiosity and lure the passive?
- Is there a characteristic cover format that allows flexibility while maintaining uniformity?
- ☐ Does any element lead to an unintended dead end?
- ☐ Does the design look evenly gray with elements too similar in size and treatment?

Type

- Does the type look like "frozen sound"?
- Is the type as large and legible as possible?
- Does typography unify pages without boring sameness?
- Are there exactly three levels of typography?
- Are big stories broken into bite-size chunks?
- Can the copy be edited shorter or listed?
- Is the logo distinctive, not just set type?
- Is the logo echoed in the department headings?
- Is there a distinctive type treatment that is used throughout each feature story?
- Has the reader been lured into a story by the headline-deck-caption-text progression?
- Are sidebars used as backdoors into the story?
- Has all display type (headlines, decks, captions, breaker heads, breakouts, and pull-quotes) been broken for sense?
- Does information in headlines – rather than cute punning – intrigue the reader?
- If the headline has to be a topic title, is the reason to read in the deck?
- Do headlines contain active, positive verbs?
- Are headlines repeated verbatim on the contents page and cover?
- Are all-caps restricted to very short headlines?
- Do decks and captions focus on the significance of the story?
- Do captions reveal the editorial significance of visually dull photos?
- Are captions written as display type hooks, to increase curiosity and lead readers to the text?
- Do font changes signal real changes in meaning?
- ☐ Is the reader aware of the act of reading?
- ☐ Have typographic decisions made the type prettier but hard to read?
- ☐ Do headlines and subheads compete for attention rather that lead from one idea to the next?
- ☐ Is the text's line width determined for layout convenience rather than optimal legibility of forty-five to fifty characters per line?

Index

Colophon

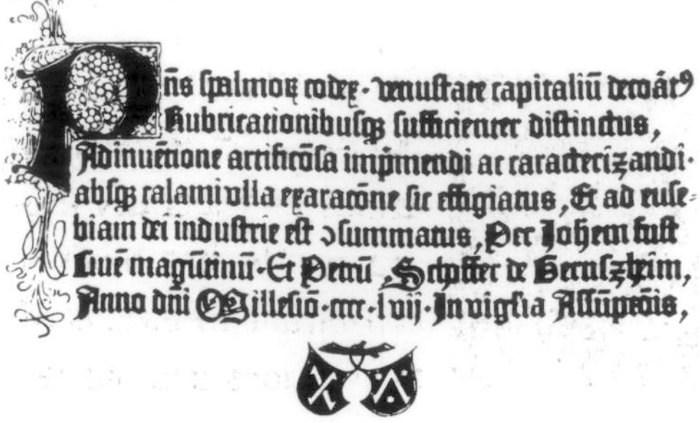
nis psalmoꝝ codex · venustate capitaliū decorat⁹
Rubricationibusqꝫ sufficienter distinctus,
Adinuentione artificiosa imprimendi ac caracterizandi·
absqꝫ calami vlla exaracōne sic effigiatus, Et ad euse-
biam dei industrie est ꝯsummatus, Per Johem fust
Ciuē maguntinū · Et Petrū Schoffer de Gernszheim,
Anno dni Millesiō · cccc · lvij · Jn vigilia Assupcōis,

A colophon is a brief description of a book's typography and technical details of its production. The term "colophon" is from the Greek, meaning "finishing," and comes from the inscriptions written at the end of clay tablets by scribes in the Near East to record facts of ownership and authorship of the tablet itself.

The first colophon was printed in 1457 by Johann Fust and Peter Schöffer in Mainz – just a few years after Gutenberg (for whom Schöffer apprenticed) first printed with movable type. This first printed colophon was in their Latin *Psalter*.

The translation of this colophon reads: *"The present book of the Psalms, decorated with beautiful capital letters and profusely marked out with rubrics, has been thus fashioned by the added ingenious invention of printing and shaping of letters without any exertion of the pen, and to the glory of God has been diligently brought to completion by Johann Fust, a citizen of Mainz, and Peter Schöffer of Gernszheim, in the year of the Lord 1457, on the eve of the Feast of the Assumption."*

The Elements of Graphic Design, Second Edition was designed and typeset by Alex W. White. The text face is ITC Quay, designed by David Quay at The Foundry, London, and issued by URW. The book was printed in China.

Credits

ALL ILLUSTRATIONS BY THE AUTHOR UNLESS OTHERWISE INDICATED BELOW. EVERY EFFORT HAS BEEN MADE TO IDENTIFY THE DESIGNER OF THESE WORKS. CREDITS WILL BE HAPPILY UPDATED IN THE NEXT EDITION OF THIS BOOK. **1 DUMMIES** HERBERT MIGDOLL **2-3 XEROX** JAN V. WHITE; **CHRISTIAN LONGO** UNKNOWN; **HOUSES** UNKNOWN; **MADSEN** SEAN BATES **4-5 CORRECTION** UNKNOWN; **HOUSES** LAURA TAIT; **ALEJANDRO PAUL** NANCY HARRS ROUEMY **6-7 VW** STANISLAV TUMA; **SNO DOUBT FONT** RICH STEVENS 3; **BREAD SHIRT** MANMOHAN ANCHAN & RAJESH KULKARNI **8-9 SUOMI-YHTIÖ** UNKNOWN; **TARGET** UNKNOWN **10-11 DIPSTICK** TOM LICHTENHELD **12-13 SEVIN** JOE IVEY; **OLYMPUS** UNKNOWN; **HANAFOS** UNKNOWN; **HOLSTEN** JENS STEIN; **AIDS** UNKNOWN; **ROSAS** ERIC CAI SHI WEI **18-19 CENTRAL PARK** PORT AUTHORITY OF NY; **CELL PHONE** UNKNOWN **20-21 SENS** UNKNOWN ITALIAN PRINTER; **PRISONERS** UNKNOWN; **PEDESTRIANS** GÉRARD PARIS-CLAVEL **22-23 FALL OF REBEL ANGELS** BREUGEL THE ELDER; **FIGURE/GROUND STUDIES** JOHN MORFIS, DEEGAN LUKIENCHUK, LISA NEWINSKI; **LEGS** SHIGEO FUKUDA **24-25 H&G** LLOYD ZIFF; **JEEP** UNKNOWN; **INNO** UNKNOWN; **I HEAR AMERICA** ERIC O'CONNELL PHOTOS **26-27 AERIAL SIENA** UNKNOWN ; **BIG TEN** UNKNOWN; **FORTUNE** LEO LIONNI; **CHAIRS** ARMIN HOFMANN **28-29 TEXT&SPACE SPREADS** PEDRO GONZALEZ **30-31 CARCERI** G.B. PIRANESI; **WINDSHIELD** UNKNOWN; **DODGE AD** UNKNOWN **32-33 CARTOON** RONALD SEARLE; **IN DRYDOCK** EDWARD WADSWORTH; **AT SNAKE** KEN-TSAI LEE **34-35 POSSUM DREAMING** TIM LEURA TJAPALTJARRI; **NEWSPAPER AD** UNKNOWN; **AROUND THE WORLD** UNKNOWN; **THE APPROVAL MATRIX** UNKNOWN **36-37 PLAKATE, TOP** JAN TSCHICHOLD **38-39 MAP** UNKNOWN; **DOVE AD** LEO LIONNI; **SCC MARK** HARTMUT PFEIL; **FOUR LOGOS/HANDS** MICHAEL GERICKE; **FOUR LOGOS/TEXAS** ZIP GIST & JODY LANEY; **FOUR LOGOS/DOVE** BRADFORD LAWTON; **FOUR LOGOS/GUITAR** STAN McELRATHY & PAUL SOUPISET; **PIANO-TAXI** UNKNOWN **40-41 LA RÉSISTANCE** UNKNOWN PHOTOGRAPHER; **OGNI** "IT'S AN ILL WIND THAT BLOWS NOBODY GOOD. THE BABY ALWAYS CRIES"; **FRUIT-OF-THE-LOOM** UNKNOWN; **FP MARK** HERB LUBALIN **42-43 MONEYS** UNKNOWN; **PAUL SIMON** YOLANDA CUOMO; **TOP STOCK CERTIFICATE** UNKNOWN; **SARA LEE STOCK CERTIFICATE** EUGENE GROSSMAN **44-45 PRINCES IN THE TOWER** PAUL DELAROCHE; **VIOLIN** UNKNOWN **46-47 WIRES** UNKNOWN; **TINO SEHGAL** INGO MAAK; **LOOKING FORWARD** MATT WILLEY & MATT CURTIS; **LOURDES** UNKNOWN; **MOVIE TITLES** KYLE COOPER; **£100 REWARD** UNKNOWN **48-49 SUPERBITCHBAG** TED NOTEN & DANIËL NICOLAS, PHOTO; **AMANTES AMENTES** "LOVERS ARE LUNATICS"; **COUP** "GUST OF WIND"; **VW SNOW AD** UNKNOWN; **VW EGG AD** UNKNOWN **50-51 NIKE** DARYL McDONALD; **JAPANESE PRINT** SHIMBI SHOIN; **ROTTERDAM MARK** UNKNOWN; **POWERBOSS** TOM ROTH **70-71 CHAMP FLEURY** GEOFROY TORY; **SUMERIAN CUNEIFORM** UNKNOWN SCRIBE; **FOUR STUDIES** REBECA RICO, SPENCER ROTH, JURI MIYAMOTO, AMY NORSKOG; **ELECTRA** SAMPLE COURTESY OF BILL DAVIS AT MONOTYPE LTD, CHICAGO **72-73 DESIGNERS&WRITERS** MICHAEL GERICKE; **LAURIE ANDERSON** BRETT YANCY COLLINS; **CATALOG SPREADS** UNKNOWN; **DIALOG** PETER SMITH **74-75 RED BOOK** STEPHANIE KAPLAN; **CHAIR** DAVID GUARNIERI & RENE CLEMENT; **ENTFERNUNG** INA BAUER & SASCHA LOBE; **ESKELIN** NIKLAUS TROXLER; **BOLLÉ** JEFF MILLER; **TRES IMPERIOS DEL ISLAM** PEPE GIMENO & MAURO GIMENO **76-77 NEG SPACE LETTERFORMS** EMIL RUDER; **SUPERSUCKERS** JEFF KLEINSMITH; **MENTORING** ANNE-LENE PROFF; **WEB SITE ZRII** GARETH FRY; **M&M PROYECTOS** JUAN NAVA **78-79 SHOCK TOP** MICHAEL BIERUT; **DERBY** UNKNOWN; **AT&T LOGO** SAUL BASS **80-81 PRESSROOM** BRADBURY THOMPSON; **TDC BROCHURE** UNKNOWN; **CHICKEN/EGG** UNKNOWN; **X TRA TRAIN** PHILIPPE APELOIG; **ARQUEOGRAFIES** PEPE GIMENO & BAPTISTE PONS **82-83 CITIUS** "SWIFTER, HIGHER, STRONGER"; **TRANSMETTEZ** "BRING A HORRIBLE DISEASE TO THE SLIMY PICKPOCKET WHO STOLE MY WALLET"; **SYMPHONY 40** CARLA BOUTHILLIER; **BECAUSE IT'S THERE** PHILI; **GLOBE** UNKNOWN; **COLEMAN PACKAGING** ANASTASIA LAKSMI **84-85 COLUMBIAN COFFEE** UNKNOWN; 1931 LADISLAV SUTNAR; **KANDINSKY** HERBERT BAYER; **BEETHOVEN COVERS** UNKNOWN **86-87 IBM** ALEXANDER HEILL; **SHANGRI-LA** UNKNOWN; **FRANCO-PRUSSIAN WAR** UNKNOWN; **CLOWN** UNKNOWN **88-89 FOUR SPOT ILLUSTRATIONS** UNKNOWN; **TIM HAWKINSON** UNKNOWN; **NUT-RITION** UNKNOWN; **VIS** STEVE PALUMBO; **CARTOON** WILEY MILLER; **AFTER PARTY** DANNY J. GIBSON; **BOTTEGA** MAN'S "FLY"; **LIBERTY'S FOOT** UNKNOWN **90-91 TRANSPARENT ALPHABET #4** KATIE SCHOFIELD; **WALLPAPER** VICTORIA AND ALBERT MUSEUM; **NEWSPAPER AD** UNKNOWN; **CUTS NOSE** HERB LUBALIN; **RAGGED RIGHT** TONY SUTTON; **EIFFEL TOWER** UNKNOWN **92-93 VALSPAR** UNKNOWN; **EGG SUNRISE** UNKNOWN; **WATER COLOURS** UNKNOWN; **ASTON MARTIN** UNKNOWN; **GARDEN BURIAL** CARL-ERIK CONFORTO **96-97 RAUM BRAUCHT** KMS TEAM; **FOUR STUDIES** JANINE ERHARDT; **MAURICE RAVEL** EMIL WEISS; **BOKER** FRED SANICOLA; **WHO AM I** PAZU LEE KA LING; **OBSESSION** ISAAC TOBIN & LAUREN NASSEF **98-99 QUASE DE VERDADE** "PARTIAL TRUTH"; **OGI FRAMES** SCOTT THARES; **LOVE** UNKNOWN **100-101 RECLINING FIGURE NO.3** HENRY MOORE; **FOUR STUDIES TOP** JURI MIYAMOTO, IGNACIO HINOJOSA, JURI MIYAMOTO, IGNACIO HINOJOSA; **FOUR STUDIES BOTTOM** JULIE TAYLOR FLYNN, DAN HORLITZ, DANA ALDRITCH, CARL JENSON; **GLASS OWL** SUMMER JELLISON **102-103 THREE MORTONS** UNKNOWN; **THREE HOUSES** CHIP ALLEN; **TROMM MARKS** UNKNOWN **104-105 EXTENSION DRAWING** JAN V. WHITE; **SUPRBOX** MADS BURCHARTH; **GREEK TEMPLE** ANNE TREMBLAY; **CORPO HUMANO** ALESSANDRA KALKO & GABRIEL SILVEIRA **108-109 SAARINEN** GOTTSCHO-SCHLEISNER PHOTO; **KOLIN AD** HE OIING HUI; **SAMRAT YANTRA** ISAMU NOGUCHI PHOTO; **DAS NEUE RUSSLAND** GYORGY KEPES; **PURPLE ROBE** HENRI MATISSE; **TWO CHICKENS** UNKNOWN; **CALLIGRAPHY** UNKNOWN; **HOTEL** UNKNOWN **110-111 THREE CASTLES** MARTIN HURLIMANN PHOTOGRAPHS; **FOUR LA SAINT-CHAPELLES** UNKNOWN; **ABSOLUT** UNKNOWN; **BROOKLYN BRIDGE** UNKNOWN **112-113 CITY CENTRE** CESAR PELLI; **INUIT** UNKNOWN; **FORD AD** UNKNOWN; **10SOCKS** WILLIAM HJORTH; **VISUAL ACOUSTICS** ALEX LEMPE **114-115 REMBRANDT** E LESSING ARCHIV FUR KUNST & GESCHICHTE/JOHN ROSS; **ST GEORGE** UNKNOWN; **PETRA** JAN V. WHITE; **GARAGE** PEPE GIMENO & RICARDO CAÑIZARES; **GUCCI** EUNYOUNG LEE **116-117 HERBARUM** OTTO BRUNFELS; **CURE-X** KLAUS TROMMER; **BALLET-TECH** PAULA SCHER; **WOODCUT ILLUSTRATION** HANS WEIDITZ **118-119 REMAIN CALM** LUKE HAYMAN & CHRIS DIXON; **MAXIMUM SECURITY** AREM DUPLESSIS & KRISTINA DiMATTEO; **PHAISTOS DISK** UNKNOWN; **BOYFRIEND'S HEAD** LEN CHEESEMAN & MIKHAIL GHERMAN **120-121 LOGONE-BIRNI** MARCEL GRIAULE PHOTO; **CANTON** L'AMBASSADE DE LA COMPAGNIE ORIENTALE; **SMETTILA SUBITO** "PLEASE STOP YOUR ACTIONS AT ONCE! I AM NOT A MELON WHOSE RIPENESS IS IN DOUBT"; **VEJA** ALESSANDRA DA SILVA **122-123 PARCHMENT GRID** UNKNOWN; **COMPOSITION WITH RED, YELLOW AND BLUE** PIET MONDRIAN; **CNBC** UNKNOWN **124-125 GUESTS RATES** KLEX; **STOP GUN TRAFFICKING** WOODY PIRTLE & DAISUKE ENDO; **FESTIVAL DE VERANO** IBÁN RAMÓN RODRIGUEZ; **JAZZ IN WILISAU** NIKLAUS TROXLER **126-127 WATER & PEACE** SUZANNE MORIN; **PA GENSYN** UNKNOWN **128-129 RED SPORTS BROCHURE** PHIL CARTER & NEIL HEDGER; **CIVIL WAR** ELAINE BRADLEY; **NEW TYPE** OSWALDO MIRANDA **130-131 PHOTO ANNUAL** STEFAN SAGMEISTER; **POLLOCK** ALEXEY BRODOVITCH; **NEW FACE** ROLAND SCHENCK & BRIAN GRIFFIN; 1979 UNKNOWN; **L'ARGENT** UNKNOWN; **GOSPEL** MICHAEL BIERUT & EMILY HAYES **132-133** 10 **TIPS** UNKNOWN; **UN TRÉSOR** UNKNOWN; **BEATLES DIAGRAMS** MICHAE DEAL; **LIGHTNING** DAN NGUYEN & SCOTT SHEINBERG **134-135 LA RAMBLA BRANDA** NAZLI YUCEL & KRYSTIAN KWIECINSKY; **TYPEWRITER** KIRSTEN DIETZ; **RUTA CONTRACT** PEPE GIMENO & JULIO ALONSO; **LAX** ROBIN PERKINS & CLIFFORD SELBERT; **MOLKEN-BRONN** DDB THE WAY CITY; **GREEN PAGES** KENNETH C. WEHRMAN **136-137 RECLINING FIGURE** HENRY MOORE; **SCULPTURE** MICHAEL R. McSHANE; **KOREAN WAR** DON DYER PHOTO; **FORMULA ONE** RON VAN DER MEER **138-139 TOYOTA** MARKHAM CRONIN & JEFF VON HOENE; **COMME DES GARÇONS** STEPHEN J. SHANABROOK & VERONIKA GEORGIEVA; **INNER CITY INFILL** MICHAEL BIERUT; **JAPAN LIGHTING DESIGN** YUJI TOKUDA; **SAMSUNG** UNKNOWN; **ESCALATOR** MARCO FUSZ; **BULTHAUP** TAY GUAN HIN & ERIC YEO; **TABARIN** PAUL COLIN; **DOGCAT** UNKNOWN; **ZOO** UNKNOWN; **BROCHURE** LEO LIONNI **140-141 BARNES&NOBLE** SIDDIQI; **PIANO** KAREN I. HIRSCH PHOTO; **M LOGO** HERB LUBALIN; **CHRIST** MASACCIO'S "TRINITY"; **NIKE** UNKNOWN; **BULL FIGHT** UNKNOWN PHOTO; **BABY** JUSTIN PIKE; **TRAIN** ARMIN HOFMANN; **142-143 GLOBALISM(S)** PENTAGRAM NY; **LIBRO ILLEGGIBILE N.Y.1** BRUNO MUNARI; **G STUDY** AFTER CARL DAIR **144-145 SWEDISH PAVERS** UNKNOWN; **PG&E** ANTONY MILNER; **EIGHT BOOKLETS** JAN V. WHITE **148-149 F** UNKNOWN; **KOREAN ALPHABETS** UNKNOWN **150-151 PELIKAN** EL LISSITZKY; **HEY VIDEO** ANONYMOUS; **SUPERSTITION** NEVILLE BRODY; **HOT SPOTS** PIET ZWART **152-153 ASICS** UNKNOWN; **SANTA** UNKNOWN; 1922 EL LISSITZKY; **CROSS COUNTRY** CHARLES S. ANDERSON; **MASTERS OF DECEPTION** ROBERTO DE VICQ DE CUMPTICH; **I AM PRETTY SURE** NICK SCHMITZ; **MUSIC NOTATION** JOHANN SEBASTIAN BACH **154-155 ESPERIENZA** FILIPPO CECCHI; **ELENA PRESSER** WILLIAM LONGHAUSER; **DASHBOARD** UNKNOWN; **HERMAN MILLER** UNKNOWN; **NIKE** UNKNOWN; **ESQUIRE – MAN AT HIS BEST** UNKNOWN **156-157 LIGHTNING** SONOKO FURUYA; **FIVE STUDIES L–R:** SONOKO FURUYA, EPHRAIM GREGOR, MARIA KARANTZALIS, YE LIU, STEVEN LONGCHALLON **158-159 TCHAIKOVSKY** KUMARI GONGAJU; **PIANO** AVIVA KAPUST; **TCHAIKOVSKY** ILYSE DAVIS; **IBM** UNKNOWN; **THREE STUDIES L–R:** PETER CASTELLANO, AMY PUTNICKI, CHRIS SILVA **162-163 THE FUTURE CITY** NEVILLE BRODY; **BIG RED ROCK** JOE ESQUIBEL & WENDY OHWILER **164-165 AUTARKY** "DICTATORSHIP"; **COUNTERS** UNKNOWN **166-167 TIME&TERRITORY** DOMENIC LIPPA & BEATRICE BLUMENTHAL; **SUN LIFE** UNKNOWN; **BANCO PORTUGAL** UNKNOWN; **LONG LIVE** UNKNOWN; **HAR MAN** UNKNOWN; **ELVIS** UNKNOWN **168-169 CROWE** JENNIFER PROCOPIO **174-175 BMW** UNKNOWN; **HO LASCIATO** "I LEFT THE BABY ALONE FOR A MINUTE IN THE KITCHEN AND FOUND HIM COVERED WITH FLOUR FROM HEAD TO TOE" **176-177 NABOKOV** STEPHEN DOYLE; **SENSES** MARK GEER; **TCHAIKOVSKY** ANNA GUILLOTTE; **DIE** SARA FAZZINO; **NEVER NEVER** UNKNOWN; **CELEBRATE** UNKNOWN; **VISA SUSHI** UNKNOWN **178-179 DODGE DAKOTA** UNKNOWN; **THINK BEFORE** MARK GEER; **ABSTRACT STUDY** JOSH ROY; **DESCEND** ROB GELB; **FSTR** KEENAN; **CNBC** CINDY GOLDSTEIN **180-181 POPEYE'S** MELANIE FORSTER & SIMON FAIRWEATHER; **BLEU** UNKNOWN; **POLAROID** UNKNOWN; **TAXI** UNKNOWN **182-183 GENETICS** UNKNOWN; **SUBHEADS** UNKNOWN; **WHAT THE HELL** UNKNOWN; **SPABEFGOMTY** ADVERTISING TYPOGRAPHERS ASSOCIATION OF AMERICA **184-185 FOUR STUDIES** CHRISTINE LEUNG, ZITA SZÁTMARY, PATRICK SCOTT, TEO THOMAS; **QUAT'SOUS** MARIO MERCIER; **MOZART** UWE LOESCH; **SIX Fs** JOHN LEUNG **186-187 MEDCAREERS** PAUL CRAWFORD; **UTAH** KEVIN PERRY; **CHARACTER** COURTNEY BLAIR **188-189 SQUARE STUDY** CHIRAG BHAKTA; **HERE WE ARE NOW** RAYMOND GRIMAILA; **COLLAPSE** PETER BIL'AK; **JAPANESE** UNKNOWN; **CINSKY** KLEX; **MIKOLÁS ALES** KLEX **190-191 ACEGMORTY** ADVERTISING TYPOGRAPHERS ASSOCIATION OF AMERICA; **WOMEN'S MAGAZINE AD** UNKNOWN; **GET PICTURE** UNKNOWN; **UNDERPINNING** UNKNOWN **192-193 VOGUE** MALCOLM MANSFIELD; **BERGDORF GOODMAN** REBA SOCHIS; **DOGS** BRADBURY THOMPSON; **DODGE RAIN** UNKNOWN; **McCALL'S** OTTO STORCH; **FISHING** BRADBURY THOMPSON; **HANGER** HERB LUBALIN; **TODAY'S HALF** UNKNOWN; **WE'RE ANTI-SHOE** UNKNOWN **194-195 NIKE** UNKNOWN; **TRACING PAPER** METADESIGN LONDON **196-197 ART IS** PAULA SCHER; **DOCKERS AD** UNKNOWN; **NIKE** UNKNOWN; **TEXT & MAP** MARK GEER; **ST-GERMAIN** STEVE SANDSTROM & SARAH HOLLOWOOD **198-199 EUROPEAN CHARACTERS** UNKNOWN **200-201 DISCOVERY** ROGER CAMP & MIKE McCOMMON; **ROLLING STONE** FRED WOODWARD; **MARAT** LUDWIG ÜBELE; **MONSTER.COM** UNKNOWN

About the Author

Alex W. White has shaped the design of many magazines and identity programs. He has been a consultant to dozens of publications and has lectured widely on typography and design to professionals in the Americas and Europe. White recently completed ten years  of service on the Board of Directors of the Type Directors Club in New York, retiring as Chairman. He has taught design for thirty years at all levels of undergraduate and graduate education at programs that include Parsons the New School for Design, FIT, The Hartford Art School,  the State University of New York, City College of New York, and Manhattanville College. He is the award-winning author of *Advertising Design and Typography*, *Thinking in Type: The Practical Philosophy of Typography*, *Type in Use*, and *Really Good Logos Explained* with Margo Chase, Rian Hughes, and Ron Miriello. White lives in Westport CT.